Marilyn Hopkins was born in Totnes, E~~~~
studying various forms of Christianity a~~~~
has contributed to many seminars, talks a~~~~
She is co-author (with Tim Wallace-Murphy) of *Rosslyn: Guardian of the Secrets of the Holy Grail.*

Tim Wallace-Murphy was born in Ireland and studied medicine at University College, Dublin. He is co-author of *Rosslyn: Guardian of the Secrets of the Holy Grail* (with Marilyn Hopkins), *The Mark of the Beast* (with Trevor Ravenscroft), *An Illustrated Guidebook to Rosslyn Chapel,* and *The Templar Legacy and the Masonic Inheritance Within Rosslyn Chapel.*

Graham Simmans has been actively involved in historical and archaeological research on Rennes-le-Château, where he lives, for many years.

by Tim Wallace-Murphy and Marilyn Hopkins
Rosslyn: Guardian of the Secrets of the Holy Grail

by Tim Wallace-Murphy
The Mark of the Beast (with Trevor Ravenscroft)
An Illustrated Guidebook to Rosslyn Chapel
The Templar Legacy and the Masonic Inheritance Within Rosslyn Chapel

Rex Deus

*The True Mystery of Rennes-le-Château
and the Dynasty of Jesus*

Marilyn Hopkins, Graham Simmans
and Tim Wallace-Murphy

ELEMENT

Shaftesbury, Dorset • Boston, Massachusetts • Melbourne, Victoria

© Element Books Limited 2000
Text © Tim Wallace-Murphy, Marilyn Hopkins and Graham Simmans 2000

First published in the UK in 2000 by
Element Books Limited
Shaftesbury, Dorset SP7 8BP

Published in the USA in 2000 by
Element Books, Inc.
160 North Washington Street
Boston, MA 02114

Published in Australia in 2000 by
Element Books and distributed
by Penguin Australia Limited
487 Maroondah Highway, Ringwood, Victoria 3134

Tim Wallace-Murphy, Marilyn Hopkins and Graham Simmans have asserted their right under the
Copyright, Designs and Patents Act, 1988, to be identified as the authors of this work.

All rights reserved.
No part of this book may be reproduced or utilized in any form or by any means, electronic or
mechanical, without prior permission in writing from the Publisher.

Cover design by Mark Slader
Designed and typeset by The Bridgewater Book Company
Printed and bound by Creative Print & Design (Wales)

British Library Cataloguing in Publication
data available

Library of Congress Cataloging in Publication
data available

ISBN 1 86204 834 7

Contents

Plate Section Illustrations

Pictures 1, 2, 3, 6, 7, 8, 9 and 10 are © Graham Simmans; 4, 11 and 12 © Tim Wallace-Murphy; 5 © Marilyn Hopkins; 13 is used courtesy of the Supreme Council, 33rd degree, Scottish Rite Freemasonry, USA

Maps and Charts

Acknowledgements

The authors did not bring this work to fruition alone and unaided. We received information and encouragement from a variety of sources. All who have contributed in this way have done so freely and happily in the sure knowledge that we would use their insights and information according to our own conscience. No contributor, other than the authors, can therefore be held responsible for the opinions expressed in this work.

We gratefully acknowledge the help and encouragement received from Stuart Beattie of the Rosslyn Chapel Trust; Laurence Bloom of London; Robert Brydon of Edinburgh; Nicole Dawe of Spreyton; Baroness Edne di Pauli of London; Michael Halsey of Auchterarder; Biorn Ivemark of Gramazie; Guy Jourdan of Bargemon; Georges Kiess of the Centre d'Etudes et de Recherches Templières, Campagne-sur-Aude; Frederic Lionel of Paris; Robert Lomas of Bradford; Michael Monkton of Buckingham; James Mackay Munro of Penicuick; Andrew Pattison of Edinburgh; Stella Pates of Ottery St Mary; Alan Pearson of Rennes-les-Bains and David Pykitt of Burton-upon-Trent who, as always, shared his personal research with such generosity.

The team at Element Books led by Michael Mann have earned our respect and deep appreciation for all the support they have given to us from the inception of this work to its final publication. In particular we wish to thank John Baldock, their editorial consultant, Florence Hamilton, our editor, Matthew Cory, and all who have aided this very communal effort.

Lastly we wish to pay homage to our two spiritual brothers, Pat Sibille and Niven Sinclair, without whose sustained support, guidance and encouragement, none of this could have happened.

Introduction

Rennes-le-Château, a name equated with mystery, intrigue and stories of buried treasure, was virtually unknown until 1972 when a television documentary presented by Henry Lincoln[1] first brought this small hilltop village in south-western France to the attention of the British public. In three programmes presented over several years, this masterly storyteller recounted a series of interlinked mysteries.[2]

The television programmes were followed by a book, *The Holy Blood and the Holy Grail*,[3] written by Michael Baigent, Richard Leigh and Henry Lincoln. To say that this book caused a sensation is putting it mildly. Described variously as 'a brilliant piece of detective work',[4] as a work 'which will infuriate many ecclesiastical authorities'[5] and, more simply, as blasphemous, it rapidly attained bestseller status and was translated into most European languages. It contained a revelation regarded by many as the single most shattering secret of the last 2,000 years.

The starting point for Lincoln's investigation was the strange story of Bérenger Saunière, a gifted parish priest who was banished to Rennes-le-Château for some undisclosed misdemeanour in the later part of the 19th century.[6] On his arrival he lived in abject poverty but then suddenly became immensely wealthy, spending literally millions of francs. The story, which begins with hints of buried treasure, turns into an in-depth historical investigation, a modern Grail quest with all the accoutrements of mystery: cryptically coded documents, political intrigue, tales of secret societies, a conspiracy that spans the centuries, the activities of the Knights Templar, the Cathars, the Inquisition and a secret which could rock the Christian Church to its foundations – the marriage of Jesus and his founding of a dynasty that is still with us today.

As a result, Rennes-le-Château now receives more than 20,000 visitors a year from all over the world. By 1988, two English bibliographers had counted over 473 books, essays and articles devoted to this remote village.[7] *The Holy Blood and the Holy Grail* was followed by *The Messianic Legacy*,[8] written by the same authors, and a plethora of other works, all more or less based on the foundations laid down by Baigent, Leigh and Lincoln. The worldwide fascination with Rennes-le-Château is sustained by the foundation of a variety of clubs and associations devoted to further investigation of its mysteries. For example, there are more than 565 websites on the Internet which focus, in whole or in part, on the enigma first brought to our attention by Henry Lincoln.

To add to the tales of buried treasure, sacred bloodlines, historical conspiracy, persecution and genocide, we must now add forgery, fantasy and outright fiction. This startling assertion was made by a prestigious BBC television programme,[9] which set out to refute yet another well-publicized book, *The Tomb of God*,[10] which claimed that Jesus was buried on a mountainside near Rennes-le-Château.

Yet bizarre though it may seem, when the mists of fabrication and questionable research are stripped away from the works centred on Rennes-le-Château, several very real mysteries remain. When we discard the various distractions we discover a real historical basis for the most unlikely claim of all, the existence of a group of families who have repeatedly conspired together in an attempt to alter the course of European history. These interlinked families all claim descent from the 24 High Priests of the Temple in Jerusalem. This is the story told in this book, which forms the true mystery of Rennes-le-Château.

PART

I

The History and Mythos of Rennes-le-Château

1

The Turbulent History of a Hilltop Village

The 20,000 visitors a year who come to Rennes-le-Château[1] arrive by car, bicycle, on foot or horseback, and occasionally by coach. They all arrive and depart by the same route: the narrow, twisting road that climbs up from the town of Couiza, traverses the northern face of the mountain for the first few kilometres before turning to the west for the final and most precipitous part of the journey. The visitors climbing this hill are entranced by the view over the rolling countryside, which is liberally peppered with reminders of the turbulent history of the area. Clearly visible on a smaller hillside to the north at Coustaussa are the substantial ruins of a château dating from the 12th century.[2] Nearby, at the village of Cassaignes, are the equally impressive remains of a 16th-century castle and a 12th-century Romanesque church. Almost due east of the road at this point are the remnants of the medieval Château de Blanchefort. As one ascends the final kilometre or so of twisting road the village itself becomes visible. The short traverse that leads from the first houses to the sandy car park, which occupies a considerable proportion of the village, is a vivid reminder that this hamlet is so small that its mere existence, despite its superb location, cannot explain why it has such vast international appeal.

Situated in the middle of the car park is a strange water tower, and to the right, facing the precipice at the edge of the area, is an architectural oddity, a rectangular structure with a rounded, turreted tower, overhanging the precipice at one corner. To the south-east can be seen a peak which is surmounted by the ruins of the medieval fortress of Bézu, and beyond that the purple foothills of the Pyrenees. On the distant horizon are the outlines of the mountain range that separates France from Spain, its jagged peaks topped with snow, even in the month of May.

From Celts to Cathars

Evidence provided by megalithic remains in the countryside surrounding Rennes-le-Château indicates that this district has been inhabited for at least 4,500 years,[3] with a neolithic cemetery near the village dating back over 3,000 years. The site of the village was regarded as a sacred place by the early Celts, who named it Rhedae after their principal local tribe.[4] Like many districts situated near natural borders such as the Pyrenees, it has been fought over many times and occupied by successive waves of invaders from other cultures. The Greeks, who colonized the port of Agde immediately after founding the port of Marseilles in 639 BCE, also reputedly settled here, while during the Roman occupation the area surrounding Rennes-le-Château increased in importance. The Romans mined for gold at Bugarach[5] and also exploited the thermal baths at Campagne-sur-Aude and Rennes-les-Bains;[6] Rennes-le-Château lies midway between these three points.

At the time of the collapse of the Roman Empire, Rhedae is believed to have been a large town of some 30,000 inhabitants. At the time of Dagobert II (died 679), the Merovingian King of France who married a Visigoth princess,[7] it became an important city and centre of power of the Visigoth Empire, which was founded in 418 CE and which straddled the Pyrenees and occupied a vast swathe of present-day Spain.[8]

The Visigoths were a warlike Teutonic people whose tribes swept westwards from central Europe, devastating everything in their path. They besieged and conquered Rome in 410 CE, stripping it of its accumulated treasures, and toppled the Roman Empire before creating one of their own which included Rhedae.[9]

After the collapse of the Visigoth Empire the site of the present village became the seat of an important county, that of Razès.[10] By the beginning of the 13th century this was part of the Languedoc, the western part of the larger province of Provence. Inspired by a religious group known as the Cathars, this entire area developed in such a manner that its culture and prosperity were unique in Europe. At that time the Languedoc was so prosperous that many authorities believe that, had the Catholic Church not instigated a brutal crusade of extermination against the 'Cathar heresy', the Renaissance might well have occurred 200 years earlier, and in the Languedoc rather than in northern Italy.[11]

THE ALBIGENSIAN CRUSADE AND THE KNIGHTS TEMPLAR

To most people the word 'crusade' evokes memories from school days, recalling the series of wars to liberate the Holy Land from the infidel. The concept of a crusade against fellow Christians in Europe seems strange, yet early in the summer of 1209, at the behest of the Pope, an army of northern knights descended on the tolerant and peaceful people of the Languedoc to extirpate the Cathar heresy.[12] These knights were given the same ecclesiastical rights and privileges as those granted to the crusaders in the Holy Land; absolution for all the sins they had committed or might commit, and the right of expropriation of all property belonging to those deemed as heretics by Holy Mother the Church.[13] The Cathar, or Albigensian, Crusade lasted for over 60 years and was of a brutal and genocidal nature that was not matched until the Holocaust against the Jews during the Second World War.[14] During the crusade, which ended with the fall of Montségur in 1244, the town of Rennes-le-Château was captured and recaptured several times.

Neither of the two knightly crusading Orders, the Knights Templar or the Knights Hospitaller, took any military part in this crusade, a fact that has puzzled historians for many years.[15] The most likely explanation was that neither Order wished to bite the hand that fed them, for they owed the gift of their land in many cases to Cathars or to nobles who were Cathar sympathizers.[16] Templar holdings abounded throughout the Languedoc, Roussillon and in the eastern part of Provence proper. Within these districts lay the vast majority of Templar properties in mainland Europe.[17] From the commanderie at Campagne-sur-Aude, about 10km from Rennes-le-Château, to the coast at Baccares one is never out of sight of Templar holdings, commanderies, castles and fortified farms.[18] The southern route to the medieval centre of pilgrimage at St James of Compostela passed nearby, bringing pilgrims in their thousands from the Mediterranean coast, Italy and beyond.[19] Here, as elsewhere in Europe, the Templars policed the routes to protect the pilgrims. The Templar role in the pilgrim trade, policing the routes and acting as bankers to both the pilgrims and the ecclesiastical establishments *en route*, was of such importance that it is now regarded as the earliest demonstrable activity of what we might call today a multi-national conglomerate. The Order, with its holdings in farming land, vineyards, quarrying, banking and the pilgrimage business, became immensely rich, and its activities spanned all of Christian Europe and the Holy Land.[20]

After the Albigensian Crusade, Rennes-le-Château, with all of the Cathar country, was subjected to the unwelcome attention of the Inquisition. In the 1360s an outbreak of plague, or the Black Death, decimated the local population. To add to its troubles the hilltop town, despite its superb defensive position, was virtually destroyed by Catalan bandits.[21] One major political result to flow from the crusade against the Cathars was that the whole of the present provinces of the Languedoc and Roussillon, which had previously been independent counties of considerable power, became part of France under the direct rule of the king and were administered by his feudal lords.[22] The principal building within Rennes-le-Château, the Château d'Hautpoul, the one-time residence of the family d'Hautpoul who lived here for centuries, reflects this change in feudal administration. From the time of the crusade until the middle of the 20th century, Rennes-le-Château steadily declined in importance until it became yet another insignificant hilltop village solely dependant on scratching a living from the surrounding land. Its modern revival as a centre of interest dates from some strange events that began with the installation of a certain Bérenger Saunière as the parish priest on 1 June 1885.[23]

Saunière, the Parish Priest

Bérenger Saunière knew Rennes-le-Château extremely well, having been born and raised in the village of Montazels only a few kilometres away.[24] This highly intelligent, active, handsome and scholarly man at first seemed destined for a promising career in the Church but, for reasons that have never been explained, lost the confidence of the hierarchy. It would appear, therefore, that his appointment to the insignificant and poverty-stricken parish of Rennes-le-Château was either a punishment or a form of banishment.[25]

Parish records show that between 1885 and 1891 Saunière's stipend averaged the equivalent of about £6 sterling per year; hardly an opulent income for a priest who had once been deemed a potential high flyer. He supplemented his diet by hunting and fishing, and with his small income and the meagre gratuities provided by his parishioners he seems to have led a pleasant and productive life.[26] During this time he engaged Marie Denarnaud, an 18-year-old peasant girl, as his housekeeper, lifelong companion and confidante.[27] He spent the evenings productively, reading voraciously and perfecting his Latin. He also learnt ancient Greek and studied Hebrew in order to increase his understanding of the Scriptures.[28] His nearest friend, whom he visited frequently, was the priest of the nearby village of Rennes-les-Bains, the Abbé Henri Boudet. With Boudet as his tutor he began to gain a profound knowledge of the complex and turbulent history of this region of France.[29]

The ancient and dilapidated village church in Rennes-le-Château, like so many others in the area, was built on the foundations of a far older place of worship. It is claimed that the earlier structure, dating from the 6th century, was built by the Visigoths.[30] By the time Saunière was installed as the curé of the village, the church, which was dedicated to Mary Magdalene in 1059, was in a state of almost hopeless disrepair, for the roof leaked to such an extent that it rained on the heads of priest and parishioner alike.[31] Not surprisingly he wanted to restore it, so with the encouragement of his friend the Abbé Boudet, he borrowed a small sum from the village funds and, in 1891, began a modest restoration. During the course of this he removed the altar stone which was supported by two ancient Visigothic columns. One of these was found to be hollow and contained four parchments which had been rolled up and inserted into sealed wooden tubes. Two of these documents are said to have comprised genealogies, one dating from 1644 and the other from 400 years earlier. The other two were apparently the work of one of Saunière's predecessors, the Abbé Antoine Bigou, who had been curé of the village in the 1780s.[32]

Saunière reported his find to his immediate superior, the Bishop of Carcassonne, Mgr Felix-Arsene Billard. He was promptly sent to Paris, at the bishop's expense, to show the documents to senior ecclesiastical scholars.[33] One of these was the Abbé Bieil, the director-general of the seminary of St Sulpice, a church long associated with the study of esoteric thought. They were also shown to Bieil's nephew, Emil Hoffet,[34] who had established an impressive reputation as a scholar. Hoffet was training for the priesthood and had developed considerable expertise in linguistics, palaeography and, most importantly, cryptography. Despite his clerical position he was deeply immersed in esoteric thought and was in regular contact with many of the groups and individuals involved in the diverse aspects of the occult revival in Paris.[35] This illustrious circle included literary giants such as Stéphane Mallarmé and Maurice Maeterlinck, the composer Claude Debussy and the renowned operatic diva Emma Calvé.[36] The outcome of Saunière's various meetings with his church superiors during his stay in Paris is impossible to establish. It would appear, however, that this simple country priest was warmly welcomed into the distinguished circle of esotericists that revolved around Emil Hoffet, and some sources suggest that Saunière became Emma Calvé's lover. It is said that Saunière visited the Louvre and purchased copies of three paintings; one of a medieval pope, another a work of some esoteric significance by Teniers, and the third, the well-known painting *Les Bergers d'Arcadie* by Poussin.[37]

THE RESTORATION CONTINUES

On his return to Rennes-le-Château, Saunière continued with the restoration of the church and its grounds. In the churchyard was the tomb of Marie, Marquise d'Hautpoul, the last of the feudal lords of the area. The head- and flagstone marking Marie's grave were designed by the Abbé Antoine Bigou,[38] who is credited with the writing of two of the mysterious documents. He was not only the parish priest of the village but also the personal chaplain to the d'Hautpoul family. Saunière's actions at this point are somewhat odd to say the least; for reasons that are impossible to explain, he obliterated the inscriptions on the tomb.[39]

Saunière began to spend considerable sums on the restoration. Records also disclose that by 1894 he was spending more on postage than his annual stipend could possibly sustain, and that between 1896 and his death early in 1917 he spent more than 200,000 gold francs, which at that time would have been valued at £500,000 sterling, the equivalent of several million pounds today.[40]

It was not only the church that benefited from the priest's generosity; Saunière paid for the construction of a modern road leading up to the village and defrayed the considerable cost of providing running water for his parishioners. For his own use he built the strange edifice, the Tour Magdala, which overlooks the valley on the steepest side of the mountaintop, and also commissioned the building of a substantial house, the Villa Bethania.[41] The church was not merely restored but garishly redecorated in a manner that can only be described as eccentric. Over the porch he placed a strange warning – TERRIBILIS EST LOCUS ISTE – which is translated in most works about Rennes-le-Château as 'this place is terrible'.[42] Immediately inside the church door the holy water stoop is supported by a frightening statue of the demon Asmodeus, renowned in legend as the custodian of secrets, the guardian of hidden treasure and the builder of Solomon's Temple.

As in most Catholic churches there are panels depicting the Stations of the Cross, which here are brightly painted and substantially different in detail from those one would expect in a village church of this nature. The fourteenth Station, which shows the body of Jesus being carried into the tomb, is particularly notable, for here the scene is set against the background of the night sky lit by the full moon. It is as though Saunière was trying to indicate that either Jesus was buried after nightfall, many hours later than the Bible states, or that the body of the Saviour is being carried *out* of the tomb under the cover of darkness.[43] Is this a sly, symbolic reference to the age-old esoteric tradition that Jesus actually survived the crucifixion? If so, this may well be a pictorial representation of the statement made in *The Lost Gospel According to St Peter* which recounts how the soldiers guarding the tomb reported: 'And as they declared what things they had seen, again they see three men come forth from the tomb, and two of them supporting one ...'.[44] This would certainly tend to confirm the esoteric legend that Jesus did not die on the cross and that after the crucifixion he was nursed back to health by members of the Essene sect.

While the adornment of his newly restored church continued its expensive progress, this provincial parish priest did not neglect his own comfort. In the grounds of the Villa Bethania he created an orangery[45] and a zoological garden. The Tour Magdala housed a magnificent library, which is hardly surprising for a man of his intellectual talents.[46] He continued to spend extravagantly and developed a fine taste in rare china, precious fabrics and antique marbles, which he collected assiduously. He was not a selfish man and he continued to cater for the needs of his parishioners. Not only did he finance the road and the water supply but he also provided them with sumptuous banquets.[47] His lifestyle began to resemble that of a medieval oriental potentate rather than that of a humble parish priest in one of the smaller and more impoverished parishes in France. His hospitality extended far beyond the bounds of his parish; he welcomed a considerable number of important guests from the capital and from abroad, including Emma Calvé. More surprisingly was the inclusion on his guest list of the French Secretary of State for Culture and, strangest of all, he reputedly welcomed Archduke Johann von Habsburg, a cousin of Emperor Franz-Joseph of Austria, who was travelling incognito under the name of 'Monsieur Guillaume'.[48]

Saunière's profligate spending and ostentatious social life did not go unnoticed, yet the Bishop of Carcassonne who had sent him to Paris appeared to turn a blind eye to the whole affair. When that bishop died, however, his successor, Paul-Felix Beurain de Beausejour, called the priest to account for his actions.[49] Saunière was unwilling to explain the source of his wealth and flatly refused to accept the bishop's order transferring him to another parish, whereupon the bishop accused him of simony, that is illicitly selling masses and pardons. A local tribunal, called to hear the case on 5 November 1910, suspended the uncooperative priest.[50] Another priest, whose ministrations were boycotted by the villagers, was appointed in his place. The Mayor of Rennes-le-Château, who sided with Saunière, informed the bishop by letter that the church remained deserted and all religious ceremonies had been replaced by civil rites. The new priest preached to empty chairs while the devout villagers continued to attend the masses celebrated by Saunière in the Villa Bethania. Saunière appealed directly to the Vatican, not merely against his sentence but also seeking to be re-established as the priest of Rennes-le-Château. He also instructed his lawyers of his intent to sue the bishop for defamation of character. In 1915 the Vatican anulled all the sanctions imposed by the Bishop of Carcassonne. Bérenger Saunière re-entered his presbytery with his head held high and with an ironic and mysterious smile upon his face.

THE DEATH OF SAUNIÈRE

The events surrounding the sudden illness and death of Saunière are very strange. He suffered a major stroke on 17 January 1917, the same date as that inscribed on the tombstone of the Marquise Marie d'Hautpoul.[51] Yet on 12 January, five days before, it is said that his parishioners declared that their priest seemed to be in an enviable state of health for a man of his age. Death is the great leveller. The rituals attending the death of rich and poor alike in early 20th-century France were the same. As Saunière lay dying, a priest from a neighbouring parish was called in some haste to hear his last confession and to administer the last rites. On his arrival the priest went straight to the dying man's bedside. In *The Holy Blood and the Holy Grail* it is claimed that, according to eyewitness testimony, he emerged shortly in a state of considerable agitation and refused to administer extreme unction, presumably on the basis of Saunière's deathbed confession.[52]

Saunière died unshriven on 22 January 1917. The ritual that followed his death was inexplicable by any ecclesiastical standards and completely foreign to local custom. On the morning of 23 January, his body, dressed in an ornate robe adorned with numerous scarlet tassels, was seated upright in an armchair and placed on the terrace beside the Tour Magdala. A number of unidentified mourners solemnly filed past the corpse, one by one. For reasons that have never been explained, many of them plucked a tassel from the dead man's garment, perhaps as some ritual token of remembrance. Even today, the residents of Rennes-le-Château are as mystified by this strange rite as everyone else.[53]

Saunière had spent money in such a profligate manner that there was understandable curiosity as to how much he possessed and to whom he had bequeathed it. When the terms of his will were made public they caused a sensation, for the priest had died without a penny! It would appear that he had transferred his money to Marie Denarnaud, his companion of 18 years.[54]

MARIE DENARNAUD

Marie Denarnaud lived in considerable comfort at the Villa Bethania until 1946 when her fortunes underwent a dramatic change. The French Government issued new currency after the war, and all who wished to exchange any considerable quantity of old francs for new were subjected to severe questioning in order to establish the source of their wealth. This measure was designed to expose tax evasion, war profiteers and various other illegal activities. Marie was not going to be accountable to anyone; she was seen in the garden of the Villa Bethania making a bonfire of vast sheaves of old franc notes.[55] She survived for seven years, living on the proceeds from the sale of the Villa Bethania. The premises were purchased by a Monsieur Noel Corbu who, with his family, looked after her until she died. She told him many times that he was walking on great riches and that before her death she would disclose to him alone a secret that would make him extremely rich and powerful. Sadly for Monsieur Corbu, Marie suffered a sudden and unexpected stroke on 29 January 1953, which left her speechless. She took her secret with her to the grave.

Marie's comments stimulated a wave of highly destructive treasure hunting in the guise of archaeological excavation. French law on buried treasure, put simply, reinforces the childhood concept of 'finders keepers'. This situation has been exacerbated by the ready availability of explosives, which are used extensively in wine growing regions to clear deep-rooted vines. One casualty was the dynamiting of an ornate tomb in the near vicinity which was reputed to be the one depicted by Poussin in *Les Bergers d'Arcadie*. The hilltop on which Rennes-le-Château stands is literally honeycombed with tunnels, some natural, many man-made, some ancient and others very recent. A large and rusting notice at the entrance to the village declares to this day that unauthorized excavations are strictly forbidden under a local by-law of 1966. This notice is reinforced by one posted outside the Mayor's office, dated 1998, which reminds the villagers that the by-law of 1966 is still valid and will be rigorously enforced – which, like all French laws, is honoured more in its breach than in its observance.

2

The Story Breaks

While travelling in France in 1969, Henry Lincoln bought a copy of a paperback by Gérard de Sède, entitled *Le Trésor Maudit*. The 'accursed treasure' of the title was the one discovered by the Abbé Bérenger Saunière who had apparently deciphered certain coded documents found in his parish church. Lincoln was intrigued by a strange omission in the story. While the texts of two of these documents were reproduced in the book, the secret messages referring to the treasure were not. He was fascinated by the discovery of a concealed message within one of the published documents, a message to which de Sède made no reference whatsoever.[1] If he had been able to discern the message, surely the author could have done so too? Why this curious omission? Would not a reference to a coded message of this nature have helped to sell the book?

Captivated by the story, he presented it to the executive producer of the 'Chronicle' series of programmes for the BBC as a possible theme for a television documentary and, with the producer's approval, he travelled to France to meet Gérard de Sède. Lincoln asked de Sède, 'Why didn't you publish the message hidden in the parchments?' At first de Sède teased him by responding 'What message?' Lincoln pressed the point repeatedly and eventually de Sède gave a most intriguing answer:

'Because we thought it might interest someone like you to find it for yourself'.[2] Later de Sède began to feed Lincoln with further tantalizing fragments of information. The first major disclosure was the text of a coded message which spoke of the painters Poussin and Teniers. De Sède informed Lincoln that the cipher for the code was incredibly complex and had only been broken by the computer experts of the cipher department of the French army. Lincoln checked the story with experts from British Intelligence who confirmed his suspicions that the cipher was unsolvable by computer. This led Lincoln to believe that this complex code was unbreakable and that someone, either de Sède or someone else, must have the key.

The two parchments, whose authorship was attributed to Saunière's predecessor, the Abbé Antoine Bigou, were excerpts from the New Testament written in Latin. However, neither is quite what it seems. In the first, the words are run together with no spaces between them and, in a number of places, some utterly superfluous letters appear to have been inserted. The second is completely different, for lines of text are oddly truncated, sometimes in the middle of a word, and certain letters are obviously raised above the others. The two extracts are not simply Latin texts, but include a sequence of ingenious and highly complex codes. These have been deciphered and the following transcription has been published in French books devoted to Rennes-le-Château and in two of the TV documentaries made for the BBC.

BERGERE PAS DE TENTATION QUE POUSSIN TENIERS GARDENT LA CLEF PAX DCLXXXI PAR LA CROIX ET CE CHEVAL DE DIEU J'ACHEVE CE DAEMON DE GARDIEN A MIDI POMMES BLEUES

(SHEPHERDESS, NO TEMPTATION. THAT POUSSIN, TENIERS, HOLD THE KEY; PEACE 681. BY THE CROSS AND THIS HORSE OF GOD, I COMPLETE – [OR DESTROY] – THIS DAEMON OF THE GUARDIAN AT NOON. BLUE APPLES.)[3]

While one of the ciphers is so complex that it might have baffled Einstein, the other is almost childishly simple. In the second parchment the raised letters simply spell out the message:

A DAGOBERT II ROI ET A SION EST CE TRESOR ET IL EST LA MORT.

(TO DAGOBERT II, KING, AND TO SION BELONGS THIS TREASURE AND HE IS THERE DEAD.)[4]

Claiming, not unreasonably, that the second message must have been spotted by Saunière, Lincoln expressed his doubts that this parish priest, intelligent though he was, would have had the slightest chance of deciphering the more complex code.

Poussin's most famous painting was *Les Bergers d'Arcadie*. De Sède informed Lincoln that a tomb resembling the one in the painting had been found not far from Rennes-le-Château and sent him several photographs of it.[5] With this added information, a full-length documentary was broadcast early in 1972 under the title *The Lost Treasure of Jerusalem?* The programme created wide public interest and controversy and Lincoln immediately began working on a sequel which was broadcast in 1974 as *The Priest, the Painter and the Devil*.

The increasing complexity of the story began to exceed any one man's capacity and in 1975 Lincoln began to collaborate with Richard Leigh and Michael Baigent. Together they wrote a third documentary, *The Shadow of the Templars*, which was broadcast in 1979.[6] This programme provoked an avalanche of correspondence. One letter, from a retired Anglican priest, aroused the authors' curiosity, as it made bald assertions with apparent indifference as to whether they believed them or not. The correspondent simply stated that the treasure did not consist of bullion, jewellery or articles of value, but of a secret that proved beyond all doubt that the crucifixion was a fraud and that Jesus of Nazareth was alive and well as late as 45 CE.[7]

The Holy Blood and the Holy Grail began by recounting the story of the priest Saunière and the coded documents, and continued with an account of the authors' investigations into the source of Saunière's wealth, power and influence. Their starting point was to see if the history of the area provided a rational explanation which might give some indication of this; their provisional conclusions suggested three important, potential sources: the Visigoths, the Cathars and the Knights Templar. It was while researching the origins and actions of the Templars that they began to suspect that there was far more to this mystery than simply a hunt for buried treasure.

THE KNIGHTS TEMPLAR

When Baigent, Leigh and Lincoln studied the accepted historical accounts of the founding of the Knights Templar, or the Order of the Poor Knights of the Temple of Solomon, they found that these raised far more questions than they answered. The earliest record, written by Guillaume de Tyre sometime between 1175 and 1185, claims that the Order was founded in 1118.[8] It describes how a nobleman, Hughes de Payen, sometimes known as Hughes de Payne, a vassal of the Count of Champagne, presented himself with eight companions to Baudouin (Baldwin) I, the King of Jerusalem. The nine knights declared their intention to 'as far as their strength permitted, to keep the roads and highways safe … with a special regard for the protection of pilgrims'. They were granted quarters built on the site reputed to be that of the ancient Temple of Solomon, from which the new Order derived its name[9] and, according to Guillaume de Tyre, no further candidates were admitted to the ranks for the first nine years of its existence. The knights were warmly received by the Patriarch of Jerusalem, who granted them the right to use the double-barred Cross of Lorraine as their heraldic device.

Baigent, Leigh and Lincoln remarked that it is strange that the official royal historian employed by King Baudouin, Fulk de Chartres, made no mention whatsoever of Hughes de Payen or the Knights Templar or, to use their popular name, la Milice du Christ (the Militia of Christ). Nor is there any contemporaneous record of the nine knights exerting themselves in the protection of pilgrims to the holy places. Nonetheless, within ten years the Templars had acquired a certain degree of renown. St Bernard, the Abbot of the Cistercian Abbey of Clairvaux, wrote a highly complimentary document in 1128, *In Praise of the New Knighthood*, in which he declared the Templars to be the epitome of Christian values.

The Knights Templar were given their rule in 1128 at the Council of Troyes, which was dominated by the thinking of the Abbot of Clairvaux.[10] Hughes de Payen was the Order's first grand master and the knights themselves were to be warrior monks, combining the discipline of the cloister with a courage that bordered on fanaticism. In 1139, Pope Innocent II, a protégé of St Bernard, issued a papal Bull which declared that the Templars owed no allegiance to any secular or ecclesiastical power other than the Pope himself. In other words, they could act independently and, if necessary, in defiance of the rule of kings, emperors, princes or prelates.[11]

The investigations made by Baigent, Leigh and Lincoln suggest that the Order had been founded not in 1118 but at least nine years earlier, as the 'front men' of a far more mysterious and secretive group known as the Priory of Sion.[12] They also indicate that the true motive for its foundation was to travel to Jerusalem to locate the hidden treasure of the Temple of Solomon.[13] Apparent confirmation of a third Order behind the scenes, manipulating both the Templars and the Cistercians, to use the authors' words, 'soon thrust itself upon them'.[14]

The Secret Dossiers

The wealth and variety of documentation relating to Bérenger Saunière and the mystery of Rennes-le-Château that appeared in France from 1956 onwards implied that the subject was of great, if unexplained, importance to someone. This material appears to have been released systematically to stimulate further investigation, and presented so that it seemed to have originated from some highly privileged source. It covered many topics that directly or indirectly relate to Rennes-le-Château, such as the Cathars, the Templars, the Merovingian kings, the Rose-Croix and, of course, included several books on Saunière and Rennes-le-Château.

Publicly available books and articles tell only a small part of the story. The most interesting and perhaps the most important information appeared in documents which were deposited at the Bibliothèque Nationale (National Library) in Paris and which did not seem intended for general circulation. The identity of the authors of many of these works are often disguised by pseudonyms.[15] One, entitled *Les Descendants Merovingiens et l'Enigme du Razès Wisigoth* (*The Descendants of the Merovingians and the Enigma of the Visigoth Razès*), claims on the title page to have been published by the supreme Masonic Lodge of Switzerland, the Grande Loge Alpina, which is the equivalent of the Grand Orient Lodge in France and Grand Lodge in Britain. At least two people of repute have made enquiries about this book from officials of the Grande Loge Alpina; the response they received is somewhat disturbing, for the officials denied all knowledge of the work.

The most important collection of papers relating to the mystery of Rennes-le-Château which are deposited in the Bibliothèque Nationale are known as the Secret Dossiers,[16] a loose collection of rather odd items – newspaper clippings, cheap pamphlets, occasional printed pages that might well have come from some other published work, letters pasted to backing sheets and numerous genealogical documentations – kept within a stiff-covered document holder. From time to time some pages were removed and others freshly inserted. Additions and amendments were occasionally made in small copperplate handwriting and, some time later, these corrected pages were replaced by printed ones that incorporated all the handwritten alterations.

The bulk of the section devoted to genealogical research is supposedly written by a certain Henri Lobineau. Additional information in the Dossiers indicates that Henri Lobineau is a pseudonym, perhaps derived from a street which passes St Sulpice in Paris, the Rue Lobineau, and that the work may have been written by someone called Leo Schidlof. Baigent, Leigh and Lincoln contacted Leo Schidlof's daughter, who protested that her parent had no interest in genealogy, none whatsoever in the Merovingian dynasty and had not even heard of the mystery of Rennes-le-Château. There was soon apparent confirmation of Miss Schidlof's story which claimed that Henri Lobineau was not Leo Schidlof at all, but a distinguished French aristocrat, the Comte Henri de Lenoncourt.[17]

The events at Rennes-le-Château at the turn of the century began to resemble a puzzle shrouded in layers of mystery, protected by a minefield of misattribution and misrepresentation. The material which has been appearing piece by piece since 1956, supposedly the work of people with perfectly plausible names, has almost inevitably proved to be the work of an untraceable authorship. Addresses quoted for publishing houses and organizations that appear to have significance have been proven not to exist. Books have been cited which cannot be traced and which no one, to the best of our knowledge, has ever seen. Even within the confines of the august and sedate establishment of the Bibliothèque Nationale certain documents have been altered, some have disappeared, others have been miscatalogued, and one document which the authors sought with some persistence seemed untraceable.

The Merovingian dynasty was mentioned in *Le Serpent Rouge*, one of the privately printed books deposited in the Bibliothèque Nationale. The date on this volume is symbolic; it is 17 January, the date of the death of the Marquise d'Hautpoul and that of the stroke suffered by Saunière. This strange book consists of one Merovingian genealogy, two maps of France in Merovingian times with a brief commentary, a ground plan of St Sulpice in Paris outlining the various side chapels, and thirteen short prose poems, of considerable literary quality.[18] Within them are references to the decoration of the church at Rennes-le-Château, to its curé Bérenger Saunière, to the Blanchefort family, Poussin's *Les Bergers d'Arcadie* and the motto *Et In Arcadia Ego* which is found in this painting. There is specific and dramatic mention of a red snake that is described as uncoiling its length across the centuries, as an allegorical illusion to hereditary descent, a bloodline, or a dynastic lineage.

THE PRIORY OF SION

From this wealth of material Baigent, Leigh and Lincoln discerned certain key points, which they summarized as follows: there was a secret Order known as the Priory of Sion which created the Knights Templar; the Priory of Sion was led by a series of grand masters whose names figure prominently in the history of the development of Western European culture; after the suppression of the Knights Templar in 1314, the Priory of Sion not only survived but also orchestrated certain critical events in European history; the Priory of Sion continues to play an influential role in both international affairs and the domestic politics of some European countries; to a large extent it is the organization responsible for the flood of information on the Rennes-le-Château mystery; the declared objective of the Priory of Sion is the restoration of the Merovingian dynasty to the thrones of Europe.[19]

Citing the Priory documents as their source, that is the Secret Dossiers, Baigent, Leigh and Lincoln state that the Order of Sion was founded by Godfroi de Bouillon in 1090, some nine years before the conquest of Jerusalem. However, even within these documents, there are other papers which claim that the true founding date for the Order was

1099 when, shortly after the capture of Jerusalem, it is claimed that a group of anonymous but powerful people held a secret meeting to elect a King of Jerusalem. There were several claimants for the title, among them Count Raymond of Toulouse; nonetheless the meeting offered the throne to Godfroi de Bouillon. Godfroi accepted the responsibilities but declined the royal title. He was king in everything but name, but only ruled for little over a year. His brother Baudouin who succeeded him had no hesitation in accepting the title of King of Jerusalem.

The Secret Dossiers state that Baudouin I of Jerusalem, 'who owed his throne to Sion', was 'obliged' to accept the constitution of the Order of the Knights Templar in March 1117, the founders of which were listed in the Secret Dossiers as follows: Hughes de Payen, Bisol de St Omer, and Hughes I, Count of Champagne, along with certain members of the Order of Sion who were named as André de Montbard, Archambaud de Saint-Aignan, Nivard de Montdidier, Gondemar and Rossal.[20] From the foundation of the Templars until 1188, the Order of Sion and the Order of the Temple, according to the Secret Dossiers, shared the same grand masters. In 1188 this situation changed as the two diverged dramatically. The first grand master to rule over the Order of Sion exclusively was, according to the Priory documents, Jean de Gisors.[21]

It was also in 1188 that the Order of Sion changed its name to the Priory of Sion and, as a kind of subtitle, adopted the name Ormus. This curious name occurs in early Zoroastrian and Gnostic texts, where it is equated with the principle of light. French Masonic ritual indicates that Ormus was a Gnostic adept of Alexandria who, after conversion to Christianity by St Mark, founded a new initiatory Order with the identifying symbol of a red or 'Rose Cross'. The text of the Secret Dossiers, confirmed by other Priory documents, indicates that one is intended to see in Ormus the origins of the Order of the Rose-Croix or Rosicrucians. To make this abundantly clear, the documents also claim that in 1188 the Priory of Sion adopted a second subtitle – l'Ordre de la Rose-Croix Veritas (the Order of the True Red Cross). Yet by quoting Frances Yates, who had demonstrated no known evidence of an Order of Rosicrucians in existence earlier than the final years of the 16th century, Baigent, Leigh and Lincoln tried to achieve some semblance of balance in their narrative.[22] They also pointed out, however, that if the Priory documents were authentic – which they apparently accepted they were – then Yates's opinion would have to be revised to accommodate the uncomfortable fact that this secretive Order had been in existence for nearly 400 years before its name became public.

THE THREE LISTS OF NAMES

The Secret Dossiers contained three lists of names. The first Baigent, Leigh and Lincoln did not deem worthy of detailed examination as it was merely a list of abbots who, it was claimed, presided over the Order of Sion's possessions in the Holy Land between 1152 and 1281. They paid more attention to the second: a list of the grand masters of the Knights Templar from 1118 until 1190, from the time of the Order's official foundation until the date it supposedly separated from its so-called parent Order, the Priory of Sion. When they compared this list with those cited by Templar historians, certain glaring discrepancies became apparent. According to the historians' lists, the Knights Templar were led by ten grand masters in the years between 1118 and 1190. Most include the name of André de Montbard not merely as a co-founder of the Order but also as the Templar grand master from 1153 to 1156. The Secret Dossiers indicate that André de Montbard never led the Order.[23]

Most Templar historians relate that Bertrand de Blanchefort became the sixth grand master of the Templar Order after the death of André de Montbard in 1156. Again the account rendered in the Secret Dossiers is substantially different. According to their list, Bertrand de Blanchefort, whom the authors believe resided near Rennes-le-Château, was the fourth grand master, attaining the rank in 1153. They then posed the question, 'Because it disagreed with those lists compiled by established historians, should we regard the list in the Secret Dossiers as wrong?' They rightly claim that no absolutely definitive list of the grand masters of the Knights Templar exists; the earliest one we have dates from 1342, 30 years after the dissolution of the Order and more than two centuries after its foundation. The problem was simple. Was the list of Templar grand masters in the Secret Dossiers authentic, based on inside information inaccessible to academic historians, or was it a forgery? By preferring the list in the Secret Dossiers to the authentic historical record, the authors of *The Holy Blood and the Holy Grail* made their preference plain, despite their many caveats and disclaimers to the contrary. Indeed, they went further and stated:

> Whether our conclusion was warranted or not, we were confronted by one indisputable fact that someone had obtained access, somehow, to a list that was more accurate than any other. And since that list – despite its divergence from others more accepted – proved so frequently to be correct, it lent considerable credibility to the Priory documents as a whole.[24]

They then went on to claim that if the Secret Dossiers were reliable in this critical respect then there was less reason to doubt their authenticity in others.

Their examination of the third list in the Secret Dossiers was made in the light of these conclusions. This was that of the alleged grand masters of the Priory of Sion which, in any other circumstances, they claim they would have dismissed as absurd. According to the Secret Dossiers the grand masters of the Priory of Sion, who were also called Nautonnier (an old French word meaning navigator or helmsman), included, among others, Jean de Gisors, from 1188–1220; Edouard de Bar, 1307–36; Nicolas Flamel, 1398–1418; René d'Anjou, 1418–80; Sandro Filpespi (otherwise known as Boticelli), 1483–1510; Leonardo da

Vinci, 1510–19; Johann Valentin Andrea, 1637–54; Isaac Newton, 1691–1727; Charles Nodier, 1801–44; Claude Debussy, 1885–1918 and, finally, Jean Cocteau, 1918–(date unknown).[25]

RENÉ D'ANJOU AND THE SACRED BLOODLINE

René d'Anjou, who was named as the grand master of the Priory of Sion between 1418 and 1480, had a profound influence on the development of Europe's cultural heritage. René, along with his distant relative, Earl William St Clair[26] of Roslin, was one of the major figures whose work helped to fuel the explosion of cultural and intellectual development that we call the Rennaissance. René was fascinated by the concept of knightly chivalry, obsessed with Arthurian legend, and had a strong pre-occupation with the search for the Holy Grail. From time to time he staged some highly colourful events known as *pas d'armes* which were a strange blend of chivalric tourney and masque in which knights not only indulged in the joust but also performed in a form of courtly drama or play. His most famous *pas d'armes* was called by the evocative title of the '*pas d'armes* of the shepherdess', an idyllic *mélange* of Arcadian romantic themes, chivalric Arthurian pageantry and the mysteries of the Grail quest. One motif which was extremely rich in symbolic and allegorical references was the theme of an underground spiritual stream. To René it encompassed the entire esoteric tradition of Pythagorean, Gnostic, Hermetic and Cabalistic thought. According to the Secret Dossiers it also had a deeper and more hidden meaning; the underground stream, in this context, did not merely convey a general body of esoteric teaching but, more particularly, specific factual information, such as a secret of some description, which was transmitted in this hidden manner from one generation to another. It is also implied that the underground stream might refer to an unacknowledged, subterranean bloodline descending through the centuries.[27]

It was from ideas such as this, supported by evidence largely derived from the Secret Dossiers and the so-called Priory documents, that the authors of *The Holy Blood and the Holy Grail* justified what was to become the most controversial theme in the book. Described by the devout as blasphemous, and by non-Christians as highly unlikely, it was by its very nature incapable of absolute and incontrovertible proof. The claim was that, despite the evidence of the Scriptures and the teachings of all the Christian churches, Jesus was married and had founded not merely a family but a dynasty which was still identifiable in the 20th century. One of the supporting arguments they used, in addition to all the other evidence, was based on a phonetic variant of a term for the Grail that occurs in some of the earlier Grail romances, namely Sangraal. In a later version by Mallory this undergoes a subtle variation to Sangreal which the authors then split into two words 'Sang Real',[28] the French for royal blood. They reinforced their argument by citing the *Grail Romances* by Wolfram von Eschenbach, who repeatedly referred to 'a Grail family'. Developing this and bringing it up to date they identified the person who, in their opinion, was not only a principal personality involved in the modern Priory of Sion, but a probable descendant of Jesus himself. They named, among others, an unlikely candidate for a true descendant of Jesus. This was a certain Pierre Plantard,[29] or as he himself prefers to be known, Pierre Plantard de St Clair.

PART

II

Nearer to the Truth?

3

Action and Reaction

The idea of direct hereditary descent from Jesus provoked an uproar among Christian authorities of all denominations; among the general public of the English-speaking world it caused a sensation. Despite the fact that the authors had peppered their text with caveats, disclaimers and cautionary warnings about the validity of the Secret Dossiers and the Priory documents as sources, a vast swathe of the readership came to believe that the Priory of Sion had as much authenticity as the police or the fire brigade, for they perceived the book *The Holy Blood and the Holy Grail* as a form of modern day 'Holy Writ'.

Prior to *The Holy Blood and the Holy Grail,* many works had been published in France on subjects related to the mystery of Rennes-le-Château. The series of books, articles, essays and documentaries in the English language that followed Baigent, Leigh and Lincoln's *magnum opus* turned this substantial literary stream into a worldwide flood of verbiage. The works ranged from the pseudo-scholarly to the downright ridiculous, all based more or less on the total acceptance that the research done for *The Holy Blood and the Holy Grail* was based upon incontrovertible fact. But all was not what it seemed, and with the massive publicity that attended the publication of a work entitled *The Tomb of God*,[1] the balloon went up with a vengeance.

The Tomb of God, by Richard Andrews and Paul Schellenberger, caused a sensation for it claimed that the body of Jesus had not been assumed into heaven as Church teaching has insisted for nearly 2,000 years, but had been disinterred from a grave in Jerusalem and reburied on a mountainside near Rennes-le-Château. Shortly after publication, dispute over this controversial concept increased enormously as the result of a BBC documentary in the 'Timewatch' series, entitled *The History of a Mystery*.

This documentary refuted the claims upon which *The Tomb of God* was based and was highly critical of earlier research. The allegations made by Bill Cram, the producer, which are relevant to the mystery of Rennes-le-Château, can be summarized as follows:

1   That the coded documents that were published as the work of
      Antoine Bigou, later discovered by Saunière during the
      restoration of the church, were modern forgeries.
2   That these documents were forged by a French aristocrat, the
      Marquis Philippe de Cherisey, a known associate of Pierre
      Plantard de St Clair. Knowledge of their true origin had been
      widespread in France since 1971, when Gérard de Sède had
      quarrelled with Plantard and de Cherisey over financial matters
      and de Cherisey had admitted being the author of the so-called
      coded documents.
3   That Pierre Plantard de St Clair was not the doyen of the
      Resistance he claims to be, but a man with extreme right-wing
      views whose so-called Resistance newspaper was published not
      against the wishes of the German Government of Occupation of
      France, but *with* their tacit approval.
4   That Pierre Plantard, which is his true name, received no special
      letter of commendation from General de Gaulle for his supposed

role in returning de Gaulle to power in 1958, but only a nationally distributed letter received by a large number of French citizens at that time.

5   That Pierre Plantard had a conviction recorded against him for crimes of deception.

6   That the Secret Dossiers and the so-called Priory documents were highly scholarly and intellectually astute modern fabrications which blend a profound knowledge of history with outright fantasy. The authors of these scholarly frauds were Pierre Plantard and Philippe de Cherisey.

7   The programme checked the records at the Louvre and showed beyond doubt that the priest Saunière did *not* purchase copies of the paintings by Teniers and Poussin from there, as claimed in *The Holy Blood and the Holy Grail.*

The disclosures made in the 'Timewatch' programme make it plain that de Séde knew that the documents were forged, either before his first interviews with Lincoln or very soon thereafter. Lincoln began his investigations in 1970 and continued his research for a further ten years, apparently unaware of the coded documents' true origins or of the fraudulent nature of the Secret Dossiers

BÉRENGER SAUNIÈRE

Paris in the late 1800s was a hotbed of esoteric speculation, quasi-masonic and chivalric societies, from which sprang countless new esoteric Orders. It was into this maelstrom of speculation and intrigue that the Abbé Bérenger Saunière was despatched by his bishop at Carcassonne after his discovery of an unspecified secret in the church at Rennes-le-Château. It was suggested that Saunière purchased copies of three paintings at the Louvre in Paris during his first visit there. The producers of the 'Timewatch' programme discovered that there was no record of this; the nearest recorded sale of Poussin's *Les Bergers d'Arcadie* is almost ten years too late. It is also claimed that no records exist of his visits to St Sulpice. The question that should be asked here, however, is would such a visit have been recorded considering the potentially explosive and secretive nature of his business?

In the light of the serious allegations made about the forgery of the coded documents and the fabrication of the Secret Dossiers by de Cherisey and Plantard, it is appropriate to review the story of Saunière.

It is possible to establish, beyond all reasonable doubt, that at the time of his induction as parish priest of Rennes-le-Château he was incredibly poor and lived a very simple life. After making a mysterious discovery he was despatched to Paris on the instructions of the Bishop of Carcassonne and spent some time there. After his return to Rennes-le-Château he spent vast sums of money, over 200,000 gold francs, the source of which has never been satisfactorily explained. For many years he lived in comparative luxury and received several important visitors, including Emma Calvé. After refusing to disclose the source of his wealth, he was suspended by the Vatican and not reinstated until 1915. His housekeeper, Marie Denarnaud, survived him by many years, and lived a comfortable life in circumstances of considerable affluence until the post-war issue of a new currency in France in 1946. She lived for a further seven years on the proceeds of the sale of the Villa Bethania, and spoke to Mr Noel Corbu of a secret that would make him both rich and powerful.

It is possible to come to some provisional conclusions. Firstly, Saunière did discover something that directly or indirectly brought him great wealth and a reasonable degree of protection from authority. In the light of his lifestyle and that of Marie Denarnaud, and her comments to Corbu, we can speculate that the discovery had two separate but related aspects. First, it was treasure that could be readily converted to coin of the realm without arousing suspicion; second, it pertained to some form of information of a potentially explosive nature which brought its possessor power as well as riches. It is reasonable to speculate that this may have been some documentary source attesting to the descendants of Jesus and Mary Magdalene or, perhaps, an ancient Cathar copy of *The Gospel of Love* – the original initiatory and heretical Gospel of St John.

Most of the authors who have written works touching on the mystery have followed the well-beaten path laid down by Baigent, Leigh and Lincoln. Certainly English language works on this subject seem to all be variations of the theme established by *The Holy Blood and the Holy Grail*. Nearly all accept without question the validity of the Priory of Sion, the authenticity of the Priory documents and Secret Dossiers and treat Saunière's stated contacts with Emma Calvé and members of the Habsburg family as absolute fact. We have to concede that the coded documents, the Priory documents and the Secret Dossiers, are probably clever forgeries. We accept that Saunière had repeated contact with Emma Calvé both in Paris and at Rennes-le-Château but it is less certain that he entertained the French Minister of Culture in his remote hilltop village. However, when we examine the alleged contacts between this rural parish priest and the Habsburgs, the senior ruling family in Europe, we are on much shakier ground.

Saunière's contacts among Parisian esoteric society may well be a highly sanitized and somewhat edited version of the truth. His known royalist and right-wing political views may yet hold the key to this particular mystery. A respected colleague, Guy Patton, who has earned a well-justified reputation for meticulous research, has been investigating Saunière's movements in esoteric and masonic circles for some time. He is soon to publish a work which will detail Saunière's movements and contacts among right-wing masonic lodges in France and elsewhere in Europe. One further puzzling matter that may well be explained is the decidedly odd nature of Saunière's 'pre-funerary ritual'. Masonic ritual derived from some of the lodges he visited may explain the ceremony wherein his corpse was seated, enfolded in a robe decorated with golden tassels which were plucked one-by-one by the unnamed mourners who attended this final rite.

There was another bizarre twist to this convoluted story that demanded investigation, a line of inquiry that has stimulated us to re-examine the authentic and verifiable record of the activities of the Cathars and the Knights Templar in the vicinity of Rennes-le-Château. This new investigation started almost by accident, when one of us, Tim, lectured on the mystical carvings of Rosslyn Chapel to a meeting of the Saunière Society in London in 1994. After that lecture, he heard an incredible story which, if it proved to have any degree of validity, would tend to not merely support but to strengthen and expand the controversial idea of direct descent from Jesus and other important figures of his time.

4

Our First Glimpse of the 'Rex Deus' Tradition

The Saunière Society was founded in England by Derek Burton in the late 1980s as a result of the burgeoning interest in Rennes-le-Château and Bérenger Saunière. The newsletters published by the Society cover a wide range of issues directly or indirectly connected to the mystery, such as medieval esotericism, the esoteric revival in Paris in the late 19th century, the Cathars and, above all, the Knights Templar and those of their traditions that survived their suppression.

Tim Wallace-Murphy was invited to talk to a meeting of the Saunière Society about Rosslyn Chapel, near Edinburgh in Scotland. The chapel was built by Earl William St Clair, the third St Clair Jarl[1] of the Orkneys, as a memorial to the beliefs and traditions of the Templar Order. Earl William was aware that books and even their authors could be burnt for heresy, so he designed the chapel as a coded library-in-stone, in the certain knowledge that it would last until such time that its secrets should be understood by future generations. Tim was to share the platform with Richard Leigh, who was to speak on the mystery of Rennes-le-Château.

Sadly Richard Leigh was unable to attend, so at short notice the format of the meeting was changed. Tim presented an illustrated lecture on Rosslyn Chapel and the rest of the meeting was devoted to a brainstorming session on esoterics in general and the themes of *The Holy Blood and the Holy Grail* in particular. The interchange of views and information that took place in the stimulating atmosphere created by the participants' varying perspectives and levels of knowledge resulted in a very productive afternoon. During the discussions Tim mentioned that he hoped to travel to Jerusalem with the intention of exploring some of the excavations under the Temple Mount if permission could be obtained. At the end of the meeting he was approached by a middle-aged man who introduced himself as Michael, and who proceeded to describe and explain the meaning of certain symbols that Tim might see under the Temple Mount. When Tim asked where this information came from, Michael replied, rather mysteriously, 'It is part of the secret traditions of my family for the last 2,000 years.' Highly intrigued, Tim questioned him further, but due to time restraints Michael was only able to give a very brief synopsis of the story.

He began by stating that the publication of the idea that Jesus may have founded a dynasty had been a matter of great relief to him, for he was a member of a group of families who claimed descent from the Davidic and Hasmonean royal families of biblical Israel, or from the 24 High Priests of the Temple in Jerusalem at the time of Jesus. The families passed down this information from father to selected son or daughter, each father choosing either the eldest child or the most spiritually gifted as the recipient of the secret. Apparently the genealogies of the early generations of these families had been inscribed on the walls of underground rooms below the Temple in Jerusalem. After the fall of Jerusalem and the destruction of the Temple, the surviving families fled but kept the tradition alive. Each family member privy to the secret was sworn to secrecy; they had to swear that if they disclosed the family traditions to outsiders 'may my heart be torn out or may my throat be cut' – hence Michael's earlier fears. After the publication of *The Holy Blood and the Holy Grail*, which had brought the idea of direct descent from families in biblical Israel into the public domain with a vengeance, he felt safe in disclosing the bones of the family tradition. The families also had the obligation to keep accurate genealogies from the time of the fall of the Temple. Michael claimed that they frequently inter-married to preserve the bloodlines and increase the likelihood of the continuity of the tradition. The families were known amongst themselves as *Rex Deus*.

FURTHER INVESTIGATION

Tim was only too aware that this story was impossible to prove. Even if it were true, there would still be enormous gaps in continuity. During Roman times there might be records that could be used as verification if, and only if, the families concerned were of sufficient notability or notoriety. However, although documentary record keeping had a long history in the Near East, with some Egyptian and Sumerian records going back for several centuries BCE, effective forms of bureaucracy did not develop in Western Europe until the 10th and 11th centuries. The systematic keeping of meticulous records developed first in France and Italy, where it was well-established by the 10th century, spread to Spain, the Low Countries and then to the German states. It only spread to England, albeit imperfectly, after 1066 and the invasion of William the Conqueror. Genealogy can, therefore, only be accurately studied in most of Western Europe from the 10th century onwards. It is unreliable or impossible from the time of the fall of the Roman Empire until then. The one possible exception to this, which is of very variable quality, lies in the records of the self-appointed great and good of the Church. Even the ecclesiastical record, however, is flawed by well-intentioned hagiography of certain of its leading figures and by the understandable temptation of Church historians to fill gaps in the record with a sort of 'holy fiction' in their sincere, if misguided, attempts to prove continuity of Church authority from the time of St Peter to their own.

While Michael's story seemed incredible, he was rational, sane and totally sincere, and Tim was fascinated by it. When Michael mentioned that according to the family sagas he was a direct descendent of Hughes de Payen, who was the co-founder of the Knights Templar and a relative by marriage to the St Clairs of Roslin and the Dukes of Normandy, Tim decided to investigate the matter further. Some months later, with a colleague present for verification and to assist in the questioning, Tim and Michael met once again. In an eight-hour session the two sceptical students of history, who each had a good working knowledge of medieval and biblical times, sat entranced as Michael recounted the following story.

When his father first broached the subject of Rex Deus, Michael was in his mid-teens and was therefore capable of understanding the broader terms of the story he was to hear and, more importantly, was of an age when an oath of secrecy would have some meaning. After taking the oath he heard, for the very first time, the story that we are now about to tell. He was informed that appropriate documentation in the form of family genealogies was hidden in a secret drawer in an old family bureau and that after his father's death it would be Michael's sacred duty to keep the genealogies up to date and to pass on the secret to the most suitable of his children. He was also to prepare himself and his chosen child to act in collaboration with other members of the Rex Deus families when asked to do so. His obedience to their requests was to be total and unquestioning. All this under an oath of secrecy, within which the penalty for transgression would be death. This was an enormous burden to lay on the shoulders of one so young. Sadly, Michael's father died suddenly some years later and by the time he returned to the family home he found that the bureau and all it contained had been appropriated by a brother. Bound by his oath of secrecy, he could never explain why he wanted it back and, despite his best efforts, he has not seen that piece of furniture nor its contents from that day to this and he has reason to believe that his brother sold the bureau, an antique of some value, blissfully unaware of its contents. He could not therefore recount the story in its entirety and there would be gaps and areas of imprecision within it as he could only impart the verbal account he had received from his father some 40 years before, from memory. The story begins in biblical Israel towards the end of the reign of Herod the Great.

THE BEGINNINGS OF REX DEUS

For some considerable time before the birth of Jesus, the Temple in Jerusalem had maintained two separate boarding schools, one for boys and one for girls, which were administered and taught at by the High Priests. The male graduates were destined to become priests at the Temple, rabbis or leading members of the community. All pupils at these schools were drawn from important families of proven Levitic descent. Priesthood in ancient Judaism was a hereditary function and all priests were of the tribe of Levi, whose members were allowed to marry outside the tribe with the exception of one family group, the Cohens. They were bound by law and custom to marry others from the same family, and it was from their ranks that all the High Priests were drawn. The 24 High Priests of the Herodian Temple in Jerusalem were the apex of the hierarchy of the Jewish religion. They alone had the supreme responsibility and privilege of being allowed to enter into the Holy of Holies, the inner sanctum of the Temple, and on ceremonial occasions they would stand in ascending order of rank on the Temple steps. These men were, for ritual purposes, known by the names accorded to their rank; for example there was a Melchizedek, a Michael and a Gabriel, all resounding names drawn from the archangels, angels and pivotal figures from the religious history of the Jews.

The traditions of these schools seem strange. The High Priests were not only responsible for the instruction of their highborn pupils but, when the young girls attained childbearing age, for their impregnation as well. The fate of the children of such unions is central to the story. The pregnant girls would be found suitable husbands among the highborn of Israel, which apparently contradicted Jewish customs of the time. These marriages were arranged on one inviolable condition, that the child born of the union with the priest would, at the age of seven, be returned to the appropriate Temple School for education. In this manner the hereditary principle of the royal priesthood was ensured and the bloodlines were kept pure.

One pupil at the girls' school was Miriam, or Mary as she is known to history, the daughter of an earlier pupil named Anne. Mary was impregnated by the High Priest known as the Gabriel and, when her pregnancy was confirmed, a marriage was arranged for her. She rejected the first man chosen to be her husband, and so another suitable candidate had to be selected by lot from among the appropriate families. This was a young man of Davidic descent, Joseph of Tyre, whose ancestor was Hiram, King of Tyre, known to masonic legend as Hiram Abif; this wealthy young man is known to us as St Joseph. The child of the union was Jesus who, after spending the years of his early childhood in Egypt, returned to Jerusalem and in his turn attended the Temple School.

THE REX DEUS DIASPORA

There are not only gaps in continuity in the historical record, but in Michael's story too. He moved abruptly from his account of events at the time of Jesus to sometime in the 4th century CE. It was then that circumstances were deemed safe enough for members of the Rex Deus families to return to Jerusalem and rebury the body of the Messiah in the one place no one would ever dream of looking for it, the Temple Mount[2] itself, which was deemed inviolable. According to Jewish custom it was never to be defiled by use as a place of burial. One can readily understand the illusion of safety brought about by the use of this site for the safekeeping of the body of the Messiah. What is more difficult to accept is the motivation that would have impelled families who sprang from the most orthodox branch of Judaism to contravene the prohibition of burial on the Temple Mount.

After the 4th century, the Rex Deus families continued to live in Western Europe. Their traditions dictate that they would at all times outwardly profess to follow the prevailing religion of the time and the culture in which they lived, but secretly they are bound by oath to follow 'the true way'. Quietly and sincerely Michael stated that he was a descendant of Hughes de Payen, and that as such and due to inter-marriage his family had until recently been the hereditary holders of a royal appointment within the United Kingdom. The mention of Hughes de Payen had brought to mind the mystery surrounding the foundation of the Knights Templar which had been further complicated by allusion in *The Holy Blood and the Holy Grail* to the clandestine activities of the Priory of Sion.

THE REX DEUS 'HYPOTHESIS'

Michael mentioned Rex Deus connections with certain important families in Byzantium, the successor to the eastern Roman Empire founded by Constantine the Great in 330 CE. He also spoke at length of the symbolism employed by this secretive group and stressed that their heraldic colours were green and gold. The discussion lasted for many hours and Michael answered all the questions with unfailing courtesy and honesty. Eventually Tim drove him home, a journey that took a couple of hours, and on the return journey he began to reflect on the major points raised by Michael's story. Used and analyzed with precision they might lead to indications within the historical record which could clarify some enigmas, such as those surrounding the foundation of the Knights Templar. The publication of these ideas should stimulate a further in-depth study of the life, times and culture of biblical Israel at the time of Jesus, but this time from a radically different perspective. So far such comments that have been published on these particular issues have always been grossly distorted according to the religious bias of the commentator. The best possible scenario would be to find sufficient confirmation to show that the families mentioned by Michael have repeatedly acted in concert with each other in order to obtain common objectives at different periods of history. This would hopefully lead to the identification of other families within the group, wherein archival evidence can be used to clarify matters of descent and marriage.

The earliest years covered by Michael's story, that of descent from the High Priests of Israel, would be the most difficult of all to authenticate – or so Tim thought. He knew from earlier study that the Church, in establishing the official canon of the Scriptures, had suppressed, distorted or destroyed the vast majority of early documents that cast doubt upon their highly tendentious version of events.[3] He was convinced from the beginning that no credible documentation would ever be found that would prove the existence of a Temple School for boys, much less link Mary the mother of Jesus to a similar school for girls. He also had grave doubts about the possibility of finding evidence that would convince either the general public or the devout Christian that Jesus was married. He could not have been more wrong.

5

Biblical Israel at the Time of Jesus

Most people in the Christian world derive what little knowledge they have of biblical Israel at the time of Jesus from the New Testament. Yet as a source of information about the day to day customs in Israel in this era, the New Testament is highly flawed. The vast majority of the documents included within the official canon, the four Gospels, the Acts of the Apostles, the Revelation and many of the Epistles, were not written by eyewitnesses (as is generally supposed), but by authors working from second-hand sources many years after the events they describe.[1] Most of the writers concerned were almost certainly Gentiles who wrote in Greek, not Hebrew or Aramaic, and who had little or no understanding of Jewish law, custom or lifestyle. The only author whose work is included in the New Testament who is unarguably Jewish by race and belief is St Paul.[2] As we will show later, he is probably the most unreliable source in the entire canon.[3]

Many of the disputes that have arisen over the validity of the Gospel accounts focus solely on the numerous contradictions that can be found between all four Scriptures. Biblical scholars have long been aware of the problems of authorship and the differences of culture that exist between the authors and the events they describe. Even the term 'gospel truth' has been misleading, in that the general public, be they believing Christian or not, seem blissfully unaware that the heavy hand of Holy Mother the Church has distorted and censored these Scriptures from the beginning. This malign influence is not merely manifest in matters of interpretation but in the actual composition of the Scriptures themselves.

Is the New Testament, moderated by information gleaned from two important discoveries in the 1940s (the Dead Sea Scrolls and the Nag Hammadi Library), all we have to go on? Fortunately the answer is no. Not only can we build on the work of more general historians and archaeologists to flesh out our somewhat skeletal picture, but we can also include a large body of documents of great antiquity, the majority of which are of earlier provenance than the Gospels. These include the works of Philo of Alexandria, who died about 50 CE, and the 1st-century Jewish historian Josephus. According to Josephus a certain Jesus bar Levi was executed in Jerusalem for causing insurrection against Rome. This man was a minor prince of the House of David and his name bar Levi means 'son of the priest'. Was this Jesus the Nazarene?

There were also some scriptural works which were ruthlessly excluded from the official canon of the Church as they told a story that was completely at variance with the dogma and beliefs that arose from the teaching of St Paul. Yet for many years these documents were accepted as authentic and were only rejected and suppressed with the establishment of the official canon at the end of the 4th century. Among them is one entitled *The Gospel of the Birth of Mary*,[4] frequently cited by St Jerome, an early 4th-century theologian, and also quoted by Epiphanius, Bishop of Salamis, and another early theologian, Austin. A better-known document is *The Protoevangelion of James*,[5] whose authorship is ascribed to James the Just, the brother of Jesus and the first 'Bishop' of Jerusalem, and is one of the few early documents which was actually written in Hebrew. One gospel, which appears to have been composed in Greek, is St Thomas' *Gospel of the Infancy of Jesus*,[6] which some authorities believe may have been originally connected with the

Gospel of the Birth of Mary. Another *Gospel of the Infancy of Jesus Christ*,[7] usually referred to as the *First Gospel of the Infancy*, was reputedly used by the Prophet Mohammed. As with the canonical Gospels, the Acts of the Apostles and the Epistles which were included in the official canon, all these documents need to be assessed dispassionately and without religious bias. Used judiciously these sources can provide parts of the complex jigsaw puzzle which create a clearer picture of the theocratic culture within which Jesus lived.

JEWISH LAW AND CUSTOM

One of the major problems of the Christian approach to biblical history at the time of Jesus is that, while the Gospels acknowledge that Jesus was born a Jew, they tell the Christian, gentile public little or nothing about the customs of the Jewish people at that time. Israel was a theocratic state where the Torah had been adopted as the system of law for a very long time. The Law of God, as given to Moses, was not merely God's Law but also the law of the state; its 613 strictures were binding on all Jews in Israel and the Diaspora. Under the Law, Jewish men were expected to marry and have children in obedience to God's instruction 'to go forth and multiply'. Few exceptions to this are recorded, although it would be reasonable to assume that John the Baptist and the other 'holy eccentrics' who inhabited the area between Gennesaret and the Dead Sea may have been among them.[8] All rabbis, *without exception*, were expected to be married and to father families.

When we study Jewish custom at this time we find that the traditional priestly style preserved the names of Old Testament archangels within their governing structure. Laurence Gardner, the author of *The Bloodline of the Holy Grail* who cites the biblical scholar Barbara Thiering as his source, claims that the Zadok priest was called after the Archangel Michael and that the Abiathar priest was named after the Angel Gabriel.[9] The Angel Gabriel is called in the scriptures 'the

Messenger Angel' and the title 'the Gabriel' could be applied to any High Priest chosen to deliver an important message. The Gabriel mentioned in 'the Annunciation' was the High Priest deputed to sire a Messiah, who was sent to make his 'announcement' to Elizabeth, the mother of John the Baptist, and Miriam known as Mary, the mother of Jesus. In this manner the descent of the Messiah was assured as being of the line of David and of the Aaronic line of high priests. This system of priestly reference can also be found in *The Book of Enoch*,[10] and the precise order of ranking of the priests in the angelic sense that obtained during the Gospel era is detailed in the Dead Sea Scrolls document known as the War Scroll.

THE BIRTH OF JESUS

In *The Gospel of the Birth of Mary* we found confirmation that Mary, the mother of Jesus, was educated at a Temple School:

> The blessed and ever glorious Virgin Mary, sprung from the
> race and family of David, was born in the city of Nazareth,
> and educated at Jerusalem, in the Temple of the Lord.[11]

Later in the same Gospel we read that when Mary arrived at her 14th year, like all of the virgins who had public settlements in the Temple who had reached this age, she should return home and 'as they were now of a proper maturity, should, according to the custom of their country, endeavour to be married'.[12] The Gospel goes on to recount that Joseph, of the House and family of David, returned to his own city of Bethlehem after his betrothal to Mary.[13] In *The Protoevangelion of James* we find that 'when her sixth month had come, Joseph returned ... and entering into the house, found the virgin grown big'.[14] The Christian version of what happened next is well-known and largely founded on the following passage:

Now when Jesus was born in Bethlehem of Judea
in the days of Herod the king, behold,
There came wise men from the east to Jerusalem,
Saying, where is he that is born King of the Jews?
For we have seen his star in the east,
and are come to worship him.[15]

Few of the millions of children who have thrilled to the Christmas story founded on the Gospel accounts, fewer still of the priests, pastors and preachers who tell it with such love and reverence, realize that within it lies another that contradicts much of what is now accepted orthodoxy. Now, as in the past, mainstream churches find the concept of spiritual initiation, astrology or the practice of magic an abomination. Yet at the very beginning of the Christian experience this so-called abomination is recorded for all time; initiates being praised and used to reinforce the cosmic nature of the birth of the innocent, sleeping infant in the Bethlehem manger. These three wise men from the East were believed to be initiates of one of the oldest orders in the world, the Magi of Persia, who received foreknowledge of this momentous birth by virtue of their spiritual insight. They travelled an immense distance for that time, following a star that moved steadily until it came to rest over a stable in a small Judean town. They made obeisance to the child in the manger, humbling themselves before the one they knew was the 'King of the Jews', issued a warning about Herod's unseemly interest and departed into the spiritual mists of obscurity whence they came. The Gospel accounts continue with the story of Herod's slaughter of the innocents and the Holy Family's flight to Egypt.[16] The Holy Family is traditionally described as consisting of the Virgin Mary, her consort Joseph and Jesus, our Divine Saviour. Is there any truth behind this treasured and magical piece of mythology?

Two of the Gospels, Matthew and Luke, agree that Jesus was born in Bethlehem, of a virgin, and was of the line of David.[17] However, the fourth Gospel gives no account of the nativity whatsoever, and casts considerable uncertainty on the Bethlehem story. In the Gospel of John, we discover that doubt is cast upon Jesus' claim to be the Messiah because his place of birth is said to be Galilee, not Bethlehem.[18] As for the most favoured story of them all, that of the three wise men, according to the internationally renowned Dead Sea Scrolls' scholar Hugh Schonfield, this legend, which was far from new, was first used in the New Testament era not about the birth of Jesus, but about the birth of his cousin, John the Baptist.[19] The Mandaeans of Iraq, who claim to follow John's teaching to this day, preserve the story in its original 'biblical' context.

When we examine the circumstances surrounding the 'flight of the Holy family to Egypt' to avoid 'Herod's slaughter of the innocents' we discover further serious discrepancies. While Herod was a notoriously bloodthirsty king, scholars have found that there is no documentary evidence from that period (other than the Gospels) which mentions his slaughter of anyone outside his own family and political circle. This so-called 'event' is pious fiction. Jesus and his parents probably did spend some years in Egypt prior to his attendance at the Temple School in Jerusalem, but for reasons which the Church would never dare to acknowledge. One clarification of this enigma can be found in the most common title given to Jesus, that of Jesus of Nazareth. At the time of his birth the village of Nazareth simply did not exist and he should be more correctly referred to as Jesus the Nazarene,[20] a sect that was an offshoot of the Essenes who had their roots among the Therapeutae, a far older esoteric healing sect who inhabited part of the Nile Delta near Alexandria. If Jesus and his parents did go to Egypt, and there is no evidence to contradict that, it would have been to receive esoteric religious instruction from them. It is highly likely that the Essenes and Therapeutae would have been only too well-aware of the principle enunciated by the Jesuits some 1,500 years later, 'give me a child until the age of seven and he shall be mine for life'.

THE VIRGIN BIRTH

Central to Christian doctrine is the belief that Mary, the mother of Jesus, was a virgin.[21] This patently contradictory idea is a concept that is totally foreign to Judaic religious belief, custom and practice. Far from expecting that their hoped-for Messiah would be 'a god' born of a virgin, they prayed for a Messiah who would be a human being. Justin Martyr (who died around AD 165) wrote 'if a man appears to be the Messiah he must be a man of solely human birth'.[22] In the eyes of devout and orthodox Jews of that period, and this must include Jews such as Joseph, Jesus and his brother James the Just, the concept of a human being 'divine' or a 'resurrecting god' born of a virgin was a completely alien and pagan notion. It relates more to the Babylonian traditions of Ishtar and Tammuz which, like the cults of Osiris, Dionysus and Zoroaster, claimed that their leading figures had been fathered by a god, with a human and virgin mother. This concept was also common in the Graeco-Roman world of myths and mystery cults, such as that of Mithras, so beloved of the Roman legionaries.

In the Judaic Scriptures, which most Jews admit consist of the Law and some history mixed with myth and legend, very few references are made to births that take place as a result of divine intervention. There was Isaac, the son born to the 90-year-old Sarah and her 100-year-old spouse Abraham,[23] the twin sons Esau and Jacob born to Rebekah,[24] who was supposedly sterile, and the birth of Samson.[25] In no case is Almighty God alleged to be the father, a concept which to any orthodox Jew would be viewed as blasphemous in the extreme. In the New Testament there is another birth which is ascribed to the actions of God. The priest Zechariah is reported to have had a vision that he and his wife Elizabeth, who is well past childbearing age, will have a son who will be 'the salvation of Israel'.[26] That son was John the Baptist.

Christians, Protestant and Catholic, not only believe that Jesus' birth came about by divine intervention, but that he was actually fathered by God and born of a virgin, a pagan concept often refuted at great cost by those devout men who accepted without question that Jesus' teaching was divinely inspired. Nestorius, who was appointed patriarch of Constantinople in 428 CE, was declared a heretic and banished to Edessa for daring to say that the argument as to whether Jesus was 'God' or 'Son of God' was completely irrelevant, for it was obvious that Jesus was a man, born quite normally of a father and a mother.[27]

Another confusion arising from Church teaching is the assumption that if Jesus is God then he *must* have been born of a virgin. According to a leading Catholic theologian, this is just not true. Cardinal Ratzinger, the head of the Congregation for the Doctrine of the Faith – the modern heir to the Inquisition – has stated that 'the doctrine of Jesus' divinity would not be violated if Jesus had been the product of a normal human marriage. For the divine sonship that faith speaks of is not a biological, but an ontological, fact; it is not an event in time, but in God's eternity'[28] – an explanation which, while it may satisfy theologians, would only serve to completely confuse the ordinary Christian. Furthermore it begs the question; how did this pagan mythology accumulate around the person of Jesus?

CHRISTIANITY'S ADOPTION OF PAGAN MYTH

Ancient historians, biographers and scriptural writers would colour events surrounding their central characters in a manner that would approximate to their own beliefs rather than to historical fact. They credited their heroes with sentiments, words and deeds which may well have been completely alien to them. In order to enhance the sense of magic that inevitably surrounds figures of importance in either the political or the spiritual realms, well-established mythology from existing belief structures would be seized upon and transferred without hesitation. For example, the parallels between Mithraism and Christianity are uncomfortably close. Mithraic tradition prophesied apocalyptic events, a judgement day, the resurrection of the body and a second coming of their god Mithras. Furthermore, Mithras was allegedly born in a grotto and attended by shepherds bearing gifts. This form of pious fiction distorted not only the entire historical era covered by the New Testament, but a significant part of the Christian history that followed.

The Gospels were distorted by the belief system that had arisen since the crucifixion and, paradoxically, are often in direct contradiction with other traditions and teachings that developed later. In the story of Jesus as a young man in the Temple, it is apparent that his parents do not understand what he means when he speaks of his 'heavenly father', despite the fact that this flatly contradicts the whole concept of the Annunciation. If Mary was truly aware that she had been impregnated by Almighty God then she should have known who Jesus' heavenly father really was.[29] This episode, while it proves nothing substantial about Jesus' life, does indicate that there may be considerable substance in the Rex Deus legend that Jesus was educated at a Temple School. It smacks very strongly of the traditional concept of Jewish young men being treated as equals by the rabbis and priests who teach them the application of Talmudic logic in order to bring about understanding of the Holy Scriptures.

The Jews of biblical Israel, if faced with the concept that Jesus was divine would, like Jews throughout the ages, condemn it as the ultimate blasphemy. As we shall see, this idea originated some 10 or 15 years after the crucifixion, from the fertile mind of an opportunist of highly dubious character. If we read all the words of Jesus in the New Testament, nowhere will we find any claim by him that he was divine. The title accorded to him by Christians, that of a 'Son of God', had a specific esoteric meaning and implied a status that was held to be attainable by those who followed his teaching. Jesus[30] himself never claimed this title, referring to himself throughout as the 'Son of Man'. The modern writer and scholar, A N Wilson, states that:

I find it impossible to believe that a first-century Galilean holy man had at any time of his life believed himself to be the Second Person of the Trinity. It was such an inherently improbable thing for a monotheistic Jew to believe.[31]

For Jesus to believe himself divine and co-equal with God the Father was not merely 'inherently improbable' but a blasphemy that no devout Jew of that time could possibly contemplate.

There is another blasphemous statement that is attributed to Jesus in the Gospel accounts of his life and which is celebrated daily in Christian ritual. To understand the context for this provocative statement we need to remember the rigidity with which the Law on food was applied by all devout Jews. The major dispute between the people who actually walked and talked with Jesus and the aberrant 'apostle' Paul arose over the dietary laws. James the brother of Jesus, the head of the Church in Jerusalem, insisted that all converts must keep the Law on circumcision and diet. Is it, therefore, even remotely conceivable that an orthodox Jewish teacher such as Jesus would have invited his followers, even in allegorical or spiritualized terms, to breach the Law upon which the Holy Covenant with God was based? Yet this is precisely what both Christian teaching and the words of the Gospel claim that Jesus did. The Catholic Mass and all forms of Protestant Communion service invite their communicants to partake of the bread and wine which is believed to symbolize the body and blood of Jesus. Had Jesus had the temerity to suggest to sincere and devout Jews that they drink blood, he would have been stoned to death as a blasphemer. So where did this concept come from?

Ritual meals of bread and wine were a natural and integral part of many religious groups who met in fellowship. They are part and parcel of Jewish family celebration, they were an essential part of the ritual of the Essenes, and they also obtained widespread usage among the mystery cults of Classical Greece. The Christian consumption of bread and wine as an allegory for body and blood has its roots in paganism.[32] In the Mithraic form of communion, Mithras himself is quoted as saying 'He who shall not eat of my body nor drink of my blood so that he may be one with me ... shall not be saved'. Such a concept would be welcome in the pagan world where symbolic union with God was considered desirable rather than blasphemous.

THE MARRIAGE OF JESUS

In re-evaluating the story of Jesus as described in the New Testament, we must not only learn to strip away the mythology and hagiography that has been woven into the story, but also learn to discern the truths about the life of this remarkable teacher; truths that were not deemed worthy of comment simply because they were common to all Jews of his time. We also need to use our knowledge of Jewish social custom and practice to illuminate the real nature of the relationships between Jesus and certain of his followers. This is particularly important when we explore the contentious issue of whether or not he was married.

We have referred earlier to the fact that in biblical Israel all men, especially rabbis, without exception, were expected to be married and to father families.[33] The Gospels are quite open about the forms of address used by the disciples in their conversations with Jesus. He is repeatedly addressed as a rabbi.[34] Another compelling reason for Jesus to marry is confirmed even by the somewhat doctored accounts of his life in the Gospels, all of which are quite explicit about the matter of his earthly descent. They clearly state that he was the heir to the line of kings descended from David.[35] The heir to the Davidic line was obliged *by law* to marry and to father sons in order to ensure the continuance of the hereditary line of the Royal House of Israel.

Nowhere in the entire corpus of the New Testament is there any statement that Jesus was a single man, that is unmarried. Had this been the case, this total breach of tradition and custom would have been remarked upon, as were the many occasions when his interpretation of the Law appeared to be in conflict with traditional Jewish thinking.

Thus, in the era where we least expected to have any chance of finding documentary confirmation of the Rex Deus tradition, both the Gospels and contemporaneous documents contain indications that the tradition is founded upon a highly plausible basis.

6

Jesus, the Essene Teacher of
Righteousness and St Paul,
the First Christian Heretic

Jesus and his family were all members of the Essenes which, contrary
to the views promoted by the Catholic Church, were not just a small
sect occupying the settlement of Qumran. According to the contemporary Jewish historian Josephus, who was at one time a member, the
Essenes were a large religious group that rivalled the Sadducees and
Pharisees in power and influence.[1] The Sadducees were a conservative,
priestly, property-owning group who preached strict adherence to the
letter of the Law and who co-operated fully with the Roman occupiers –
the Israelite equivalent of 'Quislings'.[2] The Pharisees, who have received
an incredibly bad press from Christian commentators, were theologians
who tried to interpret the Law and oral tradition in a liberal manner that
made its observance attainable by ordinary people.[3]

In total contrast to both these groups, who worshipped at the
Temple in Jerusalem, the Essenes were a group of ultra-orthodox Jews
who followed an initiatory path known as 'the Way'. They derived from
an earlier esoteric branch of Judaism known as the Therapeutae, who
mainly resided in the vicinity of Alexandria in Egypt. Within the Essene
movement were many sub-groups, such as the Nazarenes or Nasoreans,
the Zealots and the Sicarii. Respected by King Herod because of their

prophetic abilities,[4] they were staunch believers in the Messianic tradition and devout scriptural scholars who created a vast body of apocalyptic writings,[5] including the documents known as the Dead Sea Scrolls which were discovered in 1948. According to the Catholic Church, these were composed entirely at the Essene settlement of Qumran in the century before Christ. However, the Dead Sea Scrolls scholar Norman Golb claims that this collection of documents was drawn from origins throughout Israel and included a large number of scrolls from the Temple in Jerusalem, and a body of work from the first century CE. Thus the Qumran scrolls are, in part, evidence regarding the widespread nature of the Essene tradition and of the high regard in which the movement was held, even by their theological opponents at the Temple.[6]

THE GOSPELS

Papias, an early Church father who made a collection of the 'esoteric' and 'mythical' traditions of Jesus, reported that the author of Matthew's Gospel had originally collected the sayings of Jesus 'in the Hebrew tongue'. By 390 CE when Jerome was translating the Gospels into Latin, this 'Gospel of Matthew' was still accessible in Hebrew. Jerome admits that he was allowed to copy parts of it by the Nazarenes of Beroes and states that whenever either the evangelist or Jesus quoted from the Old Testament, they followed the original Hebrew text and not the Greek translation or septuagint. He claimed that this version of Matthew's Gospel was known in its time as the *Gospel of the Hebrews*, but never published a complete translation of the work.[7]

Jerome refused to translate it because it contained esoteric passages relating to the Essene mysteries, which he did not regard as suitable material to lay before a Christian congregation.[8] It was obviously an initiation document in true Essene tradition. Since then the original text has either been lost or suppressed. Certain esoteric sections are known only because they have been quoted by some of the early fathers of the Church[9]. Professor Morton Smith describes one extant passage from this work where 'after six days of further preparation, Jesus goes on to instruct the man who has been raised from the dead in the secrets of the "kingdom".'[10]

The Gospels of the New Testament were altered and in part rewritten to bring them into line with emerging Christian dogma based on the teaching of St Paul.[11] This process of aligning the Gospels with Christian teaching distanced them considerably from 'the Way' preached by Jesus – the Essene Teacher of Righteousness. This title was awarded to the supreme initiatory teacher of the Essene Way and there had been many who had earned this over the centuries since the time of Zadok the priest.

One Gospel that is part of the official canon, the Gospel of John, is also regarded in many respects as an initiation document. When we consider the origin and development of this Gospel, we encounter a series of enigmas. On the one hand, it is the only Gospel which appears to have been written by an eyewitness to the events it describes, by somebody who was particularly close to Jesus; on the other, it is accepted by most biblical authorities as the last of the Gospels to appear in written form, which it only did in the early years of the 2nd century. Understandably, this has led to the conclusion that the Gospel of John was written considerably later than the others.[12] It was a further 100 years after its first appearance that the Church began to ascribe its authorship to John, the son of Zebedee; a somewhat belated and doubtful attribution.

One biblical scholar, B Rigaux, whose opinions are now gaining wide acceptance, claimed that this Gospel was the written version of one handed down from master to pupil as part of an oral tradition started by Jesus: a tradition that passed from Jesus to 'the beloved disciple', and from him to his disciples and was never intended for the masses, but only for the initiated.[13] This suggestion that, despite its late appearance in writing, the Gospel of John was in fact the first of the four Gospels, is confirmed by the modern Anglican theologian, Bishop John Robinson.[14] This Gospel's tardy appearance does not indicate late authorship, as has previously been thought, but is a result of its disclosure in oral form to initiates only. The decision to publish it in documentary form can only have been taken after the evangelist's death, judging from evidence contained in the Gospel. No version exists without chapter 21, within which the editors take great pains to disabuse those who have believed that the beloved disciple would never die. Contradicting this 'vulgar misinterpretation' of Jesus' words, the editors claim that the death of the evangelist in no way detracts from the truth.[15] The initiatory nature of the Gospel of John, despite its later amendments and additions, places it squarely in an important stream of the Hebraic–Egyptian Gnostic tradition, namely 'the Way' of the Essenes. Gnosticism was a form of spirituality whereby one gained spiritual knowledge, or Gnosis, as one gained initiation into the secrets of the order.

THE EARLY CHRISTIAN CHURCH

Despite its theological divergence from the initiatory teachings of Jesus, the social structure of the early Christian Church was largely shaped by Essene teaching, tradition and practice,[16] a blend of Hebraic–Egyptian Gnosticism with strong strands of Zoroastrian tradition deriving from the teaching of the early Persian initiate, Zoroaster. The new 'Church' used a handbook known as the *Didache*, or 'the teaching of the Lord', and regulations drawn from it were often quoted in letters to new Christian communities. The similarities between the *Didache* and the *Community Rule* found amongst the Dead Sea Scrolls is quite startling – particularly in view of the Church's determined attempt to date the *Community Rule* to an earlier era. Both begin with information describing 'the two ways', of light and darkness, and proceed in a manner which leaves no doubt as to which of the two is the parent document.

The first 'Christian Church' in Jerusalem was led by a triumvirate of elders, based clearly on the model of the Essene community. The three leaders, known as 'the Pillars', were James the brother of Jesus and the senior of the three, Simon Peter and John.[17] According to the teaching of the Christian Church, Jesus devolved the succession of authority upon Simon Peter.

> ... thou art Peter, and upon this rock I will build my church; and the gates of hell shall not prevail against it and I will give unto thee the keys of the kingdom of heaven: and whatsoever thou shall bind on earth shall be bound in heaven: and whatsoever thou shall loose on earth shall be loosed in heaven.[18]

The Catholic Church based their assertion that the leadership passed from Jesus to Peter on the claim in the Gospel of Mark '... and Simon he surnamed Peter' – from the Greek word *petros*, which in turn is derived from *petra*, meaning rock. The Church used this seemingly convincing argument as the rock upon which they created, piece by piece over the centuries, the highly contentious dogma of papal infallibility and apostolic succession.

Despite the phrase used in the Acts of the Apostles to describe James and the original followers of Jesus as the 'first Church in Jerusalem',[19] Christianity itself did not originate in the Holy Land from the teachings of Jesus and his disciples, but among the Gentiles and the Diaspora from the teaching of St Paul, whose followers became known as Christians. The original followers of Jesus, under the leadership of James, called themselves the 'Ebionim', 'Ebionites' or the 'Poor',[20] and this group continued the practice of keeping the leadership of their group within the same family for more than 150 years after the crucifixion.[21]

The Ebionim are also known as 'the Poor Ones of Piety', 'the Meek' and 'the Beggars of the Spirit', terms known to all who are familiar with the Sermon on the Mount, and is a title adopted by the author of the Epistle of James, supposedly James the Just, the brother of Jesus. For reasons that will soon become clear, factual knowledge of the rites and beliefs of the Ebionim are difficult to establish, but we have one reliable informant, Epiphanius, who wrote:

> Besides a daily ritual bath, they have a baptism of initiation and each year they celebrate certain mysteries ... In these mysteries they use unleavened bread and, for the other part, pure water ... They say that Jesus was begotten of human seed ... that he was not begotten by God the Father, but that he was created ... and they too receive the Gospel of Matthew, and this they use ... to the exclusion of all others. But they call it the Gospel 'according to the Hebrews'.[22]

In the light of our earlier comments regarding the blasphemous nature of the words attributed to Jesus 'drink this, this is my blood ...' it is interesting to note that the Ebionim, the family and people who actually followed Jesus while he was on earth, used unleavened bread and water to celebrate their mysteries, not bread and wine.

Needless to say, the emerging Christian Church soon declared the Ebionites as 'heretical': after all, it could hardly be expected to tolerate the unpalatable fact that the followers of Jesus preached a very different message. In his views of the relationship between Jesus and the Ebionites, one early Church father, Iraneus, who was Bishop of Lyon during the late 2nd century, showed the mental convolutions that only a Pauline theologian was capable of. He claimed that Jesus – whom he believed was God – had been in error, practising 'the wrong religion',[23] an accusation that followed a Church tradition that described the true teachings of Jesus as recounted by John the Evangelist, as the 'Johannite Heresy'. Now if Jesus was divine, we would naturally assume that he was incapable of error and yet, according to a Pauline theologian,

God had boobed and led his flock into the wrong religion.[24] The mind boggles! Who were the real heretics, Jesus and his immediate followers, or the Church?

THE TEACHING OF ST PAUL

Christianity in all its forms, while it renders a certain degree of homage to particular selections taken from the teachings of Jesus, was actually founded on the teaching of a heretic and an *agent provocateur* known to history as Saul of Tarsus, or St Paul, 'the father of Christianity'. His own writings claim that Saul was a Pharisee who had spent considerable time persecuting James the Just and the followers of Jesus.[25] After his 'miraculous' conversion on the road to Damascus, he apparently did a complete 'about turn', changing not only his religion but also his name and status; from Saul the persecutor of the Jesus people he became Paul the Apostle and Christian evangelist. After spending three years in Arabia, a point the New Testament glosses over with considerable speed,[26] Paul joined James and his followers in Jerusalem, learning the 'true way' as taught by Jesus.

> However, I admit that I worship the God of our fathers as a follower of the Way, which they call a sect. I believe everything that agrees with the Law and that is written in the Prophets … [27]

The message preached so effectively by Paul as he traversed the known world in a spirit of fanatical evangelism was regarded as outright blasphemy by James and the disciples in Jerusalem. According to one devout and meticulous Catholic historian, Paul Johnson, Paul's evangelical endeavours were neither welcomed nor approved by them. Johnson claims that Paul's mission was steadily losing ground to the evangelists accredited by James the Just and admits that if it were not for

James' murder and the subsequent uprising of the Jews against the hated Roman oppressor, Paul's monumental effort might well have been a mere footnote to history or forgotten altogether.[28] With the destruction of Jerusalem and the Temple in 70 CE, Paul had the field to himself and his teaching and theology became the foundation of Christianity as we know it today.

Scholars agree that Paul's epistles, dating from 47 CE onwards, are the earliest documents in the official canon of the Christian Church known as the New Testament. The three Synoptic Gospels came later, with the dates given ranging from 70 CE to 120 CE. These documents were highly selective and were edited so that they only contained those teachings of Jesus which fitted in, more or less, with the preaching of Paul. The fourth Gospel was subjected to particular modification from the oral tradition which was its true origin, again to bring it into conformity with the one-time persecutor of James and the original disciples in Jerusalem.

THE GOSPEL TRUTH?

The Gospels are an extremely unreliable historical source, a statement which many devout Christians will find profoundly disturbing.[29] However, one noted scholar has made even more provocative allegations. Andrew Welburn, a Fellow of both the Warburg Institute of the University of London and New College, Oxford, states bluntly that 'Forgeries of many sorts can be found in the New Testament.[30] For example, words are put into Jesus' mouth that make him a propagandist for the Church and its powers.' One example is to be found in Matthew's Gospel, where Jesus is alleged to have said to the disciples: 'Go therefore and make disciples of all nations, baptizing them in the name of the Father and of the Son and of the Holy Spirit.'[31] As Jesus was a devout Jew with a profound respect for the Law, who had no intention of founding a new religion, this statement is unthinkable. His true orthodox feelings are clearly expressed in the same Gospel: 'Go not into the way of the Gentiles, and into any city of the Samaritans enter ye not: but go rather to the lost sheep of the house of Israel.'[32] We are also told that Jesus described the Gentiles as 'dogs' to whom he had nothing to say.

> And, behold, a woman of Canaan came out of the same coasts, and cried unto him, saying, Have mercy on me, O Lord, thou Son of David; my daughter is grievously vexed with a devil.
>
> But he answered her not a word. And his disciples came and besought him, saying, Send her away; for she crieth after us.
>
> But he answered and said, I am not sent but unto the lost sheep of the house of Israel.
>
> Then came she and worshipped him, saying, Lord, help me.
>
> But he answered and said, it is not meet to take the children's bread, and to cast it to dogs.[33]

The whole Christian mythology founded on the theology of Paul lays claim to absolute authenticity because it is supposedly 'historically accurate'. Yet many events in the New Testament used to colour the character of Jesus were indiscriminately 'borrowed' or 'stolen' from other religions. The mythology is based on an unhealthy mixture of magical fantasy, outrageous exaggeration and blasphemy. We have already demonstrated the impossibility that Jesus invented the Eucharist and, thereby, the central ritual of the Christian Church. Christian dogma and belief is built upon the foundations laid by St Paul, whose beliefs about Jesus the Nazarene were completely at variance with those held by the original disciples who had followed him during his ministry.

St Paul was, in fact, the first 'Christian heretic'. His conviction that Jesus had become a new passover lamb at the crucifixion was a prime example of this. Paul's conception that Jesus' sacrifice at Golgotha was an effective act of redemption for all time completely undermined the rationale of the Nazarene way of life. What was the point of ritual purity and strict adherence to the Law to attain a state of righteousness, if that 'state of grace' had already been obtained for them by the redemptive sacrifice on the cross? Paul had never met Jesus, but the disciples in Jerusalem who knew that Jesus came to reveal and to lead, *not* to redeem. Some biblical scholars claim that the account of the Last Supper in the Gospels must be a complete work of fiction.[34] The Synoptic Gospels claim that the Eucharist was instituted as the end-piece to the traditional Passover meal. If this were true, then the events which are described in such detail as following the Last Supper – the arrest, trial and execution of Jesus – could not have happened in either the way or the time-scale that are described. No Jew, much less the High Priests of the Sanhedrin, would have dared to breach the Law and the traditions surrounding their most sacred religious observance simply in order to put a man on trial.

JESUS' CRIME?

The passage relating to Pontius Pilate 'washing his hands' seems equally bizarre when we consider the evidence. After an earlier insurrection, one of Pilate's predecessors, the Proconsul Varus, had crucified more than 2,000 Jews without the slightest qualm.[35] It is therefore highly unlikely that Pilate would have thought twice about the expedient execution of one known trouble-maker. The idea that Jesus was crucified as a result of being found guilty of the Jewish charge of blasphemy is arrant nonsense; one leading scholar dismisses it as 'pure invention'.[36] Had he or anyone else been charged and found guilty of this crime, they would not have been brought before the Romans at all; they would simply have been executed by the Jews in the proscribed manner, by being stoned to death. One renowned classical scholar, Enoch Powell, who learnt

Hebrew in order to get to grips with the reality of the life and times of Jesus, claimed that this was what happened to him.

There is only one charge under Roman law – that of sedition – which led to crucifixion, the traditional Roman form of punishment. It must be remembered that biblical Israel was a theocratic state and only one law was held to be valid by the Jews, the Law of Moses. Therefore any new religious statement was *de facto* a political statement and, conversely, any political statement was also a religious one.[37] The teachings of Jesus were in many respects at variance with those of the Sadducees and Pharisees, who either supported, or accepted on grounds of practicality, the suzerainty of the Roman Empire. To the Jews, while there might be some dispute about his teaching, Jesus was a Jewish rabbi arguing *his* interpretation of the Law in the traditional manner to other Jews, a form of disputatious analysis which gave rise to the age-old aphorism 'where you have two Jews you have three arguments'. To the Roman occupiers, the hated Kittim, Jesus was simply a trouble-maker with the potential to cause insurrection. His descent from the Royal House of David, taken in conjunction with his Messianic title 'the King of the Jews', was justification enough, in Roman eyes, for his execution.

JESUS AND THE DISCIPLES

It is widely accepted today that the power of the oft-repeated lie in propaganda is incredibly effective. Two of the most expert proponents of this were Goebbels and Stalin, but even these masters of modern propaganda are mere amateurs when compared to the early fathers of the Christian Church. One of the most pervasive lies promulgated by those self-appointed custodians of 'divinely revealed truth' is the fallacy that Jesus and the 12 apostles were all poverty-stricken, semi-literate peasants, who sprang from an agrarian culture of some crudity and simplicity. The Bible itself gives the lie to this seductive statement; the Jewish Scriptures are one of the greatest literary masterpieces ever assembled in the world. A society that produced such a work must have been complex, highly literate, cultured and sophisticated. The Jewish Scriptures, the Tanakh which became the Christian Old Testament, is the reflection of a civilization of considerable antiquity and prosperity. The building programme initiated in biblical Israel by King Herod the Great was of such magnitude and skill that it betrays the falsity of the popular view of Jewish culture of the time. As for Jesus and his family, they came from royal and priestly stock who had exercised hereditary power and privilege among their people for generations.

Joseph of Arimathea who, according to the Gospels, was the uncle of Jesus, was one of the wealthiest merchants in the Middle East. Mary, the mother of Jesus, was educated at the Temple in Jerusalem, the most privileged school in the land. James, the brother of Jesus, was a High Priest at the Temple, a position of supreme importance within the Jewish faith of the time. On the Day of Atonement the responsibilities of the High Priest were of vital significance, for it was then that he had to enter the Holy of Holies and make atonement for his own sins, the sins of his family and all the sins of the people of Israel. In discharging this sacred duty James was acting as the spokesman for the people of Israel in their dealings with God. After the crucifixion James '... was clearly acknowledged by all the apostles, including Paul, as a much more significant figure than the later Christian Churches have ever dared to admit.'[38]

> He was of the lineage of David ... and moreover we have
> found that he officiated after the manner of the ancient
> priesthood. Whereof also he was permitted once a year
> to enter the Holy of Holies [on the Day of Atonement],
> as the Law commanded the High Priests, according to
> that which is written; for so many before us have told of
> him, both Eusabius and Clement and others. Furthermore
> he was empowered to wear on his head the High Priestly

diadem as the aforementioned trustworthy men have attested in their memoirs.[39]

The social and religious status that the position of High Priest conferred was considerable and entry to this rank, which would be the equivalent to that of a senior cabinet minister in Britain today, was restricted to aristocratic members of the Cohen family from the tribe of Levi. It would appear that many of Jesus' principal followers were of the same social class. Since 1969 archaeological excavations in Capernaum have revealed the true nature of the house alleged to be that of Simon Peter. The modern scholar A. N. Wilson in describing this find has written 'it would appear to have been a rather comfortable house, and to give the lie to the popular cliché that Peter and the early followers of Jesus were all paupers'.[40]

THE FIRST CHRISTIAN HERETIC

The fact that the teachings of Paul, which were deemed as heretical by James the Just, became the foundation of Christianity demands that we examine the character of Paul with considerable care. He first comes to notice with the account in the Acts of the Apostles that he was sent to Damascus to prosecute the followers of Jesus under a mandate from the High Priest in Jerusalem.[41] That simply cannot be true. The Jewish Sanhedrin, the highest council of priests in the Temple, had no jurisdiction whatsoever outside their own land. If Saul had any mandate to suppress or persecute the Nazarenes in the region of Syria, there could only be one source for his authority – Imperial Rome.[42] The Romans administered both biblical Israel and Syria, and it is therefore reasonable to assume that Saul, who by his own admission was a Roman citizen, was acting as an agent of the Roman occupying powers. A close relative of the family of King Herod, who were staunch allies and dependants of Rome, it is highly probable that Saul of Tarsus, or St Paul as we now know him, was an agent of the Romans throughout his entire career.

The account of Paul's arrest by the Romans on a charge of blasphemous teaching as described in the Acts of the Apostles is another marvellous example of pious fiction. Had he been indulging in this he would have been stoned to death by the Jews, not arrested by the Romans. So why was Paul taken into custody? The reason given for these events by Robert Eisenman, the Dead Sea Scrolls scholar, is both provocative and interesting. Assembling evidence from a variety of contemporaneous documents, Eisenman shows that Paul was arrested by the Romans as an act of 'protective custody'. He was undoubtedly in danger from an angry Jewish mob, who were incensed not by his blasphemous teaching but by his attempted murder of James the brother of Jesus.[43]

When we analyze the theological differences that separated James and Paul after his conversion on the road to Damascus, we find that the 'father of Christianity' had not merely committed blasphemy but started a heresy that is still extant. We mentioned earlier that the Jews of this time, if told that Jesus was divine, would have condemned that idea as the ultimate blasphemy. Jesus certainly never claimed divine status and when we search the New Testament to find the earliest proclamation that 'Jesus is God' we discover this not in the Gospels or the Acts of the Apostles, but in the Epistles of St Paul: '... while we wait for the blessed hope – the glorious appearing of our ... great God and Saviour, Jesus Christ'[44]. It was also St Paul who promulgated the offensive idea that at Golgotha Jesus had deliberately acted as a vicarious form of human 'paschal lamb' and had 'died for us'.[45] This was the first time that the concept of redemptive human sacrifice had been introduced into a religion springing from Judaic roots. All orthodox Jews would regard such an idea with abject horror. The one account of human sacrifice in the Jewish tradition was that attempted by the prophet Abraham, but God stayed Abraham's hand. Since that time no Jew could either perform a human sacrifice or become one. Despite reported instances of this among nearby tribes and cultures, for the Jews it remained anathema.

These controversial views on the actions of St Paul are supported by a document which many scholars believe pre-dates the Gospels, the *Kerygmata Petrou*, which originates from the Ebionites. In this account, the father of Christianity is described as 'an apostate of the Law', the 'spouter of wickedness and lies' and 'the distorter of the true teachings of Jesus'. The events that occurred on the road to Damascus that resulted in Paul's 'miraculous' conversion are given very short shrift, and are simply described as 'dreams and illusions inspired by devils'.[46]

If one reads the Epistles of St Paul rapidly and in order, it is possible to discern a subtext to which he is constantly responding. He repeatedly refutes accusations that he is a 'false apostle' or a liar who is obtaining some form of financial advantage from his evangelical endeavours. One passage in particular, though brief, is especially revealing. It demonstrates simply and clearly the point that Jewish men were expected to marry, thereby endorsing our view that Jesus was married and that Paul himself was probably married:

> Don't we have the right to food and drink?
> Don't we have the right to take a believing wife along with us,
> As do the other apostles and the Lord's brothers and Cephas?
> Or is it only Barnabas and I who must work for a living?[47]

This statement directly conflicts with one of his earlier statements regarding his marital status:

> Now to the unmarried and the widows I say: It is good for them to stay unmarried, **as I am**.[48] [our emphasis]

What are we to make of these contradictory statements by St Paul? Is he a liar, as is claimed in the *Kerygmata Petrou*, or is he simply a confused and highly unreliable witness? The claim that he is unmarried makes a complete nonsense of his earlier claims to be a good Jew, a Pharisee and a follower of the Law: '... circumcised on the eighth day, of the people of Israel, of the tribe of Benjamin, a Hebrew of Hebrews; in regard to the law, a Pharisee ... '[49] To qualify for any of these titles Paul would have had to conform with the Law and the traditions of his people and obey the commandments of the one true God, 'to go forth and multiply', and for that he would have had to have been married in accordance with the Law of Moses.

7

The Marriage and Dynasty of Jesus

It was not only Paul who would have been under pressure to marry because of the Law of Moses. All male Jews who were capable of earning their living would have been bound by the same law and tradition, especially those who held the position of rabbi or religious teacher. Among the Essenes, the Teacher of Righteousness, because of the hereditary nature of his priestly function, would have been under the greatest obligation of them all. Even the highly doctored texts of the Gospels contain substantial traces of reality which lead to the conclusion that Jesus was, in fact, a married man. The modern scholar A N Wilson suggests that 'the story of the wedding feast at Cana contains a hazy memory of Jesus' own wedding'. The text reveals somewhat more than a 'hazy memory':[1]

> And the third day there was a marriage in Cana of Galilee; and the mother of Jesus was there:
>
> And both Jesus was called, and his disciples, to the marriage.
>
> And when they wanted wine, the mother of Jesus sayeth unto him, they have no wine.

> Jesus sayeth unto her, Woman, what have I to do with thee? mine hour is not yet come.
>
> His mother sayeth unto the servants, whatsoever he sayeth unto you, do it.[2]

St John's Gospel continues with the story of Jesus changing the water into wine and ordering the servants to distribute it. Under Jewish custom the only person with the authority to give orders to the servants at a wedding feast was the bridegroom or his mother.[3]

Later in the same Gospel we find indications as to the nature of the relationship between Jesus and Mary Magdalene:

> Then Martha, as soon as she heard that Jesus was coming, went and met him: but Mary sat *still* in the house …
>
> … And when she had so said, she went her way, and called Mary her sister secretly, saying, the Master is come and calleth for thee.
>
> As soon as she heard *that*, she arose quickly, and came unto him.[4]

This indicates that Mary Magdalene was playing the role of a dutiful wife. On the approach of her husband a wife was expected to remain in the house awaiting his return. Others were permitted to go to greet him but her duty was to meet him in the sanctity of their own home unless, of course, he gave instructions to the contrary. The wife was also the only woman allowed to sit at a man's feet. In the tenth chapter of Luke's Gospel we read the following: 'And she had a sister called Mary, which also sat at Jesus' feet, and heard his word.'[5] When we examine these indications in the context of the strict customs that regulated the relations between man and wife in biblical Israel, it is an irrefutable indication that Jesus was married to Mary Magdalene.

The Archbishop of Mayence, Raban Maar, 776–856 CE, composed

a work on *The Life of Mary Magdalene*, a copy of which was found at Oxford University in the early 15th century. Maar claims that Mary's mother, Eucharia, was related to the Royal Hasmonean House of Israel. As Jesus was of the House of David this raises dynastic issues of particular importance at that time. A union between Jesus and Mary Magdalene of the House of Bethany would have a double claim to the kingship of Israel. It is interesting to note that Louis XI of France, who ruled from 1461–83, insisted that the French royal family were descended from Mary Magdalene, a further illustration of the widespread medieval belief that Jesus and Mary had children.[6]

The fox is a common symbol employed by those of the Gnostic tradition to denote pious fraud. There are numerous illustrations from the Middle Ages where a fox in priestly garb deceives and exploits the common people. For the heretics, the Catholic clergy were perceived as foxes; in the Song of Songs, one of the favourite scriptures of the esoteric stream, little foxes spoil the vines in the vineyard of the bride; a painting by Botticelli from the early 16th century uses this symbolism to give the lie to the Christian doctrine that Jesus was celibate. This glorious work of art, known as *St Mary Magdalene at the Foot of the Cross*, depicts the desolate and distraught figure of Mary Magdalene clinging to the cross; to the right is an angel holding a fox upside-down by the tail. The Catholic theologian, Margaret Starbird, claims, with some justification, that this symbolizes that the church was 'spoiling the vine' by denying the legitimacy of the bloodline of the dynasty of Jesus.[7]

SCHOLARLY CONFIRMATION

Margaret Starbird was horrified at some of the 'blasphemous' allegations contained within *The Holy Blood and the Holy Grail*. She began a programme of research with the intention of writing a refutation of the most blasphemous theme in this best seller.[8] But her meticulous enquiries led to confirmation of the fact that Jesus was married and founded a dynasty, and to the writing of a book of a very different order. In her work *The Woman with the Alabaster Jar,* she makes a very convincing case for the marriage of Jesus to Mary of Bethany, otherwise known as Mary Magdalene.[9] The Dead Sea Scrolls' scholar, Barbara Thiering, came to the same conclusion and said of Jesus and Mary Magdalene: 'This was not a purely spiritual relationship, but a real marriage, following the rules of the dynastic order. Jesus had to marry in order to continue his family line, and in his case it was all the more necessary in order to affirm his legitimacy.'[10] The Muslim scholar Professor Fida Hassnain, in his work *A Search for the Historical Jesus,* speaks of the wedding of Cana in the following terms:

> The question arises who is the guest and who is the bride? I would suggest Mary is the host for she orders the procuring of wine for the guests, which Jesus deals with. One wonders whether it is *his* own marriage with Mary Magdalene, and whether the whole episode has been kept under camouflage … I believe that Mary Magdalene behaved as the chief consort of Jesus, and he also took her as his spouse.[11]

The evidence[12] points overwhelmingly to the conclusion that Jesus *was* a married man who had fathered a family, not only as part of his fulfilment of the Law, but as part of his duties as a rabbi and his supreme obligation as the heir to the kingly line descended from David, and that his wife was Mary Magdalene, with whom he had at least two children, a son and a daughter.

Those who composed the Synoptic Gospels, and the editors and redactors of the entire corpus of the New Testament, were sublimely ignorant of Jewish law, tradition and practice. In their zeal to amend these documents so that they conformed to the teaching of St Paul they left in certain significant passages which further support the story that Jesus and Mary Magdalene were married. In the Gospel of Matthew we read:

> While Jesus was in Bethany in the home of a man known as
> Simon the Leper, a woman came to him with an alabaster jar
> of very expensive perfume, which she poured on his head as
> he was reclining at the table.[13]

In Jewish tradition and also according to the rituals of Sumer, Babylon
and Canaan, the ritual anointing of the king's head with oil was done by
the heiress, royal priestess or royal bride in their role as the goddess. The
Greeks called this ritual *hieros gamos,* or the sacred marriage. It was
because of his ritual union with the priestess that the king achieved truly
royal status as the 'Anointed One', or more familiarly in Hebrew as the
'Messiah'.[14] In Church iconography and in Western art it is always Mary
Magdalene who is depicted with the alabaster jar. It is significant that
traditionally the Catholic Church, when celebrating her feast day, reads
from Canticles (Song of Songs 3:2–4) of the bride searching for her
bridegroom or beloved from whom she has become separated.[15] Further
evidence for the pre-eminence of Mary Magdalene among the followers
of Jesus can be found in the various lists given in the Gospel accounts of
the women who accompanied Jesus. There are seven such lists, and the
name of Mary Magdalene occurs first in six of them, even before that of
Mary the mother of Jesus, and way ahead of any other women mentioned.[16] In this unconscious manner the authors of the Gospels are
stressing the true status of Mary Magdalene among the disciples, that
of First Lady.

THE DISTORTING LENS OF DOGMA

The Church's response to these unpalatable facts about the life of Jesus
which directly conflicted with their teaching was neither new nor
surprising. Simply ignoring the facts altogether and attempting to edit
out all trace of the Jesus family was the option chosen to resolve this
conundrum. Another tried and trusted ploy that had been used before

was also brought into play; a simple trick that had apparently worked in the case of James the Just and that of Jesus' twin brother Thomas, was used with devastating effect. To the litany of deceit which starts with outright omission were added the stratagems of marginalization and slander. James the Just, the brother of Jesus, who was the true leader of the Jesus people after the crucifixion, was marginalized by being called James the Less; The Gospel of Thomas was devalued by applying the appellation of 'Doubting Thomas'[17] to the twin brother of Jesus; Mary Magdalene, a lady of royal lineage and priestly status, was grossly maligned by the brutal and uncharitable means of the suppression of all information regarding her marriage to Jesus and by the slanderous implication found within Church doctrine, for which there is no basis in scripture, that she was a whore, a common prostitute.

The nature and mission of Jesus were also twisted beyond all recognition. The combined forces of the Scriptures of the New Testament and Christian doctrine portray him as a divine teacher in human form who promoted acceptance of the Roman rule, the spreading of God's word to the Gentiles and the turning of the other cheek. This divine and celibate 'paragon of virtue' is, furthermore, portrayed as a sacrificial lamb who offered himself meekly to the slaughter in order to redeem mankind from sin. According to the Gospels he was executed at the behest of his own people and against the expressed preferences of the Roman proconsul Pontius Pilate.[18] This version of events is still vigorously promoted under the guise of papal infallibility. If we strip away the layers of myth, legend, hagiography and downright distortion, is there anything left at all that has the ring of truth?

JESUS AND HIS FAMILY

Far from simply preaching bland and innocuous messages such as 'render unto Caesar what is Caesar's', Jesus the Nazarene led a band of Zealots and Sicarii who lived in Galilee and were dedicated to the overthrow of the hated Roman overlords – the Kittim.[19] Thus the 'gentle Jesus' was the militant and charismatic leader of what we would today describe as a right-wing nationalistic and fundamentalist sect in the Essene tradition. This courageous man was not executed by his own people but by the Roman army of occupation in a manner that clearly defined his crime; crucifixion was the official punishment for sedition and insurrection.[20]

An inevitable result of Jesus' conviction and execution on a charge of sedition was that his wife and children would have been in extreme danger. Had he merely been executed by the Jews on a charge of blasphemy, his family would have suffered little more than the loss of their breadwinner and a degree of public disdain. However, as the family of a criminal known as 'the King of the Jews', Mary Magdalene and her children would have been forced to flee in order to escape the vengeance of both the Romans and the House of Herod.[21] The Rex Deus sagas recount how the children of Jesus were parted in an attempt to ensure their security and the continuation of his bloodline. James, his two-and-a-half-year-old son, was entrusted to the care of Judas Thomas Didymus, Jesus' twin brother. They sought immediate sanctuary with King Abgar of Edessa, who was a supporter of Jesus. Mary Magdalene, who was pregnant at the time, fled in the opposite direction, to a refuge of comparative safety among a community whose silence and protection could be relied upon, the Therapeutae in Egypt.

Legend tells us that Joseph of Arimathea, a wealthy merchant, had the contacts and resources necessary to effect an immediate escape. It is not known how long Mary Magdalene resided in Egypt, but the principles of successful evasion are the same today as they were then – never stay in one place too long, never run straight, until one finds a safe hiding place. One old French legend from the mouth of the River Rhône tells us that Joseph of Arimathea was the custodian of the Sangraal in the form of a child who was described as Egyptian, which is taken to mean 'born in Egypt'. The probability is that at the time of her flight to Egypt

Mary Magdalene lingered there long enough to be safely delivered of the royal child. Due to the clandestine nature of the flight it would be unrealistic to expect to find any contemporaneous documentation confirming either the flight or birth. The story of the escape from Israel and the true nature of the children's genealogy would be a secret passed down orally within the family. To followers of the Essene sect discovery could be avoided by the use of something as natural as breathing: scriptural allegory and code.

THE FLIGHT FROM EGYPT

One popular legend that has persisted in the south of France for nearly 2,000 years, reinforced by a tradition within the French royal family that they are descended from Mary Magdalene, gives us a strong indication as to the route taken by the family and their eventual destination. Within this legend there are coded references to the royal child that are so cleverly disguised that they have fooled generations of devout believers throughout the entire Christian history of Europe. In the small seaside town of Les Saintes-Maries-de-la-Mer in the Camargue, a festival which honours the arrival in France of the child of Jesus the Nazarene and her mother Mary Magdalene[22] is celebrated every year from 23 to 25 May. In the crypt of the fortified church which is the central feature of the town, there is a strange, ornately dressed 'black madonna' that is not all that it might seem at first. For once this black-visaged and bejewelled statue does not celebrate Our Lady in any shape or form. It purports to represent a little-known saint, Sarah the Egyptian, also known as Sara Kali,[23] the black queen, venerated by all the gypsies of Europe. The festival, which started in the Middle Ages out of a long-standing oral tradition, is held to honour the miraculous arrival on the coast of a rudderless boat which carried a very strange crew. On board were Mary Magdalene, her sister Martha and her brother Lazarus, accompanied by an 'Egyptian' child.[24] The generally accepted assumption has always been that as the child is described as Egyptian she was dark-skinned and therefore must have been the servant of the family of Bethany; no other explanation has ever been put forward by the Church for her presence. Sarah has always been characterized as being young, no more than a child, yet no explanation has ever been offered as to how one so young could be usefully employed, albeit in a servile role.

The Essenes were masters of dissimulation; Jesus taught in parables. Much of the recent interpretation of the Dead Sea Scrolls has been accomplished by applying an understanding of the Essene use of peshers.[25] These were an elliptical form of coded writings which held hidden meanings under the veil of simple narrative. Another use of code found in the Dead Sea Scrolls was that of ciphers, such as the Atbash cipher.[26] Codes, ciphers and peshers were not the only means employed by the Essene scribes to disguise their true intent. An encyclopaedic knowledge of the Scriptures, plus the use of certain Hebrew terminology, was also used to hide the pearl of truth from the eyes of the uninitiated or potential persecutors. Sarah the Egyptian, the black child: a simple phrase that hides a wealth of meaning. Sarah in Hebrew is not simply a name: it is also a title and rank, and means queen or princess.[27] The term Egyptian is not an indication of nationality, but simply a link to the place of birth. What are we to make of the description 'black'? The key to this is to be found in the Old Testament book of Lamentations, which describes the princes of the Davidic line: 'But now they are blacker than soot; they are not recognized in the streets.'[28] Hidden under this form of esoteric description and symbolism is the identity of the child who was to grow up in France and continue the Davidic dynasty, the daughter of the crucified King of the Jews.

LEGENDS OF MARY MAGDALENE

Other persistent legends tie Mary Magdalene and Lazarus very firmly to Provence where Mary Magdalene is revered as 'the Saint Apostle of

Provence'.[29] According to tradition, having landed in Les Saintes-Maries-de-la-Mer she soon moved to Marseilles with her brother Lazarus to begin what the Church describes as 'her evangelical mission'.[30] After that it is reported that she moved to the vicinity of Aix-en-Provence, where she preached accompanied by Saint Maximus. Then the normally definitive Church tradition becomes a trifle vague and claims that through fear of persecution or guided by the desire to find her 'rabbouni' in silence Mary Magdalene sought a secluded refuge wherein she spent the last years of her life.[31] Not far from Aix-en-Provence is a mountain range that is to this day a geological curiosity. The lower slopes of the mountains of Sainte Baume are clothed in ancient forests; many yews found there, with hollow trunks but still verdant foliage, are claimed to be more than 1,000 years old. The oak groves that clothe the mountainside were used for ritual gatherings by the Druids and are only marginally younger, having stood there for many centuries. The whole area is pervaded with an eternal peace and it was here that Mary Magdalene is said to have spent the declining years of her life in meditation and prayer in a cave high up in this sacred range.

Tradition recounts that Charles II, Count of Provence, rediscovered the body of Ste Mary Magdalene in the crypt of St Maximin la Baume in the late 13th century. The pilgrimage to the cave of the Magdalene at Ste Baume, however, predates this discovery by several centuries. The grotto at St Baume became an important staging point for pilgrims travelling on the route from Italy, which passed close by Rennes-le-Château before crossing the border into Spain and on to St James of Compostela. It is recorded that in 1254 the French King, St Louis, made his pilgrimage to the shrine of the Magdalene on his return from the crusades. When Provence became part of the kingdom of France, all kings of the newly unified country made the pilgrimage and the route that they followed is now known as the 'Chemin des Rois', the Kings' Way.[32] It is not just the exoteric and devout Catholics who come here; members of the esoteric streams of spirituality also make regular pilgrimages to what they know is the shrine of the Bride of Christ. Members of the Compagnonnage, the medieval trade guilds of the craftmasons, especially those of the Children of Solomon and their modern counterparts Les Compagnons du Tour de France, incorporate this pilgrimage as the essential final stage that crowns their professional and spiritual initiation.

The medieval cult of relics spawned many anomalies within Church tradition. There were several churches in Europe which claimed to house the foreskin of the baby Jesus; there were at least three relics purporting to be the spear that pierced the side of Christ; and there were enough fragments of the true cross to have recreated an entire forest. The body of Mary Magdalene similarly seems to have been divinely blessed with special powers, as it has acquired the magical ability to be in at least two places at the same time, Vezelay and St Maximin la Baume.

Like the Gospels, the traditions telling the story of the Magdalene that have survived with the blessing of the Church have been edited and 'improved' by the priestly scribes and cannot be expected to tell anything like the full story. No further mention is made of Sarah the black Egyptian and none at all of her brother, James. It would appear that, like their ancient forebears the Davidic princes, they 'went unrecognized in the streets'. In all probability the only record of their fate and the lineage that sprang from them is to be found in the secret family traditions of the members of that select group of families known collectively as Rex Deus. In the story recounted to us by our informant, the immediate details of Sarah, her brother and their children were omitted but he did delineate the broad outlines of the life of James, the son of Jesus.

JAMES, THE SON OF JESUS

To a certain extent, the travels of Judas Thomas and his nephew James were based upon the same principle as those employed by Mary Magdalene – keep moving until one finds a safe refuge. After an unspecified period in Edessa, James, in the care of his uncle, travelled to the Celt-Iberian settlements in the vicinity of the present-day city of Compostela in the north-west of Spain. James's age when he first arrived in Spain is not immediately clear from the version of the Rex Deus sagas that were recounted to us, nor are the full details of his later travels. It is known that during his maturity he spent a considerable time in Britain with Joseph of Arimathea, but the Rex Deus legends recount that he died in Spain. Could it be that this visit by James the son of the Messiah was the real foundation for the later legends that James the Apostle visited the Iberian peninsula?[33] It would be ironic indeed if all the devout and orthodox pilgrims who visit Compostela and kneel in front of the tomb of the Apostle are in fact unknowingly venerating the child of a marriage that the Church denies ever took place.

REX DEUS IN EUROPE

Four main strands of early transmission of the bloodline are indicated, in Rome, Provence, Spain and Britain. The Roman and Provençal strands obviously became the route from which sprang the later important branches among the nobility and royal houses of France and western Europe. The families that sprang from the Spanish stem intermarried with other Rex Deus families and became the foundation of the nobility of the Languedoc, northern Spain, Aquitaine and Brittany. The British story of descent from Jesus links into one of the most persistent legends in English history, that of the visit of Joseph of Arimathea and the young Jesus to Glastonbury in the west of England.[34] The main divergence of the Rex Deus version of this story from the popular myth is that it was not Jesus the Nazarene whose feet were said to walk upon England's pastures green, but those of his son, James, the heir to the throne of David. In many respects this version of events is far more credible than the original, particularly when one takes into account the many places, trades and professions which make strong claims of being associated with 'Jesus' while he was in England. If these claims were all authenticated in respect of Jesus the Nazarene the conclusion must be that he spent an inordinate amount of time in England before his return to Israel. A far more credible scenario emerges if we consider that it was the son of Jesus to whom these legends refer and that, in all likelihood, he spent a goodly portion of his life in the island kingdom.

The royal family of Israel had to flee their country, split up and seek safe refuge almost immediately after the crucifixion. Other families descended from the 24 High Priests of the Temple were under no such compulsion to emigrate at that time. Some of course did and lived among the Diaspora, for at the time nearly 20 per cent of the population of the Mediterranean littoral were Jews. Those who remained in Israel who had the wit or good luck to survive the devastation that resulted from the Jewish uprising against the Romans would then have had to flee. Thus in the early years of Christianity, while the new religion was a small – sometimes persecuted, sometimes tolerated – sect, several diverse and often conflicting strands coexisted, often vying for support from among the same population.

Among the Jewish Diaspora scattered throughout the areas of Greek and Roman influence there were small pockets of 'Jesus people' who had been instructed in the Way either by Jesus himself, by the original disciples or by evangelists accredited by James the Just in Jerusalem. Also scattered amongst the Jewish communities were members of a rival and distinctly different organization, the emerging Pauline church, which found its main support among the Gentiles.[35] Little love was lost between the two groups who preached such conflicting doctrines. To add to the theological confusion there were a large number of followers of the Greek mystery cults and other Gnostic sects who happily borrowed any ideas from the new 'Christian' sects that happened to appeal to them. To this eclectic mix of squabbling theologians and 'believers' were now added members of the Rex Deus families who took no part in doctrinal disputes. They practised whatever happened to be the prevailing religion of the time or district, and secretly passed down through the generations knowledge of their descent and the true nature of the initiatory teaching of the man we call Jesus the Nazarene. After the fall of Jerusalem they had the added responsibility and the sacred duty of passing on the knowledge of the hiding places of the treasures from the Temple in Jerusalem. Within this group of families, all of which originated from the High Priests of the Temple, there was another more select group known as the Desposyni or the descendants of the Master.[36] While the families mostly operated under a cloak of absolute anonymity, from time to time certain of them would come into the open and make their situation known with apparent indifference to the potential consequences.

Their collective intent was to preserve the true teachings of Jesus until such a time as they could be propagated in the appropriate manner to properly selected disciples, without fear of persecution. History apparently had other ideas and intervened in a dramatic manner that ensured the continued suppression of the truth for nearly 2,000 years. The agent of this dramatic change was a sun-worshipping follower of a Mithraic cult and the son of a Christian: Constantine the Great, Emperor of Rome, founder of Constantinople and the man who endorsed Christianity with his imperial blessing.

8

The Council of Nicea

Many disparate and often squabbling sects who all claimed to hold some form of allegiance to Jesus the Nazarene took root throughout the eastern Mediterranean, Greece, Rome and the Iberian Peninsula. As the Pauline theologians began to consolidate their hold over the emerging 'Christian' Church they used what were by then the traditional means of falsehood and calumny to strengthen their case. The tone of debate in these theological disputes was so far divorced from any form of spiritual or intellectual purity that it became known as *odium theologicum*, a form of crude ecclesiastical verbal abuse that simply depended on slander and vituperation of the worst order.[1] One dubious claim in particular was used with devastating effect to bolster the authority of the developing Christian power structure centred on Rome.[2]

In order to legitimize its claim to divinely sanctioned authority the Church used the unjustified assertion that both St Peter and St Paul had been martyred in Rome, despite credible evidence to the contrary in the case of St Peter and none whatsoever as to the death of St Paul in Rome or anywhere else. They used these claims as the foundation for the doctrine of 'apostolic succession',[3] which purported to show a continuum of power and authority that derived from the apostolic martyrs and was then passed to successive Bishops of Rome. To protect the developing Church's reputation as the authentic 'guardians of divinely revealed truth', the gaps in the early years of this episcopal succession were filled by the use of devout fabrication. From that time to this, this fictitious nonsense has been used to support the claim of absolute authority for the Bishops of Rome – the Popes.

The pagan Roman Empire was usually extremely tolerant of the various forms of religion practised by those it ruled. Provided people made due obeisance and sacrifice to the gods of Rome on the appointed days, they were free to practise other religions.[4] The devout followers of the new 'Christian' religion, however, often refused to make the ritual sacrifices and occasionally some emperors, such as Nero, would use the Christians as scapegoats to divert attention away from their own short-comings; only rarely would systematic persecution be employed against them by the State. When this did occur, as in the 3rd century, it was often accompanied by confiscation of lands and property, actions which began to have a marked effect on a property-owning Church.[5] Salvation, when it came, did not originate from the steadfastness of the congregations nor from charismatic leadership within the Church itself, but from a pagan general who sought the imperial purple.

THE FIRST 'CHRISTIAN' EMPEROR

Constantine the Great became Emperor of Rome after a civil war which ended with his victory at the battle of the Milvian Bridge in 312 CE. Almost immediately he passed the Edict of Milan, which granted the Christian Church freedom from persecution, religious toleration and guaranteed its property rights.[6]

> With his decisive victory at the battle of the Milvian Bridge in 312 AD, Constantine the Great became the ruler of the Roman Empire. The night before the battle that decided the

religious fate of Europe for the next 1,700 years, this sun-worshipping military leader had a strange vision of the Cross of Christ and the legend *In Hoc Signo Vinces* – 'In this sign you conquer'. To commemorate this victory and to give thanks to the God who had inspired him, Constantine erected a triumphal arch in Rome inscribed with the cross of Christ and the words: 'By this saving sign, I have delivered your city from the tyrants and restored liberty to the senate and the people of Rome.'

The Emperor's motives were far from altruistic. He wished to use the Christian religion as a form of social cement to unite the divided peoples of the Empire.[7]

When a new emperor assumed the throne of Rome the entire system of government changed. He set the standards for fashion, food, social habits, intellectual adventure and religious belief and would surround himself with military, civil and financial advisers who were loyal to him personally. It was the business of all who sought power under the new ruler to win his favour by any means possible, including flattery, imitation and corruption.[8]

Constantine was no Christian, despite his professed gratitude for the Christian sign granted to him before his all-important battle. He was the follower of the Mithraic sun-worshipping cult[9] of Sol Invictus, and was biased in favour of religious toleration for a complex mix of reasons, among which may have been gratitude, as well as the influence of his mother, the Empress Helena, who was undoubtedly a devout Christian. His prime motive, however, was political. He wished to use the disciplined law-abiding traditions of the Christians and their beliefs to act as a socially cohesive force in healing the bitter divisions in the empire caused by the civil war.[10] Thus when Constantine began to show significant signs of favour for the new religion, many who sought his friendship and influence became Christian as a simple act of political advantage. Paradoxically, despite this, Christianity did not become the officially preferred state religion for a further 70 years.

The empire ruled by Constantine was divided into two parts, each with its own capital. Rome was the seat of power in the west, while in the east he founded a new capital named after himself – Constantinople. He was horrified to find that the most active source of disunity within his realm sprang from the very organization that he had chosen to act as a form of social cement. The empire was in grave danger of being riven apart by doctrinal argument, intolerance and vituperative theological debate within the Christian Church.[11] Acting in accordance with his view of the interest of the state, Constantine was anxious to bring about a rapprochement by whatever means possible. As a statesman and pagan he placed unity, order and stability far higher than religious dogma in his order of priority; the rule of law took precedence over divinely revealed truth. To impose his will on the disputatious clerics he convened the first ecumenical council of the Church at Nicea in 325 CE.[12]

THE DISPUTED NATURE OF JESUS

The main theological dispute that had to be settled by the Council of Nicea arose from the different views as to the nature of Jesus, with the Pauline theologians on one side and the followers of Arius[13] on the other. Pauline teaching, in its later developments, preached that Jesus was not merely divine, the only begotten son of God, but was co-eternal and equal with God the Father. Arius, according to his critics within the Church, preached that the Father alone was the 'One True God', inaccessible and unique. Christ, the Logos, was neither co-eternal nor uncreated because he had received life and being from the eternal father: 'If the Son is a true Son, then the Father must have existed before the Son; therefore there was a time when the Son did not exist; therefore he was created or made.' Arius went further than this when he concluded that although Christ was divinely guided, because the Father willed him

THE COUNCIL OF NICEA

to be so, he was not God necessarily and essentially. It would have been possible, according to Arius, for God the Son to have sinned. The Arian heresy caused uproar and division within the Church and showed the convoluted heights of absurdity attained by early theologians in attempting to define the ridiculous concept promulgated by Paul, that Jesus the orthodox and scholarly Jew was God. The controversy over Arianism forced the issue and, in order to refute this heresy, the Church was compelled to come up with a working definition that clarified precisely in what sense Jesus was a god.

THE COUNCIL OF NICEA

Constantine the Great was not only a successful general but also a highly skilled politician and manipulator. At the Council of Nicea he used these qualities with considerable acumen and showed clearly that he was the first man in history who had truly mastered the art of convening and corrupting an international conference.[14] The early Church father Eusebius recorded that as each delegate entered the palace.

> ... units of the bodyguard and other troops surrounded the palace with drawn swords, and through them the men of God proceeded without fear into the innermost rooms of the Emperor, in which some were his companions at table, while others reclined on couches at either side.[15]

Constantine formally opened the council and throughout the proceedings was obviously excelling himself. He devised elaborate and dramatic ceremonial entrances, and religious processions and services with considerable skill, in stark contrast to the simplicity and purity of the first Church in Jerusalem led by the 'three Pillars' and the event recounted in the Acts of the Apostles known as the Council of Jerusalem. The Catholic historian Paul Johnson claims that 'Constantine, in fact, may be said to have created the decor and ritual of Christian conciliar practice'.[16]

Most of the working sessions of the council were chaired by Bishop Hosius. The Pope, Sylvester I, did not attend but sent two presbyters as his representatives. Two hundred and twenty bishops were present, mostly from the eastern sees, with only five from the west, all of whom had suffered persecution by previous administrations in Rome, but were now under imperial protection and sponsorship.[17] They travelled to and stayed at Nicea at the emperor's expense. When the Council concluded, they were entertained at a massive banquet held to celebrate the emperor's anniversary. Presents, which varied according to rank, were distributed to each guest as they left the palace.[18]

The first ecumenical council of the Church accomplished a very necessary political objective in what was, for the time, a novel manner. The carefully chosen episcopal delegates were drawn from diverse cultural groups within the Church. Those in attendance included a country bishop, who is reported to have driven a herd of sheep before him as he made his way to Nicea, as well as some of the most learned and sophisticated bishops from the Eastern Empire.[19] The council's decisions were promulgated as declarations of Church doctrine, some of which were to have devastating and long-lasting effect. The first was directly in line with the political objectives of the emperor – the Church and the State were to be aligned with each other. The teachings of Arius were condemned as heretical.[20] Constantine also formalized the incorporation of certain Mithraic traditions and practices into Christian doctrine. These included many of the issues we mentioned earlier: the holy birth in a grotto attended by shepherds, the apocalyptic events of a judgement day, the resurrection of the body and a second coming of their god – but, this time following the teaching of St Paul, it was Jesus who was to come again and not Mithras.

The council also made decisions regarding the marital status of the men who had taken holy orders. Priests were forbidden to marry after they had been ordained, although those who were already married were permitted to continue with their family life.[21] Prior to the council, many of the Christian churches had celebrated Easter on different dates, the variations generally arising from the tradition of the evangelists who had first converted their local population. The council fixed a universal date for Easter and imposed it on all. At Nicea the decision was taken to make Sunday the holy day of the Christian week. Thus the ancient Jewish Sabbath observed by Jesus and his immediate followers, which ran from dusk on Friday to sundown on Saturday, was replaced by 'Sunday', the day dedicated to Sol Invictus, the god Constantine really worshipped. After condemning the Arian heresy, a creed presented by certain Arian bishops was rejected and a new one, the Creed of Nicea (which is not to be confused with the Nicene Creed), was declared binding on the Church. The Nicene Creed was not proposed until the second ecumenical council in 381, and was not finally confirmed until the fourth council at Chalcedon in 451.[22] The two creeds are similar in intent but are not identical. The Creed of Nicea defined as a basic tenet of belief the doctrine that Jesus the Nazarene was divine and equal to God the Father in every way. Setting a precedent that was to have bloody repercussions throughout the centuries to come, the council vowed to excommunicate anyone who did not accept that Jesus was fully divine.

Constantine's consummate skill at rigging the conference reached its peak of corrupt perfection in the way the votes of the delegates were recorded. Bishop Hosius first announced and signed the new creed, which was then taken to each bishop by a cohort of Constantine's own notaries under the leadership of Philumenus, a high-ranking imperial official. It has been argued that many bishops only signed under extreme duress, for who would dare to disagree with the emperor who had so recently granted them their freedom and whose troops ringed the palace? One of Constantine's final acts at the council illustrates the 'freedom of conscience' enjoyed by the delegates – he imposed criminal sentences of exile on those who refused to sign. In 326 he published a letter addressed to the newly defined heretical sects announcing that their places of worship would be confiscated,[23] but his intolerance did not end there. The criminal sentences against the heretics were followed by punitive church councils which were presided over by the emperor's court advisers. In 333 Constantine ordered savage actions against Arian writings:

> ... if any treatise composed by Arius is discovered, let it be consigned to the flames ... in order that no memorial of him whatever be left ... [and] if anyone shall be caught concealing a book by Arius, and does not instantly bring it out and burn it, the penalty shall be death; the criminal shall suffer punishment immediately after conviction.[24]

FANTASY BECOMES FACT?

By the creation of the first official Church/State establishment in Christian history, founded firmly on the deeply spiritual principles of corruption, fear and repression, Constantine the Great had brought about apparent unity within the empire. The horrendous price eventually paid for this includes the long litany of names of the unfortunate, the sincere and the devout who were to be persecuted, tortured and burnt on charges of heresy throughout the centuries to come. Tragically this unity was largely illusory, for this was not the last attempt to define the impossible. Throughout the first 520 years of Christian history a vast amount of time and effort was wasted trying to clarify the nature and the person of Jesus the Nazarene. Because the theologians who followed the heretical doctrines and the mythology created by Paul could not accept that Jesus was an extraordinary man, a great teacher and a devout Jew, they had to go to enormous lengths to prop up Paul's fantasy that Jesus was divine. This led them into ever more complex arguments attempting to define the indefinable.

This created further causes for dispute which eventually resulted in the great schism which still divides the Orthodox Churches in the East from Roman Catholicism in the West. Ultimately, Jesus was defined as being the **only begotten** son of God, **born of a virgin,** who was both **completely divine** and **completely human**.[25] The specious arguments brought in to bolster this incredible fantasy reached heights of total absurdity. The Jesus of Church dogma and Pauline theology was defined as having two natures and two wills yet, paradoxically, was not in any way two persons, but one. Would the disciples who followed the rabbi in Israel have recognized this deified and somewhat schizophrenic construct? The term 'only begotten' brought further complications, as did the phrase 'born of a virgin'. It indicated that God had sired no other son and that Mary had brought no other children into the world. This conclusion would be hilarious if its consequences had not been so tragic; the Gospels, those inerrant words of God, had got it wrong! How could a virgin have had a large family?

The creation of dogma rarely resulted in any degree of unanimity among the squabbling theologians of the Church, for it did not arise from any valid source of spiritual insight. Dogma was created in a similar way to the conclusions of the Council of Nicea, as a statement of the will of the majority in a vain attempt to paper over the many differences of belief that arose from a collection of churches founded on differing evangelical traditions. The Church, in the name of divinely revealed truth, simply used compromise allied to repression to control its bickering flock. Any dogma or policy that supported the fundamentally flawed theology of Paul, and that could be used as an instrument of Church governance, was built into its teaching. Any statement or fact that contradicted or devalued Church teaching was declared heretical and punished by exile, confiscation of property or death.

The phrase from the Gospels 'thou art Peter and upon this rock I will build my church' was used ruthlessly to bolster the authority of the Church and the new Church/State establishment. The Greek word *petra*, which originally related to the 'Rock of Israel', was deliberately mistranslated as if it was a play on words and was thereby related to the

Greek *petros* (or stone), an analogy for Peter. This claim was elaborated to the point where the Bishops of Rome claimed that only those who had received authority in a direct line of succession from Peter had divine validation to be the leaders of the Church. The heretical document of the Gnostics known as *The Apocalypse of Peter* described these self-same bishops as 'dry canals' and stated:

> They name themselves bishops and deacons as if they had received their authority directly from God ... Although they do not understand the mystery they nonetheless boast the secret of Truth is theirs alone.[26]

These dry canals, the bishops of Rome who were later to be called 'Popes', assumed to themselves a dramatic new role that was a complete reversal of previous practice. The Council of Nicea endorsed a much earlier claim made by Clement, the Bishop of Rome between 90 and 95 CE who was supposedly the fourth in succession after Peter. Clement forcefully promulgated the opinion that the leaders of the Church had been authorized by Almighty God to rule on earth in His name and, as they held 'the keys to the kingdom', they had divine authority to exert judgement and discipline over their congregations, which he called the 'laity'. After Nicea it became part of the dogma of the Church that the Bishop of Rome and the hierarchy who served under him were God's representatives on earth and that their pronouncements were made with divine authority. Thus the position held by the leader of the first Christian Church in Jerusalem, James the Just, had been completely negated. James, as High Priest, had been the spokesman of his people seeking forgiveness and guidance from Almighty God. Now his apparent successors had become the spokesmen of God who ruled their congregations with absolute and unquestionable authority. The transformation was devastating in the extreme; James the Just had *served* his people before God, the Bishops of Rome *ruled* their people in the name of God. When St Augustine perfected the doctrine that 'outside the Church there is no salvation', the absolute political control that was the ultimate objective of the Church hierarchy became explicit. This was made manifest by one saying in particular which arose after the Council of Nicea: 'If you want God as your Father you *must* have the Church as your Mother' [our emphasis].

All who claimed spiritual or dynastic authority that conflicted with the Church/State alliance were swept aside. The writer Laurence Gardner recorded this when he described how the Bishop of Rome, Pope Sylvester, informed a delegation of Desposyni, the true descendants of the Messiah, that they simply had no place in the new Christian order.[27] Despite the claim by the Church that it was preaching the same message as Jesus, Sylvester informed the delegation that the teachings of the Messiah had been superseded by Church doctrine and dogma which had been amended to bring it more in line with imperial desires. Despite the fact that Jesus had now been elevated to divine and co-equal status with Almighty God, the Pope, allegedly God's representative on earth, informed them that the power of salvation rested not in Jesus the Messiah but in the Roman Emperor, Constantine the Great.

Doctrinal disputes continued to exert significant pressure on the Church for over two centuries, with both Church and State continuing in their efforts to unify the Church and train it to be the obedient, respectful and fearful creature of the Pope in Rome. After Constantine founded the effective tool of the Church/State establishment, it continued to be used with increasing effect except for the brief period when the empire was ruled by Julian the Apostate.

THE MONOPOLY OF THE CHURCH

The Church not only fought venomous battles with the dissidents within its own ranks, but as it grew in power and became adopted as the official religion of the State it turned its attentions to the pagan religions. The doors were firmly shut against spiritual enquiry and insight, with all potential rivals ruthlessly swept away. The ancient Greek mystery cults were abolished and Gnostic sects within Christianity were brutally suppressed, their leaders persecuted and their scriptures destroyed.

By the middle of the 6th century, the religious establishment of Rome monopolized all access to the sacred in the Western Empire. It accomplished this by dogmatism within its own structures and the elimination of all rival religions, cults and centres of worship outside them; the ancient temples were closed and the oracles of old were silenced forever.[28] Not only did the Church exert rigorous control over all spiritual matters, but it deadened, for centuries to come, the search for knowledge and truth in the secular world.[29] It owned and controlled all centres of learning; no student was admitted who had not taken holy orders; the clergy were literate, the laity were illiterate and it was intended that they should remain so.[30] The individual citizen, who had been denied all personal access to the sacred save through the ministrations of the Church, was now kept in the perpetual slavery of sublime ignorance. What use was learning, when simple faith and obedience were all that was required for salvation? The contrast between the attitudes to education that were current in Classical Greece and the Christian 'Dark Ages' could not have been greater. This distinction was highlighted by the 20th-century English philosopher Bertrand Russell who wrote:

[Socrates] always says he knows nothing, he does not think knowledge lies beyond our reach. What matters is precisely that we should try to seek knowledge. For he holds that what makes a man sin is lack of knowledge. If only he knew, he would not sin. The one overriding cause of evil is therefore ignorance. Hence, to reach the Good we must have knowledge, and so the Good is knowledge. The link between Good and knowledge is a mark of Greek thought throughout. Christian ethics is quite opposed to this. There, the important thing is a pure heart, and that is likely to be found more readily among the ignorant.[31]

Not content to dominate just the peasants, the slaves and the merchants, the Church also sought to control the rulers of nations and repeatedly stated that as earthly kings and emperors only existed as God's chosen rulers, God's Church was of far greater authority than the State or those who ruled it. These attitudes formed the mould for European history and the brutality and intolerance that were to follow make a sad contrast to the loving precept of 'love thy neighbour as thyself'. The theology of the word of God had killed the essential, liberating truth of the word of God.

THE SPREAD OF CHRISTIANITY

At first missionary activities outside the frontiers guarded by the legions of Rome had been virtually non-existent, but with the disintegration of the empire new methods had to be found both to defend the Church and extend its influence. Europe before Charlemagne, the first Holy Roman Emperor, was an area of tribal settlement where frontiers were fluid or non-existent. The Church was the obvious repository of stability and the sole channel of culture, civilization and administrative expertise; the authoritative guardian of all that could be used to bridge the gulf between the old imperial system of Rome and the semi-barbaric condition of tribal Europe.

In the fluctuating chaos of emerging Europe, the Church was the only institution with any clear idea of where it was going, how or why. The tribal areas had been occupied by the invading hordes who had taken over lands which had lost the unifying structure and stability provided by the old empire. As the Gothic tribes settled in Italy and beyond, the Church made its first successful forays into the hinterlands and began to convert the Franks and the Burgundians. Bishops became not only spiritual leaders but also the military commanders of many districts, thus reinforcing the Church's reputation for establishing stability and order. An extensive bureaucracy sprang up in Rome which soon acquired considerable expertise in matters of civil administration.

Administrators bringing the benefits of civilization along with the blessings of the Church followed hard on the heels of the missionaries. In the emergent states, the Church became the major law-maker, with much of the customary law of the tribes being absorbed and codified into civil law by the clergy. They wrote down the oral legends, myths and stories of the newly converted peoples, adding their own gloss, omitting all that was offensive to accepted doctrine, retaining this, adding that, subtly changing the histories and forming the mould for new, essentially Christian, cultures. In this pervasive way the Church was able to distort the histories of entire peoples, devaluing for all time any potential rivals in the field of religious beliefs, thus increasing its grip not only on the current reality of the tribes but also on their ancient cultural heritage.[32] Its administrative skills were only one of the reasons for the success of the missionary activities; the other, and perhaps the most important, was its agricultural expertise. To starving people or to tribes living at subsistence level, the Church brought not only stability, law and administrative order, but more importantly good agricultural practice which provided a stable and reliable food supply.

CHRISTIAN 'LOVE' IN ACTION?

After the Council of Nicea, Constantine made it absolutely clear that the benefits and privileges which he had granted to the Christian Church 'must benefit only adherents of the Catholic faith',[33] which he defined as those who fully accepted the doctrine enshrined in the new creed and the authority of the Bishop of Rome. For those of differing belief he stated 'heretics and schismatics shall not only be alien from these privileges but shall be bound and subjugated to various public services'. Constantine's successors continued in the same vein, with membership of a heretical sect incurring a degree of legal infamy and a loss of civil rights. The Emperor Theodosius I debarred all heretics from public office and conducted purges against them.[34] The theologian St Augustine of Hippo, who created the guilt inducing doctrine of Original Sin, also formulated justification for religious coercion and the most vigorous investigation of heresy. The first person to be executed for heresy in the West was Priscillian of Avila in 383.[35]

With the effective end of the Arian faith in the 5th century a period of calm and unity of religious belief appeared to pervade Europe. With the Church's stranglehold on all forms of education, intellectual adventure was stifled and the superstitious populace remained quiescent in a state of ignorance and fear. After their rebuke by Pope Sylvester, the Desposyni and the other families of the Rex Deus group went underground in order to ensure their survival. It was not until the latter part of the 11th century that they started to act publicly and in concert in a manner that is discernible in the historical record.

PART

III

The Templar Era

9

The Resurrection of Rex Deus

Throughout the period known as the Dark Ages all heretics, dissidents and members of Rex Deus kept a very low profile. The families descended from the High Priests of the Temple in Jerusalem, including the dynasty founded by Jesus, spread throughout Europe and Asia Minor and consolidated their position among the leading members of the emerging aristocracies. They all outwardly practised the prevailing religion of their district and lived in a manner that ensured their escape from the unwelcome attentions of the 'thought police' of the Church/State establishment. In England, according to the tradition, Rex Deus became the major dynastic factor in the bloodline of the Saxon royal family. In France, while mention is made of the Merovingians as members of the Rex Deus group, this connection does not assume the almost overwhelming importance placed upon it by the authors of *The Holy Blood and the Holy Grail*. Certain of the group established themselves in positions of power well beyond the boundaries of Christian Europe and these families continued the tradition of practising the predominant religion of their district irrespective of what that may have been.

One strange story springs from this era. Our informant, Michael, told us that in about the 4th century certain members of Rex Deus disinterred the body of the Messiah from its hiding place somewhere in Greece and reburied it in the one place no one would ever dream of looking – under the Temple Mount in Jerusalem. To the best of our knowledge there is no proof of any interment whatsoever in these hallowed precincts. The only written reference linking the body of the Messiah to that site is to be found in the book *The Tomb of God*, which advanced the rather strange thesis that the body of Jesus had been disinterred from under the Mount and transported to France for reburial on a mountainside close to Rennes-le-Château. The 'evidence' produced to support this theory has caused considerable controversy and been condemned as highly speculative. One cannot doubt the sincerity of the authors, but this book nonetheless raises one important question which still remains unanswered. Where did the authors get the idea that Jesus was buried under the Temple Mount? This land was especially hallowed and no human burials were allowed there; the only reference we have found to a burial on this sacred site is from within the Rex Deus tradition and that did refer to the burial of the Messiah.

Traces of the Rex Deus families in the 11th century can be found by examining the career and known associates of one clearly identified member. Following the Norman Conquest, Princess Margaret, the daughter of the deposed true Saxon heirs to the throne of England, sought refuge in Hungary. The princess, a descendant of the Davidic and Hasmonean lines of the kings of biblical Israel, became engaged to be married to King Malcolm Canmore of Scotland. During the prolonged and dangerous journey from Hungary to her new home, she was accorded the protection of two knights, one from northern France and the other from Hungary. It is highly unlikely that this important personage would have been entrusted to the care of anyone other than fully fledged members of the Rex Deus group, who were aware of the true import of her bloodline.

These knights were granted estates in Scotland by their princess's grateful consort and founded dynasties that have exerted a major influence on Scottish history. The Hungarian knight, Sir Ladislaus Leslyn,[1] was the founder of the Leslie clan, and one event during his journey with the princess is immortalized forever in the clan coat of arms. While crossing a fast-moving river with the princess riding pillion, Ladislaus instructed her to hold fast to his buckler lest she be swept away by the current. The armorial bearings of the Leslies still display three buckles on their blazon and the motto 'hold fast'. The second Rex Deus knight was Sir William 'the Seemly' St Clair[2] from Normandy, in north-west France, who was a direct descendant of Røngvald the Mighty, the 9th-century Earl or Jarl of Möre in Norway[3]. Røngvald's son, Hrolf or Rollo, was a Viking raider who was created the first Duke of Normandy by the treaty of St Clare-sur-Epte in 912 CE.[4] After signing the treaty Rollo and his leading knights made an effortless conversion to Christianity.

THE ST CLAIRS

Rollo was warlike, prolific in breeding and shrewd in the way of the world. He extended his lands by conquest and his influence by alliance and marriage with the leading aristocratic families of the time. He sought to establish strong bonds with the local aristocracy and, in particular, matrimonial links with dynasties of the Rex Deus tradition, such as the families of Chaumont, Gisors, d'Evreaux, Blois,[5] the Counts of Champagne and the ruling House of Flanders, whose younger sons were the Counts of Boulogne. Was he also Rex Deus, from a family outside the confines of early Christian Europe? Was his effortless conversion to Christianity in accordance with the Rex Deus tradition of overtly practising the prevailing religion of their region? How else could he have had the insight to form alliances with families who were almost exclusively from the Rex Deus group? Within a few generations the various branches of the St Clairs owned vast tracts of land throughout Normandy and their alliances had embedded them firmly in the fabric of the French nobility. One St Clair, William the Bastard, a later Duke of

Normandy, successfully invaded England with the support of many of the leading St Clair knights and is now known as William the Conqueror. William the Seemly St Clair, on the other hand, made his somewhat circuitous journey to Scotland shortly after the Norman conquest of England, in which he did not play any part.[6]

The career of William the Seemly blossomed after his arrival in Scotland. Granted lands at Roslin by King Malcolm, William was appointed to the important position of the royal cupbearer.[7] The estates at Roslin were used by the Scottish king as a natural buffer in the defence of his country against the English invaders. Grants of such land were only made to people of demonstrable bravery, reliability and proven loyalty. How did a comparative stranger acquire such a reputation? The answer is simple; he came highly recommended by the new queen whose own family had had knowledge of his for over 1,000 years. The king's trust was not misplaced, for successive St Clair Lords of Roslin fought valiantly to protect their sovereign's territory against English incursions, and they became known as the 'Lordly Line of the High St Clairs'.

THE FIRST CRUSADE

Many noblemen from the Rex Deus group of families played a leading role in the planning and execution of the First Crusade. Known as 'the People's Crusade', this was called to liberate the sacred sites of the Holy Land from their Muslim occupiers. This should not disguise the fact that it was a military expedition of considerable complexity mounted by a group of noblemen of consummate military skill and dedication. The true objective was, more importantly, the re-establishment of the ancient biblical throne at Jerusalem, which was to be occupied by its rightful heir, the direct descendant of the Davidic and Hasmonean royal lines of Israel. Henri de St Clair, the son of William the Seemly St Clair and the first of his line to be born in Scotland, took part in the First Crusade and played an active role in the successful siege and assault on Jerusalem.[8]

When the crusaders entered the holy city they went berserk; Arab, Christian, Muslim and Jew alike were slaughtered. According to eyewitness accounts the invading knights' horses were wading knee-deep in blood.[9] Thus the city fell to the invaders and the sacred places were restored to Christian care.

At a conclave of knights, whose membership was secret, the throne of the newly conquered territories was offered to the rightful heir of the Davidic line and a direct descendant of Jesus, Godfroi de Bouillon.[10] Appalled at the indiscriminate slaughter of so many innocent citizens he refused the royal title but accepted all the royal prerogatives and responsibilities and asked to be known simply as the Protector of the Holy Sepulchre.[11] In this manner the Rex Deus group achieved one of their primary objectives and it was now time to consolidate their position in the Holy Land, capitalize on it and exploit it by every means at their disposal. Action was required, therefore, not only from the families who were already in the Holy Land but also from some who lived in Byzantium and others who remained in Europe. These included the Count of Champagne, several of his vassals such as André de Montbard, André's nephew Bernard de Fontaines, and Hughes de Payen.

THE COURT OF CHAMPAGNE

With Godfroi de Bouillon established as the Protector of Jerusalem, the main centre of activity for members of Rex Deus in Western Europe became the city of Troyes in eastern France, the seat of Hughes I, Count of Champagne, who was the godson of King Philippe I of France. Although nominally subjects of the King of France, the Counts of Champagne were in fact virtually independent princes who occupied lands, somewhat larger than the country of Wales, which lay to the east and south-east of Paris. They not only owed allegiance to the King of France but also the Holy Roman Emperor and the Duke of Burgundy. The family of the Counts of Champagne were linked by blood and marriage to the St Clairs,[12] the Capetian Kings of France, the Duke of Burgundy and the Norman and Plantagenet Kings of England. In 1104 the Count of Champagne met in secret conclave with members drawn from certain distinguished noble families – Brienne, de Joinville, Chaumont and Anjou[13] – all of whom were members of Rex Deus. Almost immediately afterwards he departed on the long journey to the Holy Land and did not return to his family estates until 1108. In 1114 he again set out for the kingdom of Jerusalem announcing his intention of joining *la Milice du Christ* – the Militia of Christ.[14] For reasons that are not clear he returned to Europe a year later and almost immediately made a substantial donation of land to the Cistercian Order.

Troyes was the centre for one of the most active courts in Europe, which attracted courtiers, knights and intellectuals of considerable stature. It was known for its important leather industry – the Jews of the city were renowned for their skill in making parchment – and many of the vineyards in the region were also owned by Jews. The greatest Jewish thinker in European history, Rabbi Solomon ben Isaac, otherwise known as Rashi, lived in the city and was frequently a welcome guest at the court of Hughes of Champagne. He was a man of such intellectual repute that even to this day he is held to be second in importance only to the great Jewish intellectual, Maimonides. The tolerance of the regime of Hughes of Champagne was such that Rashi was able to maintain a Cabbalistic school of considerable stature in the city.[15] The Cabbala was the principal formal method used to impart the hidden, Gnostic teachings of mystical Judaism. The origins of Cabbalistic teaching reach back to antiquity, but it only became manifest in the form we now recognize in the Rabbinical schools of Moorish Spain during the 10th and 11th centuries.

BERNARD OF CLAIRVAUX

Another important player in these mysterious events was Bernard de Fontaines, the nephew of André de Montbard, who joined the struggling

Cistercian Order under rather peculiar circumstances.[16] Founded to purify the rather corrupt monastic system and reassert the stark simplicity of the rule of St Benedict, the Cistercians were, at that time, in imminent danger of collapse. When Bernard took holy orders, over 30 of his immediate male relatives and many of his friends accompanied him; the new influx of vocations more than doubled the membership of the Order.[17] Among those who accompanied him were his uncle, the knight Gaudri de Touillon, his two younger brothers and, surprisingly, his elder brother who was married with children and who was heir to the family estate.[18] The Order was now in a position to found a new abbey. Bernard was appointed as the abbot of this daughter house of the Cistercians,[19] which was built on the donation of land made by Hughes I, the Count of Champagne. The abbey was called Clairvaux and while Bernard of Clairvaux, as he now became known, never formally led the Cistercian Order, he rose to a position of almost unbelievable power within the Church. He became a close personal adviser to the Pope and, as a churchman and diplomat, exerted great influence in temporal affairs, being the adviser of kings, emperors and leading families among the nobility. Despite his position within the mainstream of the Church, his deep commitment to the initiatory style of teaching used by Jesus and the Ebionites is made clear by the 120 sermons he preached, all based on the Song of Songs by King Solomon.[20]

THE KNIGHTS TEMPLAR

Bernard of Clairvaux played a mysterious role in the foundation of an Order of warrior monks who were to become one of the most powerful and controversial organizations in European history. They were known by a variety of names: the Poor Knights of Christ and the Temple of Solomon, the Militia of Christ or, more commonly, the Knights Templar. Detailed accounts of the founding of the Order are non-existent. The main source used by historians are the documents written by Guillaume de Tyre[21] some 70 years after the event, and while this is commonly accepted as the true account, alternative versions do exist supported by documentation that makes them seem reasonably credible.

According to Guillaume de Tyre, the Order was founded by a vassal of the Count of Champagne, a certain Hughes de Payen, acting with André de Montbard, the uncle of Bernard of Clairvaux. In 1118, the two knights along with seven companions presented themselves to the younger brother of Godfroi de Bouillon who had accepted the title of King Baudouin I of Jerusalem. They announced to the monarch that it was their intention to found an Order of warrior monks so that 'as far as their strength permitted, they should keep the roads and highways safe … with a special regard for the protection of pilgrims'.[22] The king gave them quarters which included the stables of what was believed to be the Temple of Solomon,[23] and the Patriarch of Jerusalem, another relative of Bernard of Clairvaux, granted them the right to wear the Cross of Lorraine as their insignia. The new Order took vows of personal poverty and chastity and swore to hold all their property in common. The original nine knights are generally believed to have been:

- Hughes de Payen, a vassal of Hughes I of Champagne and a relative by marriage to the St Clairs of Roslin
- André de Montbard, the uncle of Bernard of Clairvaux and another vassal of Hughes of Champagne
- Geoffroi de St Omer, a son of Hughes de St Omer
- Payen de Montdidier, a relative of the ruling family of Flanders
- Achambaud de St-Amand, another relative of the ruling house of Flanders
- Geoffroi Bisol
- Gondemar
- Rossal
- Godfroi[24]

According to Priory documents and the forged Secret Dossiers, André de Montbard, Gondemar and Rossal, plus two knights who do not figure on the above list, were all members of the secretive Order known as the Priory of Sion. No other evidence has ever been advanced to support this somewhat dubious claim. Far from being members of the Priory of Sion, brothers Gondemar and Rossal were in fact Cistercian monks who were just transferring their allegiance. Many would simply see this transfer as one that took place between the monastic and the military arm of the same Order, for the Cistercians and the Knights Templar were so closely linked by ties of blood, patronage and shared objectives that many Templar scholars believe that they were two arms of the same body.

HUGHES OF CHAMPAGNE

In *The Holy Blood and the Holy Grail* it is alleged that Hughes I of Champagne ranked among the co-founders of the Order of the Knights Templar, and his position in this whole affair is most curious. There is a letter to him from the Bishop of Chartres dated 1114, congratulating him on his intention to join *La Milice du Christ*. He certainly took up a form of lay associate membership of the Order in 1124 and thereby created a bizarre anomaly in feudal terms, for by joining it and swearing obedience to its grand master, Hughes de Payen, he came under the direct control of a man who, in the normal social order of things, was his own vassal.[25] Baigent, Leigh and Lincoln and the disputed Priory documents are not the sole source for the strange assertion that Hughes of Champagne was among the original founders of the Templars, nor were they the only authorities to claim that the Order was founded somewhat earlier than was claimed by Guillaume de Tyre.

A secret Templar archive has recently been discovered in the principality of Seborga in northern Italy, containing documents that confuse this issue still further. It is claimed that Bernard of Clairvaux founded a monastery there in 1113, to protect a 'great secret'. This monastery, under the direction of its abbot, Edouard, contained two monks who had joined the order with Bernard: two knights who took the names of Gondemar and Rossal in their profession as monks. One document claims that in February 1117 Bernard came to this monastery, released Gondemar and Rossal from their vows and then blessed them and their seven companions prior to their departure to Jerusalem, which did not actually take place until November 1118. The seven companions of the two ex-Cistercians are listed as follows: André de Montbard, Count Hughes I of Champagne, Hughes de Payen, Payen de Montdidier, Geoffroi de St Omer, Archambaud de St-Amand and Geoffroi Bisol. The document records that Bernard nominated Hughes de Payen as the first grand master of the Poor Militia of Christ and that he was consecrated in this position by the Abbot Edouard of Seborga.

Whether or not Hughes of Champagne was directly involved in the actual founding of the Knights Templar is open to debate. However, two things are certain. First, the Count of Champagne was at the very least a prime mover behind the scenes, even if he is not to be numbered among the original nine founding knights. Second, those involved in both founding and promoting the Order were linked by a complex web of direct family relationships. The ancestry of Hughes de Payen, for example, shows that his family were a cadet branch of the dynasty of the Counts of Champagne and therefore he was linked both by blood and allegiance to Hughes I. This is not the only anomaly in the whole bizarre story. The main reason given for the founding of the Templars, to protect the pilgrim routes, does not bear any close examination whatsoever for the first 10 or 12 years of their existence. It would have been a physical impossibility for nine middle-aged or elderly knights to protect the dangerous route from Jaffa to Jerusalem from all the bandits who believed that the pilgrims who provided such easy pickings were a gift from God. The recorded actions of the knights make this an even more incredible scenario, for they did not patrol the dangerous roads of the Holy Land to protect the pilgrims, but spent nine years in the dangerous and demanding task of excavating and mining a series of tunnels under their quarters on the Temple Mount.[26] These arduous tasks were apparently completed with the patronage and support of the King of Jerusalem.

THE EXCAVATIONS

The tunnels mined by the Templars were re-excavated in the early years of this century by Lieutenant Warren of the Royal Engineers.[27] The access tunnel descends vertically downwards for 80ft through solid rock before radiating horizontally in a series of minor tunnels under the site of the ancient Temple. Lieutenant Warren failed to find the hidden treasure of the Temple of Jerusalem, but in the tunnels excavated so laboriously by the Templars he found a spur, remnants of a lance, a small Templar cross and the major part of a Templar sword. These artefacts are now preserved for posterity by Robert Brydon of Edinburgh, a leading Templar scholar. Also in his keeping is a letter from a Captain Parker who took part in Warren's excavation under the Temple and several subsequent ones. Parker wrote to Robert's grandfather in 1912 and told of how, on one of these expeditions, he had discovered a secret room carved out of solid rock beneath the Temple site with a passage leading from it to the Mosque of Omar. Parker went on to describe how, when he broke through the stonework at the end of the passage and found himself within the confines of the mosque, he had to flee from a small army of extremely angry and devout Muslims. Two questions arise from the nature and position of these Templar excavations. What were they seeking? And how did they know precisely where to dig?

By the north door on the exterior of Chartres Cathedral, there is a carving on a pillar which gives us an indication of their objective. It shows the Ark of the Covenant being transported on a wheeled vehicle.[28] Legend recounts that the Ark of the Covenant had been secreted deep beneath the Temple in Jerusalem centuries before the fall of the city to the Romans. It had been hidden there to protect it from yet another invading army who had laid the city to waste. Hughes de Payen had been chosen by his fellow members of the Rex Deus group to lead the expedition mounted to locate the Ark and bring it back to Europe.[29] Persistent legends in the esoteric community indicate that it was then hidden for a considerable time deep beneath the crypt of Chartres Cathedral. The same legends also claim that the Templars found many other sacred artefacts from the old Jewish Temple in the course of their investigations as well as a considerable quantity of documentation. While there has been much speculation as to the exact nature of these documents, a reasonable consensus is emerging that they contained scriptural scrolls, treatises on sacred geometry, and details of certain knowledge, art and science – the hidden wisdom of the ancient initiates of the Judaic/Egyptian tradition[30]. One modern archaeological discovery suggests confirmation of this. The so-called Copper Scroll, one of the Dead Sea Scrolls discovered at Qumran, tends to confirm not only the objective of the Templar excavations but also, albeit indirectly, the transmission of knowledge through the generations among the members of the Rex Deus families.

The Copper Scroll, which was unrolled and deciphered at Manchester University under the guidance of John Allegro, was a list of all the burial sites used to hide the various items, both sacred and profane, described as the treasure of the Temple of Jerusalem. Many of these sites have been re-excavated since its discovery and several of them have disclosed not Temple treasure but evidence of Templar excavations made in the 12th century. The only rational scenario that can possibly explain how the Templars knew exactly where to dig is the concept that secret knowledge had been passed down the generations through families whose roots lay in the Temple precincts of Jerusalem over 1,000 years earlier. It is significant that the name Roslin, chosen by William the Seemly St Clair for his first estate in Scotland, is derived from Gaelic which, when translated into English, means 'ancient knowledge passed down the generations'.[31]

THE RETURN TO EUROPE

The discoveries made by the Knights Templar as a result of their excavations created several problems. Geoffroi de St Omer was despatched back to France with certain of the scrolls, which he took to his scholarly relative, Lambert de St Omer, who made a copy of one of them which now resides in the library of Ghent University.[32] The County of Ghent had been founded by a college of four families drawn from the ranks of Rex Deus, who chose the Count of Flanders from among their number. When the news of the first finds was relayed back to Europe, Count Fulk d'Anjou sped with all haste to Jerusalem where he took the oath of allegiance to the new Order.[33] He immediately granted it an annuity of 30 Angevin livres before returning to Anjou. When one considers that the vast majority of knights joining the Order stayed within its ranks for their lifetime, this action by Fulk of Anjou is a trifle strange. His apparent freedom of manoeuvre, despite his oath of allegiance, can be explained by his ancestry, for Fulk was not only the Count of Anjou and a Templar but also a senior member of Rex Deus who later became the King of Jerusalem.

The next notable figure to arrive in Jerusalem was the Count of Champagne who took the oath of membership in 1124. As stated earlier, this created the bizarre situation in which the count swore an oath of obedience to one of his own vassals. The only rational explanation lies in the collective loyalty of the Rex Deus families, whose own order of rank took precedence over normal feudal practice.

Behind the scenes in Europe, Bernard of Clairvaux, who had become a senior adviser to the Pope, consolidated his position within the Church. There was a pressing need for the Rex Deus members burrowing away so actively in Jerusalem to keep the true nature of their activities secret. The arrival of notabilities such as Fulk of Anjou and Hughes de Champagne in the small European population of Jerusalem could not be hidden, so a cover story had to be created. Bernard began to persuade the Pope that the new military Order which was already active in the Holy Land should be given papal backing and a formal position within the Church. For this they would need a rule, a formal charter stating the aims and objectives of the Order, the obligations of its members to it and the rules of membership, as well as the establishment of a formal command structure. No one can be sure how long this process took, but it is hardly a coincidence that the first delegation of Templars who returned from Jerusalem with their hoard of sacred treasure and holy scrolls arrived just in time to attend the Council of Troyes and receive their rule.[34] There must have been close co-operation between Bernard and the team who were organizing the council, and the successful excavators in Jerusalem.

The main excavations in Jerusalem were completed in late December of 1127. Hughes de Payen with all the knights of the new Order escorted their finds back to their associates among the Rex Deus families in France. The grand master, Hughes de Payen, and his principal co-founder of the Order, André de Montbard, then met the King of England who was visiting some of his French estates. The English king had married twice and on both occasions had chosen his bride from eligible ladies drawn from the ranks of Rex Deus. He granted safe conduct to Hughes de Payen and his companion, who crossed the Channel and travelled north across the border to Scotland where they stayed at Roslin with the St Clairs,[35] Hughes' relatives by marriage and leading members of Rex Deus. King David of Scotland, the son of the Rex Deus and Saxon Princess Margaret, made an immediate grant of land to the new Order which became their headquarters in Scotland. The new Templar lands adjoined the estates of Roslin, the property of the Rex Deus family of St Clair. The oldest Templar site in Scotland, once known as Ballantrodoch, is now called Temple after the Order.

10

The Actions and Beliefs of the Knights Templar

The Templars were granted their rule in 1128 and soon gained an exceptional degree of legal autonomy, being responsible through their grand masters to the Pope alone.[1] The grant of land at Ballantrodoch by King David was followed by many similar gifts from Rex Deus members throughout Europe, with other pious members of the aristocracy also making generous donations of land and finance to the rapidly growing Order, which soon numbered representatives from all the leading families in Western Europe among its ranks.

France, Provence, and the Languedoc-Roussillon areas became the Templar's major power centre, while the rapid growth in resources and skilled manpower enabled them to establish important bases throughout the Holy Land, to the extent that they became one of the most significant forces within the kingdom of Jerusalem. They soon acquired a well-earned reputation for bravery in battle and never willingly surrendered to the enemy. However, their reputation for generalship and strategic thinking is not rated so highly. Their extensive and costly military activities in Outremer, as Palestine became known, were financed by the profits from their estates and activities in Western Europe.

Material wealth in the early twelfth century was almost invariably based on land and feudal dues. The Knights Templar owned estates of varying size scattered throughout every climatic zone in Europe from Poland, Denmark, Scotland and the Orkneys in the north, to France, Italy and Spain in the south.[2] Their commercial interests were impressive and varied and their activities included the operation of farms, vineyards, stone quarries and mines. As a result of their two-fold interest in protecting pilgrims on the one hand and maintaining communications with their bases in the Holy Land on the other, they operated a well-organized fleet which exceeded that of any state at the time. This included a number of highly manoeuvrable war galleys fitted with rams, and for carrying pilgrims, troops, horses and commercial cargoes they owned a large number of ships which plied the Mediterranean between bases in Italy, France, Spain and the Holy Land. Their main seat of naval power was on the island of Majorca, while their principal port on the Atlantic coast was the highly fortified harbour of La Rochelle from where, it is alleged, they conducted trade with Greenland, the British Isles, the North American mainland and Mexico.[3] This seemingly incredible allegation is apparently confirmed by the sagas of Rex Deus. Within 50 years of their foundation, the Knights Templar had become a commercial force equal in power to many states; within 100 years they had developed into the medieval precursors of multi-national conglomerates, with interests in every form of commercial activity, and were far richer than any kingdom in Europe.[4]

The transformative effect of Templar activity upon European culture and commerce was remarkable, and yet many modern Church historians still accuse the Order of being formed of illiterate knights. The so-called 'illiterates' developed sophisticated and coded means of communication which transcended the linguistic barriers which otherwise would have fragmented the commercial impact of their activities.[5] Among the principal items of their trading activities were those which we would describe in modern terms as 'technology and ideas'.[6] The Templar communication network was the principal route by which knowledge of astronomy, mathematics, herbal medicine and healing skills made their way from the Holy Land to Europe. Among the technological advances brought back by the warrior knights were mouth-to-mouth resuscitation, the telescope and a financial instrument which they acquired from the Sufis of Islam, known as 'the note of hand'.

TEMPLAR BUILDING

The Templars were great builders. On their own estates they built and maintained castles, fortified farms, barns, outbuildings and mills as well as dormitory blocks, stables and workshops. Some Templar castles, particularly in southern Europe and the Holy Land, were built on defensive sites which posed incredible difficulties of construction. They were particularly renowned for building strategically situated castles with water gates on coasts and rivers. The classic round Templar church, founded on octagonal geometry and supposedly based on the design of the Church of the Holy Sepulchre in Jerusalem, became such a distinctive feature of Templar construction that it became almost diagnostic of their involvement. This type of building formed only a small part of their church construction programme, albeit of very special and cabbalistic significance.[7] The vast majority of Templar churches, especially those in the southern regions of Europe, are small, undecorated, rectangular structures, often with apsidal ends.

According to many scholars, including the ecclesiastical historian Fred Gettings, the Templars were openly involved in the financing and construction of the Gothic cathedrals.[8] The sudden flowering of the Gothic style of architecture, which enabled cathedrals to be built of far greater height with more windows, brought about a new era in church design and art that allowed larger naves and greater spaces, uncluttered by pillars, to be created within church buildings. It is no coincidence that this architectural form, which cannot be explained as an evolutionary development from the Romanesque style that preceded it, arose after the knights returned from their excavations in Jerusalem.

One cathedral above all others is a hymn to their direct involvement and belief: Chartres in France. Constructed with almost unbelievable speed, Chartres Cathedral is portrayed by the Church as the product of co-operative effort by the townspeople, financed by the pilgrim trade. This totally fails to explain the massive input of financial resources that must have been necessary to pay for the quarrying and transport of the stone, and the enormous expenditure on the huge numbers of stonemasons, sculptors and other craftsmen who would have been employed to complete such a vast and complex edifice at such speed. It is highly doubtful if the proceeds of the pilgrimage to Chartres over the period of its construction would have paid for the stained-glass windows, much less for the construction and decoration of the entire building. The only source of finance in Europe at that time which could have produced the resources necessary was the Order of the Knights Templar.

In England, craftsmen who work in stone are known as stone-masons; in France they are known collectively as members of the Compagnonage who, in the 12th century, were broadly divided into three groups, fulfilling separate functions: the Children of Father Soubise were responsible for the construction of ecclesiastical buildings in the Romanesque style; the Children of Master Jacques were also known as *Les Compagnons Passant* and one of their primary functions was the art of bridge building. The craftmasons who built the Gothic cathedrals, who were instructed in the art of sacred geometry by Cistercian monks, were known as the Children of Solomon, named after King Solomon who, according to the Scriptures, commissioned the first Temple in Jerusalem.[9] The Knights Templar, acting with the agreement of Bernard of Clairvaux, gave a 'rule' to the Children of Solomon in March 1145, which laid down the conditions required for living and working. The preface to his rule contains words which have been intimately associated with the Knights Templar ever since:

> We the Knights of Christ and of the Temple follow the destiny that prepares us to die for Christ. We have the wish to give this rule of living, of work and of honour to the constructors of churches so that Christianity can spread throughout the earth **not so that our name should be remembered, Oh Lord, but that Your Name should live**[10] [our emphasis].

It was not only the Order of the Knights Templar who attained immense wealth, property, power and prestige in the years that followed the completion of their excavations in Jerusalem. Under the guiding hand of Bernard of Clairvaux the once struggling Order of Cistercian monks expanded at a similar rate. Within his lifetime the Cistercians established over 300 abbeys throughout Europe, a truly outstanding era of growth that was never even approached by any other monastic Order. The Cistercians became known as the 'apostles of the frontier' from their habit of refusing donations of land near major centres of population and opting instead to site their new establishments in marginal lands in the mountains and barren reaches of Christian Europe. The Templars, on the other hand, sited their possessions within cities, at centres of pilgrimage and sea ports as well as in the countryside, with a special emphasis on estates strategically situated near major trade and pilgrimage routes. In England and Wales they had over 5,000 properties and they also owned a considerable number in Scotland, Ireland, Poland, Denmark, the Low Countries and the German states; they even had estates in Hungary guarding the overland routes to the Holy Land. Spain, long a centre of devout pilgrimage to the shrine of St James of Compostela, was liberally adorned with Templar strongholds and the Order played its part in defending Christian Spain against Moorish incursions.

Similar Orders arose and achieved some degree of renown by modelling themselves on the Templars. Two such in Spain were the Knights of Calatrava and the Knights of Alcantara.[11] Both were founded shortly after the Templars and Bernard of Clairvaux is known to have played a part in this. Were these also outward manifestations of Rex Deus? There were many Templar establishments in Italy, which was one of the major embarkation points on the sea routes to the kingdom of Jerusalem, but their most important power base in Europe was the present country of France. In the south are the regions of Provence and the Languedoc-Roussillon which, in the Templar era, were separate entities from the kingdom of France. Throughout these southern regions Templar holdings were plentiful, with over 30 per cent of the total estates owned by them throughout Europe situated in the Languedoc-Roussillon alone.[12]

IN THE VICINITY OF RENNES-LE-CHÂTEAU

Much play has been made about Templar lands surrounding the village of Rennes-le-Château. Archival records in the region are remarkably comprehensive and, according to George Kiess of the Centre d'Etudes et de Recherches Templières, the only authentic Templar site mentioned which is near to Rennes-le-Château is the village which is now the site of the permanent exhibition of CERT, Campagne-sur-Aude. The allegation that the Templars had a commanderie at Bézu which escaped the attentions of the Seneschals of King Philippe le Bel at the time of the suppression of the Order is pure invention. The Templar commanderie at Bézu never existed. The assertion that Bézu was Templar property was made by the Abbé Mazières, a historian whose work is highly questionable; when questioned about his sources the abbé became somewhat embarrassed and claimed that the archives upon which his research was based had been destroyed. No other local historian of note has ever had sight of this documentation. Bézu is recorded in the local archives as once being the abode of medieval 'coiners' who forged currency for many years.

The claim that Bertrand de Blanchefort, whom Baigent, Leigh and Lincoln were convinced was the fourth grand master of the Knights Templar, lived at the Château de Blanchefort within sight of Rennes-le-Château, is inaccurate. There are many places in France called Blanquefort, Blancafort or Blanchefort. As French noblemen were invariably known by the names of their estates and not by their family surnames, there is great opportunity for confusion. Bertrand de Blanchefort, who was the sixth grand master of the Knights Templar and not the fourth, did not originate from, live or own land in the region of Rennes-le-Château. He came from Guyenne in Aquitaine,[13] which had been a major centre of Rex Deus settlement since the fall of the Roman Empire and was still dominated by their nobility. How, therefore, could he donate the estates of Bézu, which he did not own, to the Order he commanded?

The true extent of Templar activity in the Languedoc-Roussillon was very considerable and can still be substantiated from archival records and by archaeological examination of the substantial remains of Templar buildings that abound in the district. A considerable body of work has been completed under the auspices of the Centre d'Etudes et de Recherches Templières which has authenticated a large number of Templar properties in the Languedoc and Roussillon districts.

THE TRANSFORMATIVE
ACTIVITIES OF THE TEMPLARS

Prior to the Templars, Europe was a hegemony of squabbling feudal fiefdoms, counties and kingdoms. Long-distance trade was largely non-existent, except by sea, and all travellers were vulnerable to attack by brigands and extortion by feudal lords who charged a toll for safe passage through their lands. Towns were small and relatively powerless, being subject to the all-pervading will of the Church/State establishment or the arbitrary rule of the seigneur, or lord, of the district. With the advent of the Knights Templar all this was about to change dramatically.

The Templars' declared objective of protecting the pilgrimage routes was not restricted to travel within the Holy Land. Not only did they control the routes spreading like a fan northwards from the Mediterranean coast, which were used by the devout in their attempts to reach the birth place of the Saviour, they also policed all the other pilgrim routes. A complex series of communication networks linked every part of Europe to the major international sites of pilgrimage in Jerusalem, Rome and, most important of all in the 12th to 14th centuries, St James of Compostela in Spain.[14] The district surrounding Compostela in northwest Spain had, like the province of Aquitaine, been administered by Rex Deus families since the time of the Roman occupation. These routes alone linked all the major population centres in Europe. In addition to these were all the national sites of pilgrimage, such as Canterbury in England and Chartres, Mont-St-Michel, Rocamadour and the many other sites of veneration of the Black Madonna in France. Mont-St-Michel was closely linked to St Michael's Mount off the south coast of Cornwall in the Rex Deus sagas, which also give a strange insight into the cult of the Black Madonna; the sagas describe the Hasmonean family as 'black'. With Templar protection, travel by pilgrim or trader alike along the major routes of Europe was now possible in comparative safety and freedom from extortion or assault. One other innovation was made by the Templars which further enhanced the safety of trade and accelerated the change in the balance of power between the feudal lords and the towns, the creation of a complex and highly efficient banking system.[15]

The Templars used their immense wealth with skill and wisdom. Not only did they make substantial strategic investments in land and agricultural pursuits, they also invested in basic industries which provided the essential ingredients for the massive expansion in building, both lay and ecclesiastical, which began to change the face of Europe. Using their own commercial insights as well as techniques which they adopted from their Muslim opponents in the east, they developed the concept of financial transfer by 'note of hand' into something like its modern equivalent, developed the bankers' cheque and the precursor of the credit card. This latter development arose from the financial needs created by the medieval equivalent of the 'package tour industry' – the pilgrimage trade. Pilgrimage was a long, arduous and expensive enterprise for the pilgrim and a source of immense profit for the Church and innkeepers, ferrymen and others *en route*. The pilgrim would be wary of carrying large sums of money as he travelled, for fear of robbery, extortion or accident. The answer was simple; seek out the master of the local Templar commanderie and deposit sufficient funds with him to cover the estimated cost of the return journey, including travel, accommodation and ancillary costs such as alms and gift-giving. In return for the financial deposit, the Templar treasurer would give the traveller a coded chit as a form of receipt and a means of exchange. At each overnight stop, or where alms or offerings had to be given, the pilgrim would hand his chit to the local Templar representative who would pay any dues outstanding, recode the chit accordingly and return it to its owner. When the pilgrimage was over and the weary traveller had returned home, he would present the chit to the treasurer who had first issued it. Any balance of credit would be returned in cash, or if the pilgrim had overspent he would be presented with the appropriate bill. The entire pilgrimage trade policed by the Templars bears a startling resemblance to the modern package tour industry. The modern equivalent of the Templar chit is, of course, the credit card.

Templar banking practice was not restricted to the pilgrimage trade, they also arranged safe transfer of funds for international and local trade, the Church and the State. In the medieval era it was forbidden for Christians to charge interest on loans and therefore money-lending as a profession had been traditionally restricted to the Jews. This did little to enhance their reputation as a racial group, which was already jeopardized by the persistent allegation that they were 'Christ killers'. The Knights

Templar found a way round this which allowed them to lend considerable sums of money at interest without being subjected to the charge of usury. It was quite permissible to charge rent for the leasing of a house or land, so the Templars used this principle in their money lending and charged 'rent' rather than interest for the services they rendered. The rent was payable at the time the loan was granted and was added to the capital sum borrowed. By this euphemism they avoided being brought before the courts on the un-Christian charge of usury. Their wealth was such that their financial services were not only sought by the merchants and landowners of feudal Europe, but by the princes of the Church and State. They lent to bishops to finance church building programmes; to princes, kings and emperors to finance state works, building programmes, wars and crusades.[16] Within the twin embrace of financial security and safe travel, Europe began to transform itself. Safe and effective trade over longer distances led to the accumulation of capital and the emergence of a newly prosperous merchant class, the urban bourgeoisie. The new-found wealth of the city merchants changed the balance of power still further in favour of the towns and cities. With the peace and tranquillity of the countryside now ensured the feudal lords began to lose the *raison d'être* on which their power was based.

The Order of the Knights Templar, despite its relatively short life span, was the major instrument of transformative change in medieval Europe. From their Arab opponents in the Holy Land, the Templars brought many blessings of knowledge and technology that conferred immense benefits on the European population. The Gothic cathedrals that arose from their knowledge of sacred geometry still adorn the European landscape and form a permanent series of 'prayers in stone' that raise their spires skyward in silent supplication. When taken as a whole the various activities of the Knights Templar are like a huge mosaic of individual pieces which together form a picture that accurately predicted the future. The Order was not merely the medieval precursor of the modern multi-national conglomerate but was in many respects an early embryonic form of the European Union. When we compare the effects of the activities of the Templar Order on European culture with those of its rivals, the question that inevitably arises is: What was it about the Knights Templar that made them so markedly different from any other religious or military Order of that time? Why was it this Order and no other that effected such a profound and transformative change that touched the lives of nearly everyone living in Europe? To gain some understanding of what motivated these warrior monks, we must examine the true nature of their spiritual and religious beliefs (something academic historians have been very reluctant to do), some indication of which can be found in the carvings and iconography of the cathedrals of Chartres and Amiens.

CHARTRES CATHEDRAL
AND THE BLACK MADONNA

In Chartres Cathedral, a major centre of Christian worship, there is not one carving that originates from within the first 200 years of the cathedral's existence which makes any reference to the central tenet of Christian belief, the crucifixion.[17] The only reference from the 12th century to what St Paul describes as this 'redemptive sacrifice' is to be found in a stained-glass window in the west front, which is one of the last surviving parts of the previous cathedral erected by Bishop Fulbertus in 1150 and destroyed by fire in 1194.[18] The west front of Fulbertus' cathedral was incorporated into the present building, which was begun after the fire and was completed within a span of 30 years.

Long before the advent of Christianity, a fire-blackened Druidic Madonna and Child, described by Caesar as Virgini Parturae, was venerated on the site that was later used by the Christians for their cathedral.[19] The ancient Druidic statue was preserved for centuries in the crypt of the cathedral and, along with the robe of Mary, was regarded as a particularly sacred object of veneration by many thousands of pilgrims.

Bishop Fulbertus had a particular reverence for the Virgin Mary and played a major role in the spread of Mariolatry in medieval Europe. This veneration was given visual representation by the carving of a replica of Virgini Parturae, in the guise of Mary the mother of God, on the main portal of the west front of the cathedral.

The Templars used Mariolatry as a vehicle to disguise a central heretical tenet of their own beliefs under the guise of the cult of the Black Madonna. This form of veneration rapidly spread from Chartres throughout France, Spain and much of Europe, so that under the guise of worshipping the Black Madonna, the Templar cult of Isis and the Horus child and the heretical and feminine principle of divine wisdom was practised under the noses of the unsuspecting clergy.[20] Isis was the black Egyptian goddess associated with wisdom and gnosis, traditionally depicted as the divine mother of the god Horus. This cult is also linked to the respect and veneration accorded to the true role played by Mary Magdalene, the wife of Jesus. The English author Ean Begg has recorded that there are no less than 50 centres of devotion dedicated to St Mary Magdalene which also contain shrines to the Black Madonna.[21] If one studies a map of these sites of dual interest, the greatest concentration is to be found in the Lyons, Vichy, and Clermont-Ferrand districts, which contains a range of hills known locally as 'the Mountains of the Madeleine'. Wherever one finds a shrine to the Black Madonna, one can immediately associate two groups with its veneration, the Knights Templar and Rex Deus. We have mentioned earlier that Bernard of Clairvaux had preached 120 sermons on the Song of Songs. Traditionally the Song of Songs has been associated with the Magdalene and the link with the cult of the Black Madonna is quite explicit when the female lover says 'I am black but comely'. Bernard of Clairvaux enjoined the Cistercians, the Templars and the Children of Solomon to make 'obedience to Bethany and the house of Mary and Martha'.[22] Many authorities believe that the majority of the new Gothic cathedrals dedicated to Our Lady that arose as a result of Templar activity were not dedicated to Mary the mother of Jesus, but to the wife of Jesus, Mary Magdalene or Mary of Bethany.

In many of the churches with proven Templar connections, direct artistic references to Jesus himself are rare, and in the few that do occur he is always shown as a teacher or a guide, never as a sacrifice. Paradoxically, for knights supposedly dedicated to the Christian cause, two Johns seem to take preference over Jesus in both artistic and religious terms. One of these is depicted with unfailing regularity in every major site of Templar influence; the other is rarely depicted at all and yet seems to have been the principal source of Templar beliefs. These two characters were John the Baptist, and John the Evangelist – the disciple whom Jesus loved and the prolific author of many scriptural documents long since lost or suppressed by Holy Mother the Church, such as the *Acts of John* and the *Gospel of Love*.

AMIENS CATHEDRAL AND JOHN THE BAPTIST

The importance of John the Baptist to the Knights Templar is indicated in a variety of ways. Amiens Cathedral in the north of France, which is accepted as the finest example of Rayonnante Gothic architecture in the world, was constructed to house the only relic of any true significance to the Knights Templar, the head of John the Baptist.[23] The stone partition separating the choir from the ambulatory is superbly carved in bas relief with incredibly detailed panels throughout its length. Depicted on these panels are episodes from the life, not of Jesus the Messiah and the supposed Son of God, but of John the Baptist, the Priestly Messiah and the man who many claim initiated Jesus into the spiritual mysteries. One panel in particular graphically illustrates events immediately after the execution of the Baptist when his head is being presented to Salome on a salver. Salome is shown piercing the skull with a knife, virtually trephining it in a manner that was repeated in Templar and masonic burials for centuries to come.

The feast day of St John the Baptist was celebrated with considerable fervour in Templar lands, a tradition that continues in the one-time Templar villages of Provence today. Hovering almost intangibly over what can be reconstructed of the Templar belief system is the shadowy and insubstantial form of the other John, John the Evangelist. According to one modern Pope, Pius IX, the Templars 'were followers of the Johannite Heresy from the very beginning'.[24] There is considerable dispute about the true nature of the so-called Johannite Heresy and one modern speculative historian claims that it arises from those who followed the beliefs of John the Baptist. This completely misleading conclusion is promulgated with considerable force and skill but absolutely no proof whatsoever. The Templar habit of veneration for John the Baptist was well known and perfectly acceptable even in those repressive times. It was their secret adherence to the true teachings of Jesus carried down through the centuries in the form of the original Gospel of St John that gave Holy Mother the Church good cause to be worried.

The Knights Templar were eventually suppressed after being tried on charges of heresy. All convicted of this charge by the Inquisition became 'non-persons' and all incriminating documentation belonging to them was either destroyed or suppressed by the Church authorities. As a result, modern historians have no authentic documentation on which they can base an assessment of the belief structure of the Knights Templar, for the only records that exist are those of the trial which were preserved by the prosecution. Indirect evidence such as that we have already mentioned abounds, and for the last two centuries a consensus has begun to emerge arising from the detailed detective work that has been done to expose the truth. The Templars existed without interference from the Church authorities for nearly 200 years. How did they keep their heretical beliefs a secret for so long?

PRESERVATION OF THEIR BELIEFS

The Knights Templar, like the Rex Deus group from which they sprang, hid their true beliefs behind the mask of Christian conformity. They were a Gnostic sect that preserved and passed on the initiatory teachings used by Jesus and recorded by John the Evangelist. As we have already mentioned, their round churches had profound cabbalistic significance and from this it is reasonable to deduce that among the secrets they preserved were those of the Cabbala. According to the 19th-century esoteric scholar, Magnus Eliphas Levi, the Templars classed themselves as 'the sole repository of the great religious and social secrets … without exposing them to the corruption of power'.[25] It was his belief that their prime intention was to preserve the true teachings of Jesus, unchanged by the vagaries and uncertainties of political necessity. The families of Rex Deus had learnt a harsh lesson from the Council of Nicea and used the Templar Order as one of their means of preserving the truth. Magnus Eliphas Levi wrote:

> The successors of the old Rosicrucians, modifying little by little the austere and heirarchic methods of their precursors in initiation, had become a mystic sect and had united with many of the Templars, the dogma of the two intermingling, as a result of which they regarded themselves as the sole depositories of the secrets intimated by the Gospel according to St John. [26]

Albert Pike, the American masonic scholar, writing in 1871, said that the Order 'adopted St John the Evangelist as one of its patrons, associating with him, in order not to arouse the suspicions of Rome, St John the Baptist'.[27] John the Baptist was not only the patron saint of the Knights Templar but became the patron saint of the later Freemasons. In *The Hiram Key*, Knight and Lomas suggest that a medieval work by a certain

Lambert de St Omer (a close relative of Godfroi de St Omer, one of the nine founding knights) entitled *The Heavenly Jerusalem* contains an illustration which '... apparently shows the founder [of the heavenly Jerusalem] to be John the Baptist.[28] There is no mention of Jesus at all in this so-called Christian document.'

The British author and researcher into ancient civilizations and belief systems, Graham Hancock, wrote:

> ... the research that I had conducted into the beliefs and behaviour of this strange group of warrior monks had convinced me that they had tapped into some exceedingly ancient wisdom tradition ... [29]

HRH Prince Michael of Albany confirmed this when he described the scrolls discovered by the Templars in their excavations in Jerusalem as 'the fruits of thousands of years of knowledge'.[30]

Gnosticism is all about the preservation of secret knowledge by passing it down through the generations using a system of teaching and initiation. The renowned British mythologist and poet, Robert Graves, claimed that the longest unbroken record of accurate transmission of such knowledge is to be found in the initiatory system of the Sufis. According to Graves, the Sufis predate Islam by several millennia and he has dated Sufic signatures on constructions from as early as 2500 BCE. He also stated categorically that the Sufis were the people commissioned to construct the first Temple in Jerusalem and that their modern heirs derive from the Craftmasons Guild of England and Scotland which arose at the time of the Saxon king Athelstan.[31] One of the strands of transmission of the Rex Deus bloodline was through the Saxon royal family. The Rex Deus founders of the Knights Templar used the knowledge passed down in this manner to pinpoint the site they used for their excavations in Jerusalem, and this arcane knowledge became part of the secrets passed down through the initiates of the Templar Order.

THE INNER CIRCLE

The Knights Templar rapidly grew in number so that at any given time there were several thousand knights in the ranks backed up by foot soldiers known as 'serjeants', and a host of ancillary tradesmen and labourers. To become a Templar of knightly rank one had to be of legitimate and noble birth and to have already attained knighthood. It is axiomatic that only certain knights would have been deemed reliable enough to have been entrusted with dangerous knowledge that could have provoked charges of heresy. The original founders became a tightly knit inner circle from which, during their lifetime, the leadership of the Order was carefully selected. The French researchers and writers, George Cagger and Jean Robin, state:

> The Order of the Temple was indeed constituted of seven 'exterior' circles dedicated to the minor mysteries, and of three 'interior' circles corresponding to the initiation into the great mysteries. And the 'nucleus' was composed of seventy Templars ... [32]

Thus it is highly probable that those of knightly rank within the Order covered a wide spectrum of belief. It is possible that many of the knights were the professed Christians they claimed to be, but within this outward or exoteric circle of Christian warriors were hidden graded concentric circles, each professing esoteric beliefs and levels of knowledge dependant upon the degree to which they had been initiated into the Gnostic arcana of the Templar Order. We have no doubt that its Rex Deus members entered as of right into the higher echelons of the three inner circles, to which, from time to time, other well-qualified and suitable initiates from the outer circles might be admitted. To maintain continuity and control, the nucleus would have consisted of Rex Deus members alone who had attained the highest degree of initiation and trust.

The nucleus of the Order and the inner circles appear to have indulged in active research into esoteric and religious matters that sprang from the twin roots of the Rex Deus traditions and the many scrolls discovered in Jerusalem. The arcane scholars of the Templar Order did not seek knowledge for its own sake like some modern academics, but were essentially practical and pragmatic men. Unlike the simple Christians among whom they moved, they did not, as a central tenet of their belief, waste time seeking eternal salvation. Sacred knowledge was the object of their research and such spiritual knowledge was held to be of direct and practical application in the real world in which they lived. Like the Gnostic initiates of old, the fruits of their knowledge and the practical applications that flowed from it were to be used here in the phenomenal world for the direct benefit not only of the Order, but also of the communities within which they moved.[33] Thus the benefits that flowed from the storehouse of knowledge that the inner core of Rex Deus Templars preserved and extended were used to transform the face of medieval Europe. Direct action by the Templars was not the only instrument that Rex Deus used to influence European culture and thought, they also used popular legend and myth to influence European perceptions of spirituality and history in a way that is still effective as we approach the new millennium.

11

⚍

Myths and Legends of the Middle Ages

The secrecy of Rex Deus was such that no one outside the group began to gain any knowledge of its existence until the final decades of the second millennium. Yet people from every country within Western European culture knew of its legends and stories from their earliest years, without recognizing their true origins. The dissemination of the Arthurian legends and the story of the search for the Holy Grail was the master stroke that truly immortalized Rex Deus traditions. The mystery, idealism and drama of the story of King Arthur and his Knights of the Round Table has only been equalled in its effect on the public imagination by the fascination of the quest for the Holy Grail.[1] Both legends were deliberately and successfully created to serve the purposes of the descendants of Jesus.

The Grail is variously described as a chalice, a cup, a stone within a cup, a stone or a magical bowl[2] capable of restoring life to the dead or good health to the wounded. The pre-Christian origins of the Grail claim that it is not a cup but a dish or a cauldron.[3] It has also been described as a salver, an altar or a stone, and has been sculpted in the north door of Chartres Cathedral as the stone in the cup carried by Melchizedek.[4] Legends associating many of these artefacts with mystical and magical powers are to be found in many early European cultures, particularly those of Celtic origin. The romance of the Grail acquired its 'Christian' gloss under the skilled guidance of two remarkable men, Chrétien de Troyes, and Wolfram von Eschenbach,[5] who had visited the Holy Land and is believed to have spent some time there with the Templars; some authorities believe he was a Templar himself. Their stories wove pagan beliefs into a seemingly Christian context that was acceptable, but only just, to the ecclesiastical hierarchy of the time. Thus the Grail romances are a strange synthesis of pagan legend, Celtic folklore, Jewish symbolism, Rex Deus tradition and alchemical, cabbalistic nuance glossed with a thin veneer of orthodox Christian veneration for the holiest relic of them all.

The romantic story of 'the search for the Holy Grail' is one well known to every schoolchild and historian who has ever studied the medieval era of the Knights Templar and the ideals of chivalry. The most popular versions of the Grail stories are based on the rather sanitized ones written by Thomas Mallory in 1469, which make the tale into one of chivalric and Christian virtue in which the central character, a knight, is seeking a holy relic usually depicted as the cup used by Jesus at the Last Supper.[6] Why should any knight seek any relic, however holy, when in every church and chapel he had, through the miracle of transubstantiation, access to the body and blood of Christ himself? These dubious Church versions of the story are a series of variations which disguise hidden themes that are heretical in the extreme.[7]

The first of the Grail romances burst upon European consciousness around 1190, in the form of an unfinished epic, *Perceval* or *Le Conte del Graal* by Chrétien de Troyes.[8] Like so many of the principal actors in the complex drama of Rex Deus during the 12th century, Chrétien originated from Troyes, the principal seat of the Counts of Champagne in France. He trained to be a priest but, having learnt Latin, became a translator and a writer of note. He is reputed to have written a tale of Camelot entitled *Erec and Enide*, and another romance, *Lancelot* or *The*

Knight in the Cart, which told the story of the adultery of Queen Guinevere, the wife of King Arthur. He dedicated three romances to Marie, Countess of Champagne, who was not only the wife of his patron but also the daughter of Louis VII of France and Eleanor of Aquitaine.[9] It is claimed that Countess Marie made the Court of Champagne the vineyard of culture and chivalry, but when her husband, Count Henry, died almost immediately on his return from the Crusades, she retired from public life. Chrétien immediately sought a new patron, Philippe d'Alsace, the Count of Flanders,[10] who was a son of a cousin of Payen de Montdidier,[11] one of the co-founders of the Knights Templar and a relative of the King of Jerusalem. It was to this leading member of the Rex Deus group that Chrétien dedicated his last and unfinished work, *Le Conte del Graal.*

It was not simply in their origins that the legends of King Arthur and the quest for the Holy Grail became inextricably mixed. Each shares the same sense of idealism and a desire to seek spiritual perfection played out against a backdrop of brutal reality. It is ironic that so many commentators and modern scholars have remarked that the entire medieval genre of Grail and Arthurian romances seem to share some common source that has long since been lost. Parallels have been drawn between the relationship between this common source and the romances it spawned and the so-called 'Q' document and the Synoptic Gospels that derive from it. We do not dispute that there may well have been some common documentary source linking the work of the principal Grail sources, Chrétien de Troyes and Wolfram von Eschenbach, and the various English authors of the Arthurian genre. However, we know that the true, common source for all of this mystical mythology arises from the teachings and traditions of Rex Deus. The enduring and all-pervasive power of this particular myth is described by Malcolm Godwin:

THE LEGEND OF THE GRAIL, more than any other western myth, has retained the vital magic which marks it as a living legend capable of touching both imagination and spirit. No other myth is so rich in symbolism, so diverse and often contradictory in meaning. *And at its core there exists a secret which has sustained the mystical appeal of the Grail for the last nine hundred years, while other myths and legends have slipped into oblivion and been forgotten* [our emphasis].[12]

The Grail has been described as taking many forms: the most popular legend claims that it is the cup used by Joseph of Arimathea to collect the blood and sweat of the crucified Jesus.[13] If this were true, this could only have taken place after Jesus had been taken down from the cross and was, according to one of the central tenets of the Christian faith, already dead. There are three reasons why this cannot be true. Firstly, the Jewish religious aversion to its menfolk handling corpses, much less blood, would have been a barrier to this occurring in the manner so popularly described – had Joseph handled Jesus' corpse he would have had to undergo a prolonged period of ritual purification which could not have taken place on the eve of Passover. Second, the orthodox Jewish tradition of burial at that time, which is continued in the beliefs of the modern Hassidim, demands that the entire body and blood had to be buried in as complete a manner as possible so as to guarantee life in the hereafter. This reverential practice would absolutely prohibit the taking of blood from any Jewish corpse. Finally, the modern science of forensic pathology tells us much about post mortem bleeding that was not known at the time of the crucifixion, which contradicts this story. Dead men don't bleed! Therefore, there can be only two viable explanations; either the entire story is pious fiction or, more likely, it did happen and indicates that Jesus was alive when taken down from the gibbet at Golgotha, a theme that is visually celebrated in the Stations of the Cross at Rennes-le-Château and described in *The Lost Gospel of Peter*.

In the repressive era of 12th-century Christian Europe, to be perceived as spiritually different provided a one-way ticket to the stake.

Therefore the Grail romances purported to describe a long and dangerous search for the supreme holy relic, the cup of Christ, with the searcher being subject to temptation and physical danger while *en route*. This was, after all, nothing more than a romanticized image of a well-known medieval reality, the perils of the pilgrimage trail. It was accepted custom for the devout to make great sacrifice of time and resources in order to complete a long and arduous pilgrimage to venerate the relics of some long-dead saint in distant lands. So what was so different about the search for the Holy Grail? It was not a search for a physical relic at all but an allegorical description, in acceptable Catholic terms, of a heretical and alchemical quest.[14] The romances of Chrétien de Troyes and Wolfram von Eschenbach are guides to a pathway of spiritual perfection wherein the 'base metal' of fallible humanity can ultimately be transformed into the 'pure gold' of spiritual unity with the divine, thus *Parzival* is nothing more nor less than a coded guide to an ascending pathway of initiation.

The Grail romances carry other coded clues to belief systems that contradict the monolithic power of Holy Mother the Church. The King of the Grail Castle is described as the Fisher King and his well-being, or lack of it, reflects the spiritual and physical state of the nation he serves.[15] The wounded Fisher King imperfectly serves an impoverished land just as the usurpers who lead the Christian Church despoil the spiritual life of those they claim to serve. When the Fisher King is restored to health by one pure enough to see the Grail, the fortunes of his wasted kingdom will be restored. When the true teachings of Jesus triumph once more over greed, lies and hypocrisy, the reinstitution of heaven upon earth that is the ultimate objective of Rex Deus teaching will be brought into being. This is the whole point of the Grail, according to one mythologist of international repute. Professor Joseph Campbell, writing of the importance of the Grail, cites one particular passage from the *Gospel of Thomas*: 'He who drinks from my mouth will become as I am, and I shall be he'.[16] In Campbell's view this was the ultimate form of enlightenment, which arose from a successful search for the Holy Grail.[17] Other clues to Rex Deus and Templar belief can also be found in the Grail romances. The sight of a bleeding head being carried into festivities[18] on a platter symbolizes the importance of the head of John the Baptist, and the references to Sophia, the feminine principle of Wisdom, are too numerous to recount.

The insightful initiate of the early 20th century, Rudolf Steiner, believed that esoteric symbolism could be interpreted in up to nine different ways depending upon the degree of illumination or spiritual insight attained by the observer. The exoteric interpretation of the Grail stories is that of the search for a holy relic, as we have already mentioned. In the 12th century, when the cult of relics was at its height, relics directly associated with the person of Jesus were held to be of the highest significance. This interpretation, therefore, could hardly become the object of suspicion by a hierarchy that encouraged the veneration of objects such as the numerous foreskins, reputedly those of Jesus, that were displayed in so many churches and cathedrals across Europe. King Louis IX of France, St Louis himself, built Sainte Chapelle in Paris, the most beautifully decorated medieval building in Europe, to house one particular relic that was sanctified by direct contact with the body of the Messiah, the Crown of Thorns. St Louis purchased this relic from one of the Rex Deus rulers of Byzantium, who was far more interested in the money he could gain for it than in the Christian mythology that surrounds the spurious redemptive sacrifice at Golgotha.

The esoteric interpretation of the search for the Holy Grail, that of a mystical pathway or ascending initiatory way that led to spiritual enlightenment, was at best suspect but, more likely, heretical. The various interpretations of the term Holy Grail did not stop at 'gradual' or spiritual ascent, but took another even more blasphemous twist with the publication of *The Holy Blood and the Holy Grail*. Paradoxically it was within the Secret Dossiers that the interpretation of the Holy Grail or Sangraal took a further evocative twist that stumbled inadvertently upon *the* truth. A new meaning was now superimposed upon all previous interpretations of the Holy Grail. Sangraal was no longer to be considered as a contraction of Sainte Graal, but was held to be a disguise for another term entirely, Sang Real – the holy blood.[19] This was the first time that a 'non-fiction' book was published in the English language which openly claimed that there was a bloodline that could trace its descent from Jesus the Nazarene. This book burst upon the Christian world like a bombshell, inspiring revulsion and adulation amongst its readers in almost equal proportions.

Myth and legend have, since time immemorial, been used to carry spiritual allegory and uncomfortable truths into the public domain in an acceptable manner. Until fairly recently they were contemptuously dismissed by the academic establishment as simply a form of inspired fiction that only appealed to the semi-literate or the credulous. In their arrogance such academics ignored the simple fact that all the truly meaningful activities of mankind, be they social, religious or political, have always tended to create their own mythology. Thus the great and the good of the distant past, the important figures in all the major religions and the heroes of prehistory have generated a vast and colourful mythology of their own. In recent years, thanks to the work of people of inspired genius such as Joseph Campbell, the value accorded to myth and legend has undergone significant change.[20] Like religious and artistic symbolism, myth and legend can usefully be interpreted at many levels and, in the historical context, can often be signposts that lead to the discovery of previously hidden truths. This confirmation of their value was echoed by Professor Campbell who claimed that 'Mythology is the penultimate truth – penultimate because the ultimate cannot be put into words.'[21] This point was further reinforced by the poet Kathleen Raine, who stated that 'Fact is not the truth of myth; myth is the truth of fact', [22] and by the Indian scholar, Ananda Coomeraswamy, who wrote 'Myth embodies the nearest approach to absolute truth that can be stated in words.'[23] Bill Moyers, in conversation with Joseph Campbell, remarked that 'Myths are stories of our search through the ages for truth, for meaning, for significance.' Campbell replied that 'Myths are clues to the spiritual potentialities of human life.'[24]

If, as psychologists suggest, a personality is the by-product of the stories a person tells himself, then the same is true for tribes, nations and peoples. Nowhere is this more true than with the English, a mongrel people whose culture has been influenced over time by waves of invasion from other countries. Myth and legend were useful tools that were often employed by English rulers to bolster their own power, status and legitimacy. In the English tradition one legend above all others has been used to bring about social cohesion and to inspire the people to strive for an almost idealistic level of behaviour. The values with which it is imbued, those of loyalty, courage and service to others, have served the English psyche well. This is the legend of King Arthur and his Knights of the Round Table.[25]

The earliest references we could find to any character in British history who had a remote similarity to Arthur were written by St Gildas, the 5th-century ecclesiastical historian, who described the bravery of a tribal leader in the west of England whom he called Aurelius Ambrosianus.[26] Four centuries later another monastic scribe, Nennius of Bangor, renamed this tribal leader Arthur.[27] These early references to a courageous and warlike leader called Arthur describe a significantly different character from the one in the popular legends of Arthurian romance. The first publication describing the idealistic king that we know as Arthur came to public notice in 1136, some 18 years after the formation of the Knights Templar. This work was called *The Matter of Britain*, and in it the legendary King Arthur is described as a proponent of chivalry and courage who became something of a Messianic saviour of his people.[28] It is believed that when danger threatens he, like Jesus before him, will come again. The author of this magical work was Geoffrey of Monmouth, who was a secular canon in the City of Oxford. Geoffrey's story made no reference whatsoever to the Holy Grail,

Lancelot or the Round Table. It was translated into Welsh, French and Anglo-Saxon, and became so widespread in Europe that for centuries people believed it to be provable historical fact.[29]

Geoffrey claimed to have translated the story from an ancient document passed on to him by his uncle. It is claimed that this uncle was an archdeacon of Oxford called Walter Map, but the only Walter Map who became archdeacon in that city did not occupy that post until some 40 years after Geoffrey's death. Most scholars conveniently ignore this discrepancy but, nonetheless, dismiss the existence of this unknown document out of hand. It is perhaps not coincidental that at the time Geoffrey was writing his masterwork, Payen de Montdidier, one of the co-founders of the Knights Templar, was grand master in England, and that the most important Templar preceptory in the kingdom at that time was at Oxford. The masonic scholars Knight and Lomas have linked Montdidier and Geoffrey of Monmouth and made a highly plausible case demonstrating that the Templar grand master was the most probable source for the fundamental outlines for the Arthurian story.[30]

Another English monk and historian, William of Malmesbury, made the first written reference to the Holy Grail in 1140, some four years after Geoffrey of Monmouth's Arthurian stories had been published.[31] He also wrote the *Gesta Regum Anglorum*, a chronicle of the kings of England from the time of the Saxon invasion up to 1126, and the *Historia Novella*, charting the royal house up to 1143. The Saxon kings were, as we have mentioned earlier, one of the roots of transmission of the Rex Deus bloodline. The Norman kings of England from 1066 to 1143 were all descendants and relatives of William the Conqueror, the one-time Duke of Normandy and a bastard son of the St Clair family. William of Malmesbury's tale does not include any reference whatsoever to the legend of King Arthur recounted by Geoffrey of Monmouth and the two stories only began to merge some considerable time later. One might expect that two devout monks working in similar fields might have displayed a degree of brotherly love and mutual respect. William of

Malmesbury, however, was publicly highly critical of the work written by Geoffrey of Monmouth.[32] An all too familiar form of internecine strife, common in academic circles, ensued with accusations and denunciations aplenty, especially over the validity of the sources for these stories.

Within three years of this dispute Geoffrey of Monmouth was denounced by three further aggressive authors, all of whom denied that he had authoritative information. Three other versions of the Arthurian story were now composed by William of Malmesbury, Henry of Huntingdon and Caradoc of Llancarfan, all of whom were supported by the same patron, Robert of Gloucester, the illegitimate son of King Henry I of England and the half-brother of Princess Matilda. It is interesting to note that the land upon which the Templar preceptory at Oxford was built had been donated by Matilda. A considerable row, which focused on the accuracy of the sources for the tales, began between them and Geoffrey of Monmouth, who claimed that their work was bogus because he alone had access to the ancient document that proved the true history. Knight and Lomas were convinced that the three later versions and the row over sources were used as a public rebuke to Geoffrey of Monmouth, and to try and repair the damage caused by his work to the secrecy about the Rex Deus descent.[33] Knight and Lomas came to the following conclusion:

> The story of Arthur appears to be a description of the history of Rex Deus and the Holy Grail represents a separate line of apostolic succession from Joseph of Arimathea that has precedence over the lineage claimed by the Vatican through St Peter.[34]

Perhaps Payen de Montdidier had been indiscreet in passing on details of secret Rex Deus tradition to an outsider such as Geoffrey of Monmouth, who had not been in a position to write the story with the appropriate level of accuracy. If so the ensuing strife and alternative works may well have been an attempt to put the record straight.[35] In December 1135 King Henry I died and a state of virtual civil war ensued between Matilda, who was supported by her half-brother Robert, Earl of Gloucester, and her cousin Stephen of Blois, and it has been suggested that it was to influence the outcome of this civil war and to legitimize the claims of Matilda that the three new stories had been written. It is significant to point out that Matilda carried Rex Deus blood in her lineage as did her husband, Geoffrey of Anjou. It was their bloodline in the form of their son that started the Plantagenet dynasty which held the Royal House of England for the next 300 years. Henry II is undoubtedly one of the leading figures of Rex Deus at the time. He was, on one side, the great grandson of William the Conqueror and, on the other, of St Margaret of Scotland, the Rex Deus bride of King Malcolm Canmore. At the time of his coronation his uncle was the Fisher King, Baudouin III, King of Jerusalem.

According to the Grail romances of this period the Grail is kept by the family of Perceval or Parsifal, who is described as a direct descendant of Joseph of Arimathea. The direct bloodline linking these two characters is always described as being highly significant. Christian teaching would have us believe that Jesus appointed Peter as his successor, 'the Rock' upon which he founded his Church. Yet in the Grail romances Jesus appoints Joseph of Arimathea as the guardian of the Grail. Is this, as some commentators suggest, simply the 'visible, tangible symbol of an alternative apostolic succession',[36] or does it imply something far more significant, that Joseph of Arimathea was given custody of one of Jesus' children?

According to the Rex Deus tradition, the son of Jesus first fled to Edessa with Jesus' twin brother Judas Thomas, before travelling as a young man to Spain and England in the company of Joseph of Arimathea. The Grail stories were not warmly welcomed by the Church. As the stories themselves were not blatantly heretical and their authors worked under the protection of men of power, the Church could neither suppress the stories nor burn the writers. Yet it did not remain idle. With the aid of a group of Cistercian monks, a highly sanitized and censored version of these legends, that was in line with Church thinking of the time, was created. This 'official' version was known as the Vulgate Cycle,[37] which in its turn provided the foundation of later writers such as Thomas Mallory, who created *Le Mort d'Arthur* in around 1469. The concept of this enduring myth was long-lasting and has stimulated variants by the Victorian poet laureate, Arthur Tennyson, and served as an inspiration to William Morris and the Pre-Raphaelites of the same era. It has even reached into modern times with the film *Monty Python and the Holy Grail*.

THE TAROT

The divinatory pack of cards known as the Tarot, which was used by initiates to impart spiritual insights of a heretical nature through its symbolic coding, displays mysterious connections with the Grail search and certain of the leading families of Rex Deus. The true origins of this form of prophecy are unknown but it is believed that it came from the Orient to the Mediterranean littoral in the 13th century. At that time, the original Eastern pack was transformed by influences traceable to the Cathars, Gypsies, Knights Templar, Jewish Cabbala and Hermetic magical beliefs. There are even some who claim that the Tarot originated with the Knights Templar and, not surprisingly, when they were tried for heresy and suppressed, the four cards representing knights suddenly disappeared. The Grail scholar Malcolm Godwin claims that '… it is possible that the Templars learned their use from their Saracen rivals'.[38] He also claims that the Tarot, with all its Gnostic and Rex Deus implications, was a significant factor in the hostility of the Church to any form of playing cards. According to many priests, the Tarot pack was the 'Devil's breviary' or 'the rungs of a ladder leading to hell'. The Church was right to be uneasy, for the use of visual symbolism as a teaching board was central to Templar tradition and continues in Freemasonry and the modern Templar Orders.

The Tarot pack teaches a very different form of spirituality to the Church, stressing the cyclical themes of reincarnation, renewal and transformation.[39] In the card known as 'temperance' is the figure of the goddess Isis[40] who was venerated by the Templars in the form of the Black Madonna. Perceval, the Grail hero, is symbolically represented in the bottom left of this card as a valley between two peaks – Perce à Val. The whole Tarot pack recounts in symbolic form the quest of a pilgrim who undergoes initiatory trials and a symbolic death and resurrection before he meets the goddess. There are many correspondences between the cards and the Grail legends. The card known as the 'fool' is Parzival; the 'hermit' represents the Grail hermit; the 'hanged man' depicts the Fisher King; the 'tower' represents the wasteland and the 'moon', the Grail bearer.[41] Most of the others either relate to the Grail quest or the Arthurian romances. One of the four suits represents the House of Pendragon, a direct reference to the Arthurian stories. Another, the south, represents one of the leading Rex Deus families of northern Europe, the House of the Spear and the House of Lothian and Orkney[42] – a direct reference to the St Clairs of Roslin and Lothian, who were also the Earls of Caithness and Orkney.

Rex Deus were wise in their use of myth, legend and the Tarot to spread their hidden message to the populace at large. The atmosphere in Europe was changing and the Church was beginning to react unfavourably to the undercurrents of subversion and heresy that were surfacing so frequently. The Church could brook no rivals and by the late 13th century was under threat from the cynicism of its own flock over Church corruption on the one hand and a more simple and purer form of Christianity which had spread half-way across Europe, on the other. Holy Mother the Church was soon to reap a brutal and public vengeance on this rival organization, who claimed to follow 'the true teachings of Jesus' enshrined within a Johannite document, the *Gospel of Love*, allegedly written by St John the Evangelist.

12

The Albigensian Crusade

GENOCIDE IN THE NAME OF JESUS

During the 12th and 13th centuries, a truly dazzling civilization arose in the Midi in southern France, illuminated by the principles of democracy, love and religious toleration.[1] It developed under the guidance of a nobility who permitted the growth of economic stability, prosperity and creative freedom unequalled anywhere else in Christian Europe.[2] The political structure of the Languedoc was well advanced for its time, with the feudal rule of the counts being subject to a large degree of democratic moderation by the well-established wealthy bourgeoisie aided by a group of privileged lawyers in the prosperous towns and cities.[3] For once, the Catholic Church no longer ruled supreme, but was in a state of decline.[4] The tolerant Languedoc nobility had long been renowned for their encouragement of prosperous pockets of Judaism[5] within their territories, and now extended their protection to the Cathars, who practised a form of Christianity that claimed to follow the true teachings of Jesus.[6] The laity were known simply as the hearers; the priests as 'les bonshommes', or good men,[7] who were dedicated to perfecting the ideals of their Essene precursors. It was their critics who called them perfecti, a corruption of the Latin term 'hereticus perfectus', also known as the Cathari – the pure ones.[8]

Despite the fact that Count Raymond IV of Toulouse had raised and led the largest single force to take part in the First Crusade to the Holy Land, by the mid-12th century the literate and sophisticated local nobility were predominantly anticlerical. Raymond VI, who died in 1222, was particularly favourably disposed to Catharism and took a member of the Cathar perfecti with him whenever he travelled. The family of the Count of Foix were noted for their tolerant attitude to the Cathars and the count's wife, after raising her family, became a member of the perfecti.[9] The Viscount of Carcassonne and Béziers, Roger Trençavel, had Cathar perfecti as his tutors and became a heroic defender of the Cathars in all his lands – a crime for which he ultimately paid with his life. According to Guiraud, the Catholic historian, the minor nobility of the Lauragais, the prosperous and densely populated area that links Toulouse and Carcassonne, were almost completely Cathar.[10] Pierre des Vaux-de-Cernay, a supporter of the Church, wrote 'the lords of the Languedoc almost all protected and harboured the heretics … defending them against God and church.'[11]

The dedicated commitment of the Languedoc nobility to the First Crusade and their tolerance for the Cathars derives from the fact that the aristocracy of the entire area was largely drawn from the families of the Rex Deus tradition. Just as Jews had been well tolerated and encouraged to establish themselves at the seat of the Count of Champagne at Troyes, large and prosperous Jewish communities had existed throughout the Languedoc for centuries and their intellectual and commercial skills contributed to the prosperity of the area. The spiritual impact of the Jewish communities in Narbonne, Carcassonne and Béziers assisted in the spread of Cabbalistic studies in Europe.[12] This tolerance extended to the Cathars who deliberately encouraged the establishment of a class of skilled craftsmen within the society in which they moved. The perfecti took an active role in these creative activities and supervised the operation of the workshops which specialized in the manufacture of textiles, leather work and paper.[13]

CATHAR BELIEFS

The Cathars were members of a dualist school of Gnosticism with roots in early Zoroastrianism,[14] the teachings of Pythagoras and the Mithraic cult transformed by contact with early Christianity. Some authorities claim that Catharism was a derivative of Manichaeanism, the initiatory Christian cult based on the teachings of a Persian mystic called Mani.[15] Cathar society had distinct echoes of the Druidic era of the Celts, where the perfecti were the equivalent to the Druidic priests and the troubadours of the Languedoc, wandering minstrels who extolled the spiritual value of courtly love. Celtic Christianity was also an initiatory religion that is often described as having Gnostic and strong dualist tendencies.

The perfecti were men and women, easily identified by their distinctive robes, who lived in working communities irrespective of their previous social status. They travelled the countryside in pairs tending to the pastoral needs of the communities they served, preaching to their growing flock and administering healing.[16] Their healing was based upon spiritual insight moderated by their expertise as herbalists and, in this, they consciously replicated the duties of the first apostles and the Essenes.[17] In *The Gospel of Thomas* it is recorded that Jesus had informed his disciples that they too would become capable of doing all that he did.[18] The perfecti, as true initiates of Jesus' teaching, knew this to be true and, like the supreme initiate they followed, lived a simple life, travelling everywhere on foot to discharge their sacred duties to the community they served. They believed that sacred knowledge came from God through the true teaching of Jesus and that spiritual union with God would be the ultimate result of their Gnosis. This Gnosis, or body of sacred knowledge, had been passed on by Jesus to his disciple, St John the Evangelist, and thence to the Cathars, whose sacrament of the 'consolamentum', a form of spiritual baptism granted to believers who had undergone a three-year novitiate, was the outward sign of the attainment of this enlightenment. By this spiritual baptism believers of either sex then attained the rank of a perfectus.[19] The consolamentum was also granted to believers who had reached the point of death.

The Cathars believed in reincarnation and the transmigration of human souls into animals and, since an animal might contain an unperfected soul awaiting revelation, perfecti ate no meat, only fish were allowed. As the creation of more tunics of imprisoning flesh could only delay the perfection and liberation of souls, they also abstained from all sexual relations.[20] The ordinary believers, or hearers, were exempt from these demanding strictures and were permitted to eat meat, marry, engage in sexual relations, go to war and live perfectly normal lives; indeed one of the many Christian criticisms of the sect centred around the alleged immorality of the Cathar believers. Their real role was to prepare themselves for the ultimate sacrament of spiritual baptism in their final hours on earth. Believers greeted perfecti with a ritualized form of respect known as the 'melhorer' to which the perfectus would respond with a blessing.[21]

There were four Cathar diocese established in the Languedoc in 1167: Agen, Albi, Carcassonne and Toulouse,[22] with a fifth later founded at Razès.[23] In view of our earlier comments about the lineage of many of the noble families of the Languedoc, it will come as no surprise to learn that another diocese was founded in the County of Champagne, to which was added that of France as a separate episcopal district. The northern provinces of Italy, Lombardy and Tuscany contained a further six episcopal sees, with six more in the Balkans which came under the control of the Rex Deus rulers of Byzantium. As within the Catholic Church, each diocese was headed by a bishop; however, each Cathar bishop had two assistants, a 'major son' and a 'minor son', elected from the deaconate of senior perfecti. When the bishop died he would be succeeded by the major son, whereupon the minor son was promoted and a new minor son elected.[24] Ranked beneath them were the deaconate and communities of the perfecti. These had a monastic, residential function and were also schools of initiation and healing centres.

The award of the consolamentum was only the beginning of an initiatory progress that the perfecti continued throughout their lives as they ascended through the various degrees of enlightenment, receiving increasing levels of esoteric knowledge as they progressed.[25] This led to the development of specialist skills and abilities according to the level of their spiritual development and their own innate spiritual talents. One teaching that they held in common with the Knights Templar derived from the secret passed down through the generations by the Gnostic families of Rex Deus, that Mary Magdalene was the wife of Christ.[26]

Until recently, gaining any realistic understanding of the Cathar beliefs was virtually impossible as the only references available were those of their oppressors, the Catholic Church. However, in the light of recent discoveries, such as the Nag Hammadi Scrolls, some degree of clarity can be established enabling us to interpret the records of the Inquisition in a more accurate and dispassionate manner.

THE CATHARS AS HERETICS

One early reference to the Cathars can be found in an appeal made by Prior Eberwin of Steinfeld to Bernard of Clairvaux. Eberwin is complaining of a group he calls the 'Cologne Heretics' and in particular about the actions of one of their leaders, an apostate monk called Henry. As a result of Church pressure Henry wisely thought it time to move his preaching mission into more tolerant territory.[27] Acting in answer to Eberwin's appeal in 1145, Henry was followed to his new refuge in Toulouse by Bernard of Clairvaux. In a letter to the Count of Toulouse, who had given Henry his protection, Bernard wrote about the religious conditions he had experienced on his travels through the county.

The Churches are without congregations, congregations are without priests, priests are without proper reverence, and, finally, Christians are without Christ.[28]

He went on to say of Henry that in Toulouse 'he revels in all his fury among the flock of Christ'. Despite encountering strong anticlerical and heretical attitudes in Toulouse and among the Languedoc nobility, St Bernard admitted that the Cathars were a people of simple and devout spirituality led by a gifted priesthood: 'No one's sermons are more spiritual.'[29] During this time the Pope was informed by anxious clergy in Liège that a new heresy had arisen which appeared 'to have overflowed various regions of France. One so varied and so manifold that it seems impossible to characterize it under a single name.'[30] This heretical community was comprised of grades of listeners and believers with its own hierarchy of priests and prelates and was described as militantly anticlerical, that is anti-Catholic, in character, with adherents in the Low Countries, Lombardy and the Languedoc.[31] The question is 'Where did this form of heresy come from?'

The most probable precursor of Catharism had arisen in Eastern Europe and Byzantium when, in around 930 CE, a priest known as Bogomil preached a dualistic, Gnostic gospel in Bulgaria.[32] Contact between the Cathars and the Bogomils of Constantinople, Asia Minor and the Balkans is highly probable, for after the crusades Byzantium had strengthened the trade routes with Venice and Genoa, thereby creating viable means of communication with the east. Thus the movement to Christianize the Holy Land had served to strengthen the routes through which heretical, initiatory Gnostic teaching travelled easily from the east to the west. The new heresy was a pure form of initiatory Christianity which revered the *Gospel of Love*, the secret *Gospel of St. John*[33] which preached the simple message that Jesus came to reveal the true way to sacred knowledge and not to redeem mankind from sin. The Cathars knew that the true teaching of Jesus was the sole route to spiritual union with Almighty God and that they were the guardians of a form of Gnosis which had been handed down from its roots in the Egyptian temple mysteries, through the Therapeutae, the Essenes, the revelations of John the Baptist and on to its peak of perfection in Jesus' initiatory teaching. The true spiritual parent of the Cathar religion can be found in the first 'Church' in Jerusalem led by James the Just, the brother of Jesus.

Despite the fact that Catharism and Christianity were both supposedly founded on Jesus' teaching, there were many fundamental differences of belief between the two religions. The Cathars resolutely denied the validity of all the Christian sacraments, especially the eucharist with its cannibalistic overtones.[34] They completely refuted all claims made by the Catholic clergy and the Pope in Rome to any form of authority and argued against the Christian concept of grace that was so central to Catholic dogma and papal control.[35] They refused to venerate the cross, asking why they should worship the rack on which their teacher had died. The so-called sacrifice at Golgotha was dismissed out of hand, for to the initiates of the Cathar faith Jesus was not a redeemer at all but a divinely inspired teacher who brought with him the supreme gift of Gnosis.[36] Later the Inquisition accused the Cathars of practising 'sorcery' on the feast day of John the Baptist, 24 June, a charge also used in the trials of the Templars, reflecting that the Church perceived a degree of community of belief existed between them.[37]

THE ALBIGENSIAN CRUSADE

As the Cathar religion grew in power and influence throughout the Languedoc it began to rival and, in many districts, completely displace the Church of Rome. This posed a threat to the Church that could not be tolerated under any circumstances. In response, the Church first despatched a preaching ministry to the Languedoc headed by a fanatical Spanish priest, Dominic Guzman.[38] His preaching fell upon deaf ears and his pastoral activities were spectacularly ineffective, for a house for repentant Cathar women which he founded at Prouille in 1206 was little used.[39] The terrifying finale to his fruitless evangelical mission was to issue a brutal warning.

> For years now I have brought you words of peace, I have preached, I have implored, I have wept. But, as the common people say in Spain, if a blessing will not work, then it must be the stick. Now we shall stir up princes and bishops against you, and they, alas, will call together nations and peoples, and many will perish by the sword. Towers will be destroyed, walls overturned and you will be reduced to slavery. Thus force will prevail where gentleness has failed.[40]

Those who heard this message were utterly incapable of understanding the harsh reality that lay behind it. The Cathars and the people of the Languedoc lived in a society which treasured the concepts of tolerance, love and pacifism and could not visualize the brutal methods which the Christian Church used in the extirpation of 'heresy'. They were soon to be rudely awakened. In 1209 the Pope, inappropriately named Innocent III, declared a religious war against the Cathars. He gave this dubious expedition the title of a crusade, which meant that every devout Christian who participated for a minimum of 40 days was granted a papal indulgence giving absolution for all their past sins and any they might commit during the crusade.[41] These noble crusaders were also entitled to seize all property of any heretic, be he prince or peasant; a papal licence to murder, steal, rape and pillage in the name of 'the Prince of Peace'. Knights, nobles and soldiers alike flocked to the papal banner of the crusade in their thousands, and fought with venomous vigour. Along with the crusading army came the clergy, who treated any suspected heretic with torture and the warm embrace of death at the stake. Yet despite this being an official crusade, neither the Knights Templar nor the other crusading Order of the Knights Hospitaller took any significant part in the action[42] and the French king only engaged himself near the end of the campaign, in 1229, when he saw the chance to annexe the Languedoc into the kingdom of France.[43]

In July of 1209, the crusaders advanced upon the prosperous and populous city of Béziers. Viscount Raimon-Roger Trencavel, the Lord of both Béziers and Carcassonne, was certain that the city was indefensible and left in some haste for the superbly fortified city of Carcassonne. The large Jewish community of Béziers, who knew only too well the intolerance and persecution that their fellow Jews had suffered in the north of France, fled with him. The community of Béziers took little notice of the appeals of their bishop, who sought an immediate surrender, and decided to defend the city.[44] The siege was short and on the eve of the final assault the leaders of the besieging army asked the advice of the papal legate. They knew that the majority of the citizens of Béziers were Catholic, so they sought the legate's guidance on how to treat their co-religionists in the battle to come. Far from suggesting that they follow the precept of love thy neighbour as thyself, this man of God ordered the crusaders: 'Show mercy neither to order, nor to age, nor to sex ... Cathar or Catholic – Kill them all ... God will know his own when they get to him!'[45]

The crusaders followed his advice to the letter; over 20,000 civilians were said to have been slaughtered without mercy, with 7,000 of those murdered in the sacred precincts of the cathedral where they had fled for sanctuary. Pierre des Vaux-de-Cernay claimed that the massacre was a punishment for the sins of the heretics in the city and for the Cathar blasphemy against Mary Magdalene, on whose official feast day, 22 July, the massacre of Béziers took place. He claimed:

> Béziers was taken on St Mary Magdalene's day. Oh, supreme justice of providence! ... The heretics claimed that St Mary Magdalene was the concubine of Jesus Christ ... it was therefore with just cause that these disgusting dogs were taken and massacred during the feast of the one that they had insulted ... [46]

The massacre was intended to terrify the occupants of all the other strongholds into surrendering without a battle. The immediate result was the unconditional surrender of Narbonne, whose leaders, both the viscount and the archbishop, not only offered material support to the crusaders but also promised to surrender any perfecti in the city and any property that the Jews from Béziers owned within it.[47]

After the fall of Béziers the principal city of Carcassonne, the seat of the Trencavel family, was besieged. After a week the crusaders offered Viscount Trencavel and 11 of his companions safe conduct out of the city but insisted that the garrison, the inhabitants and all the contents of the town were to be left to the mercy of the besiegers. The viscount refused this offer and the siege continued for a further week, by which time the wells within the city walls were running dry and access to the waters of the river was blocked by the crusading armies. On 15 August the viscount was offered safe conduct by the crusaders in order to discuss the terms of surrender but, despite this assurance, Viscount Trencavel was imprisoned[48] and the rights of inheritance of his son were set aside. He died in prison in November 1209 and, according to most historians, his death was the result of foul play. When Carcassonne surrendered the lives of its inhabitants were spared without religious discrimination, but they were forced to exit the city in their underclothes and leave their homes and possessions to the mercy of the crusading army.[49] One of the leaders of the crusade, Simon de Montfort, was awarded all the rights, feudal privileges and lands of the Trencavel family.[50]

TORTURE, DEATH AND REPRESSION

As Simon de Montfort tightened his grip on the Languedoc, the cruel deaths of the heretics were marked by tongues of flame flickering skywards. The first public burning of perfecti was at Castres, while after the siege and fall of Minerve 140 perfecti, both men and women, were burnt alive and this became the inevitable fate of all perfecti who were captured.[51] All who fought against the crusaders ran enormous risks. In 1210 Simon de Montfort, who was now the leader of the entire crusade, inflicted a terrible punishment on the surviving defenders of the fortress of Bram by selecting 100 of their number at random and gouging out their eyes and having their lips, ears and noses sliced off. One prisoner was only blinded in one eye and ordered to lead his maimed companions to the Castle of Cabaret[52] as a warning to the defenders of the fate that awaited those opposing the crusading army. This appalling example of Christian 'love and generosity in war' hardened the defenders' will to fight on; the castle of Cabaret remained in Cathar hands. Rennes-le-Château, which at that time was a fortified town of approximately 10,000 inhabitants, was captured in 1210 by Simon de Montfort, who dismantled its fortifications.

Having clearly established a code of chivalry for the crusaders, de Montfort's army marched on to further conquests. In 1211, after the siege and fall of the Castle of Lavaur, the 80 knights who had valiantly defended the town were sentenced to be hanged. The gallows collapsed under their combined weight and as an act of mercy Simon de Montfort ordered that their throats be cut. The Chatelaine of Lavaur, Lady Guiraude, was handed over to the victorious soldiery and repeatedly raped. In true Christian conformity to biblical law, when this chivalrous sport was exhausted her bleeding body was cast into a well and she was stoned to death as an adulteress.[53] It is recorded that, to the great joy of the crusaders, 400 Cathars were burnt on a huge fire; shortly afterwards 60 more perfecti were burnt at Les Casses.[54]

The King of Aragon joined the battle in support of the Cathar cause and was mortally wounded at Muret, on 12 September 1213, where the slaughter exceeded that of Béziers.[55] To add to the terror of the crusade and the routine execution of the heretics, a scorched-earth policy was employed by the crusaders, who ordered that the crops be burnt so that the population would be starved into submission.[56] The war lasted 30 years. The true nature of the brutality that was endemic in this crusade was graphically described by Guillaume Tudelle, who wrote that 5,000 men, women and children were simply hacked to pieces after the fall of Marmande in 1226.[57] All these routine acts of barbarity were justified by the crusaders, who claimed that they were defending the true religion against heretics who, by definition, had no rights. This was deemed to justify a brutal war of expropriation which was blessed by the official encouragement and endorsement of successive Popes and vigorously supported by local churchmen who benefited hugely from the requisition of the property of the heretics they hated.

The long-drawn-out agony of the Albigensian Crusade effectively ended in 1244 with the surrender of the last Cathar stronghold of Montségur after a siege of nearly a year. For once, the crusaders behaved with some semblance of chivalry, for the fighting men of the garrison and all within the castle walls, with the exception of the perfecti, were spared. The surrender terms called for a fortnight's truce before the crusading army entered the fortress.[58] It is alleged that several perfecti made their escape down the mountainside under cover of darkness during the truce in order to smuggle out the Cathar treasure,[59] whatever that may have been. When the truce ended and the defenders marched down from the castle, crusader tradition ensured that their path was lit by the flames arising from a vast funeral pyre where 225 perfectae (women) and perfecti (men) were being burnt alive.[60] Despite the brutality, only three perfecti are known to have recanted during the crusade and the prolonged era of repression that followed. The nature of the Cathar beliefs were such that the vast majority of perfecti and perfectae were willing to die for them.

THE KNIGHTS TEMPLAR AND HOSPITALLER

The 30 years of brutal, intermittent warfare in the Languedoc had been dignified with the official title of a 'crusade'. As a result of the plenary indulgences granted for the remission of all sins committed during its campaigns, this war tended to replicate the brutality, intolerance and indifference to the rights of the peasantry and the Jews that had characterized the original crusades. There were, however, two notable exceptions to the parallels that can be drawn between the campaigns in the Holy Land and that in the Languedoc. The two crusading Orders of warrior monks who had fought so valiantly against the Saracens in the Holy Land took little or no part whatsoever in the crusade against the Cathars.[61] While we have no record of the papal criticisms against the crusading Orders of the Knights Templar and the Knights Hospitaller for their singular reluctance to participate in this orgy of bloodletting, we do have records of some of the justifications they used for their curious inaction.

The Languedoc-Roussillon area was home to nearly 30 per cent of Templar holdings in mainland Europe and also housed many extensive holdings of the rival Order of the Knights Hospitaller. Despite their prolonged and traditional rivalry, we find that there was a suspicious degree of unanimity from the two Orders when they tried to explain their seeming neutrality in such a holy war. They claimed that many of the donations of land in this region specifically forbade them from using these bases for any warlike activity. They also argued that the vast majority of their holdings were purely commercial, understaffed and not garrisoned in the military sense, unfortified and therefore completely useless either as bases or defensive strong points in time of war.[62] Bearing in mind the intense rivalry that lasted throughout their lifetime, this unanimous justification for their peaceful stance is bizarre to say the least. The central core of leading Templars was drawn from the Rex Deus group of families and many of the local nobility in the Languedoc who had donated lands to either or both of the Orders were drawn from the same group. Earlier we have shown the Rex Deus allegiance of many of the families who either protected, participated in or granted lands to the Cathar Church, so it is not hard to see why these Orders refused to join in the crusade against the Cathars.

There are clear links between the Knights Templar and the Cathars that seem to extend well beyond the bonds of family loyalty and blood. At the height of the crusade it is well recorded that the Templars gave assistance to knights who actively defended the Cathars against the crusaders.[63] If one reviews the names of leading Templars from this period and compares them to the names of the Cathar families recorded by the Inquisition, there is a remarkable degree of correspondence.[64] The Templars not only gave shelter to fleeing Cathars but even allowed them to be buried in consecrated ground. The records also disclose that certain of these burials were later violated on the orders of the Inquisition, with the exhumed corpses being tried, convicted and burnt for heresy. Our colleague, Nicole Dawe, has proof that the Templars gave refuge to many Cathars and Cathar sympathizers who had been dispossessed and at a later date exerted their influence to ensure that the dispossessed regained their property. Nicole also claims that this crusading Order went even further in its position of so-called 'neutrality', by allowing hostile activity against the crusaders by Cathar knights to whom they had given refuge.[65] However, despite the clandestine support or tolerance exerted in the Cathars' favour by the Templars, the 30-year war of attrition finally came to its bloody conclusion at Montségur.

THE INQUISITION

The Church did not rely on the crusade alone to stamp out the Cathar heresy. A new institution, the 'Holy Office of the Inquisition', was created to serve the interests of the papacy. Founded in 1233, led and largely staffed by the Dominican Order, its aim was to create a climate of fear within which heresy would not dare to rear its head. The principal objective of this new organization was to extinguish the Cathar heresy for once and for all.[66] Under the guidance of this new institution, the Christian gift of peace was as terrifying as the horrors of the recent war. The Inquisition used torture as a routine part of their interrogation techniques and the accused, as heretics, were denied any form of legal representation. Torture, harassment and fear of the stake were the means by which the Dominican fathers implemented the precept of 'forgive your enemies'.[67] The crusade was over but not the mass burnings; at Moissac, for example, 210 'heretics' were publicly burnt on the orders of the Inquisition. The last perfectus was burnt in 1321 at Villerouge-Termenes and the last mass burnings of the Cathar faithful took place in Carcassonne as late as 1329.

A heretic was not necessarily sentenced to death if he abjured his faith after interrogation. The sentences that could be imposed against such a heretic included imprisonment for life, confiscation of all property or being condemned to have a yellow cross sewn on one's clothes which effectively debarred him or her from any form of social contact. Anyone who was seen to help, employ, feed or speak to a person who wore the yellow cross could be charged with heresy themselves or with harbouring heretics. To be sentenced to wear the yellow cross was a sentence of slow death. Even associating with a heretic during childhood was considered as proof of guilt. The inquisitors demanded details of a suspect's family and social life and all who were named as associates of the suspect were interrogated in their turn. Under this ruthless regime all suspects were deemed guilty of heresy simply because they were charged with it and the Inquisition became an instrument of terror that has haunted Europe for 700 years.[68]

But even the Inquisition could not completely extinguish the Cathar faith. While many perfecti were burned and an innumerable number of believers were persecuted by the Inquisition in the 60-year period of repression that followed, some fled into exile and others learnt the arts of dissembling and disguise. The Cathar religion as a visible entity vanished completely in the 14th century. Many Cathars joined the Templars in the final years of the crusade and after the fall of Montségur;[69] many fled to Tuscany where they were assimilated into the tolerant local society. Their descendants may well have given refuge to

Templars who took flight after the later suppression of that Order. Some Cathars from the Languedoc travelled to Scotland to the St Clair lands near Roslin and established a papermaking industry; here, once more, we can discern the influence of Rex Deus. The Cathars who fled to Lombardy and to Roslin were seeking the protection of the families of the bloodline that originated with Jesus and the priests of the Temple of Jerusalem. Sadly, the Order of the Knights Templar, where so many of the persecuted Cathars sought refuge, offered only a temporary respite, for they in their turn were soon to be added to the list of innocent victims of the Inquisition.

13

The End of the Templars?

The persecution of heretics had been intermittent from the 3rd century onwards and, prior to the crusade against the Cathars, had been conducted in a haphazard and somewhat *ad hoc* manner by local bishops whose attitudes varied from the lazy and seemingly tolerant on the one hand, to the fanatical and over-zealous on the other. They would only usually mount a concerted attack on the heretics when pressed to do so by Rome or impelled to do so by the political needs of the Church/State establishment.[1] During its operations against the Cathars, the Inquisition had gained a profound degree of experience in the noble arts of arrest, torture and secret trial and refined its interrogation techniques to a degree that was not excelled until the mid-20th century by the KGB. The priests of the Inquisition refused to soil their hands with the execution of their victims, and the unfortunates condemned after a trial without legal representation, knowledge of the charges or sight of the witnesses brought against them, were handed over to the State for the final ignominy of burning at the stake. Thus the men of God absolved themselves from the responsibility of killing their victims.[2]

The Inquisition enabled the Church to mount a sustained campaign against dissidents and heretics that is still, in somewhat subtler form, invoked on a worldwide scale today. The Inquisition, now called by the innocuous name of the Congregation for the Doctrine of the Faith, is headed by Cardinal Ratzinger.[3] Woe betide those who come to his attention and do not submit to his draconian discipline, for excommunication is still used to silence any theologians who have the temerity to question the 'infallible' doctrines of Holy Mother the Church.

The extirpation of the Cathar heresy and the growing power of the Inquisition boded ill for the Templars. For some years their increasing power and wealth had caused concern, not only among the kings who were so heavily in debt to them but also, and more importantly, to the one man outside the Order to whom they owed obedience, namely the Pope. A suggestion was made to amalgamate the crusading Orders of the Knights Templar and the Knights Hospitaller and make them more accountable to external authority, a move which was firmly resisted by both.[4] In 1291 the fall of Acre, the last stronghold and port in the Holy Land, began to cast further doubts as to the need for either Order, leaving Spain as the only country where their usefulness was beyond doubt, for their military prowess was valued by the Spanish kings and clergy in the fight against the Moors, Islamic invaders who had occupied southern Spain since 711 CE. Elsewhere the growing wealth and arrogance of the Knights Templar was creating ever-increasing resentment and enmity.

LE ROI MAUDIT?

Philippe le Bel, the grandson of St Louis the crusading king, acceded to the throne of France in 1285. The newly crowned king had three burning reasons to resent the Templars: they had been very reluctant to pay his grandfather's ransom during the crusades,[5] he had applied to join them and been refused,[6] and he had inherited a debt-ridden kingdom. To rebuild his personal finances the king seized all Jewish property and expelled the Jews from his kingdom, imposed a harsh tax on the Lombard and Florentine bankers and re-minted his coinage with a far lower precious metal content – the first recorded instance of currency devaluation.[7]

Philippe's intervention on behalf of a French candidate for the papacy resulted in the election of a French archbishop, Bertrand de Goth of Bordeaux, who was crowned Pope Clement V at Lyons on 17 December 1305. The king imposed certain conditions for his support, including the right to retain the tithes of the clergy of France for a period of five years, and insisted that the new Pope reside in France, which placed him under the direct political and military influence of the king. As a sign of gratitude the new Pope appointed 12 of Philippe's henchmen as cardinals. Prior to the papal election Philippe had imposed a secret condition that he disclosed less than six months after Clement's coronation.[8] As a result, in 1306 the new Pope wrote to William de Villaret, the grand master of the Knights Hospitaller, and to Jacques de Molay, the grand master of the Templars, requesting them to meet him in France to consider amalgamating their Orders. According to the Pope's instructions these two powerful men were to 'travel as secretly as possible and with a very small train as you will find plenty of your knights on this side of the sea'.[9]

The grand master of the Hospitallers replied that as he was in the middle of a major assault on the Turkish island of Rhodes, he could not attend. It is obvious that both Pope Clement and King Philippe were well aware of this from the outset. Jacques de Molay had no such excuse and, despite the Pope's request that he travel with a very small train, set out for La Rochelle with a fleet of 18 ships. The fleet carried 60 of the senior knights of the Order,[10] presumably the inner circle of initiates, 150,000 gold florins and 12 pack-horses carrying a large quantity of silver bullion.[11] The grand master knew that Pope Clement was Philippe's puppet and was prepared to bribe the king in order to avoid the proposed coalition. After landing at La Rochelle the Knights Templar and their baggage train travelled to their headquarters in Paris where the king greeted them with great ceremony.[12]

Jacques de Molay had prepared his case against the amalgamation well and suggested that as both Orders had done good service for Christianity, why initiate change? He also argued that as they were spiritual as well as temporal, it might not be a matter of indifference for the members to leave the Order they had chosen under God's guidance only to be forcibly enrolled in another. There were also grounds for considerable disagreement over the wealth and influence of the Orders, as well as the matter of who was to lead them in the event of a merger. The grand master could not, however, disclose that the Templars were the military arm of the descendants of the high priesthood of the Temple in Jerusalem.

THE PERILS OF FRIDAY THE 13TH

The proposed joining of the Orders was simply the excuse that the king used to tempt Jacques de Molay to leave his safe haven in Cyprus. On Thursday 12 October 1307, Jacques de Molay occupied a place of honour at the funeral of Catherine de Valois, the sister-in-law of the king. At dawn on Friday 13 October, the Templar grand master, the 60 knights of the inner circle and all but 24 of the members of the Order resident in France were arrested on the orders of the king.[13] The orders had been dispatched in secret on 14 September, instructing the royal seneschals throughout France to make the arrests on a charge that was described as 'a bitter thing, a lamentable thing, a thing which is horrible to contemplate, terrible to hear of, a detestable crime, an execrable evil, an abominable work, a detestable disgrace, a thing almost inhuman, indeed set apart from all humanity'.[14] The Knights Templar were arrested for heresy and accused of causing Christ 'injuries more grave than those he underwent on the cross'.[15] Gerard de Villiers, the preceptor of France, was the only leading Templar to escape.

To justify these controversial actions, Philippe le Bel was careful to explain that he was acting on the due and proper request of the chief inquisitor in France, Guillaume de Paris,[16] who was nominally a deputy of the Pope and also held the position of the king's confessor. In order to meet the needs of the Church/State establishment he permitted the inquisitors under his command to become just another arm of royal power. The arrested knights were deliberately terrorized by threats and torture prior to their first appearance before the inquisitors. The rack and the strappado were the most common tortures used but many also had flames applied to the soles of their feet. One Templar knight, the 50-year-old Gerard de Pasagio, claimed that they tortured him 'by the hanging of weights on [his] genitals and other members'. Bernard de Vaho, a Templar priest from the city of Albi, had his feet burnt so badly that after a few days the bones dropped out of them.[17] Yet the inquisitors had the gall to state at the end of each deposition that the victim had 'told the pure and entire truth for the safety of his soul' and not as a result of 'violence … fear of torture, of imprisonment, or any other reason'.[18] In February 1310, one knight, Jacques de Soci, claimed that he knew of 25 members of the Order who had already died 'on account of tortures and suffering'. The tortures used were successful; of the 138 depositions from the hearings which took place in Paris in October 1307, which included the confessions of Jacques de Molay and his leading knights, only four record that the victims were able to resist the torment to which they had been put. Similar success was achieved throughout France. The treatment of the Templars was truly appalling and the 70-year-old Jacques de Molay was undoubtedly tortured, but there is no credible evidence to support the claim that this included any form of crucifixion.

Despite the fact that the arrest of the Templars was nominally effected under the orders of the official inquisitor, Pope Clement saw the brutal actions of the king as an assault on the power of the papacy, for the Templars were solely responsible to the Pope. However, he lacked both the power and the will to reverse them. In an attempt to regain the initiative he issued a papal directive on 22 November 1307 ordering all Christian rulers to arrest the Templars[19] in their domains and to confiscate their property in the name of the Pope.[20] When the English king first heard of the initial arrests in France, he replied that he could not give 'easy credence' to the charges and he sent letters to the kings of Portugal, Castille, Aragon and Naples, strenuously defending the Knights Templar. When he received the papal directive, however, he was left with little room to manoeuvre and replied that due action would be taken against the Knights Templar 'in the quickest and best way' which, in this instance, was distinctly different from that used in France. Few Templars were actually arrested, most were allowed to stay within their preceptories and at first torture was forbidden for those under interrogation with the result that no one confessed to any charge of heresy. The trial in England seemed to be inconclusive until June 1311, when one Templar, Stephen de Stapelbrugge, confessed to denying Christ and claimed that homosexuality had been encouraged. Under papal pressure, ecclesiastical law was now being applied and torture frequently used, resulting in further confessions.[21] The trials in Scotland and Portugal produced different results yet again; the Portuguese knights were found not guilty, while in Scotland the verdict was 'not proven'[22]. A letter was sent by the Archbishop of Compostela to the Pope, pleading that the Templars be spared in the light of their usefulness in the campaigns against the Moors.[23] The Order offered to submit to the Pope and enquiries began which again convicted the Templars of idolatry, in that they worshipped heads. In Lombardy, ruled by the Rex Deus family of Savoy, certain bishops favoured the Templars and claimed that they could find no incriminating evidence; others were less favourable and obtained convictions; results were equally varied in Greece and Germany.

THE DEATH OF DE MOLAY

The final drama in the demise of the Knights Templar took place on 18 March 1314. The Archbishop of Sens and three papal commissioners took their places on a specially erected stage in front of the Notre Dame in Paris in order to announce the fate of the four leading Templars. The Bishop of Alba read out the confessions that had been forced from the Templar knights under torture and pronounced sentence on them all – perpetual imprisonment. At this point Jacques de Molay intervened and, under the assumption that the grand master was prepared to confess his guilt, he was allowed to speak freely.

> It is just that, in so terrible a day, and in the last moments of my life, I should discover all the iniquity of falsehood, and make the truth triumph. I declare, then, in the face of heaven and earth, and acknowledge, though to my eternal shame, that I have committed the greatest of crimes but ... it has been the acknowledging of those which have been so foully charged on the order. I attest – and truth obliges me to attest – that it is innocent!
>
> I made the contrary declaration only to suspend the excessive pains of torture, and to mollify those who made me endure them.
>
> I know the punishments which have been inflicted on all the knights who had the courage to revoke a similar confession; but the dreadful spectacle which is presented to me is not able to make me confirm one lie by another. The life offered me on such infamous terms I abandon without regret.[24]

De Molay's words were greeted with roars of support. Geoffroi de Charney stood beside his grand master to demonstrate his agreement.[25] The proceedings halted abruptly. The papal commissioners gave orders to clear the square and then sped to report the situation to the king, who immediately condemned both Templars to the most horrible death. On the following day on the Ile des Javiaux the Templars were executed by being roasted over a hot, smokeless fire to ensure that their suffering was prolonged. De Molay's last words cursed the Pope and the king and called upon them both to appear before the supreme judge in heaven within the year.[26] History records that both heeded that prophetic call. Pope Clement, who had never enjoyed good health, died first on 20 April and King Philippe expired on 29 November of the same year. Finally, the Order of the Knights Templar was officially suppressed and its properties in different parts of Europe were handed over to either the Knights Hospitaller or to the ruling monarch. The two exceptions to this were Scotland, where the Order continued openly for a period of time before going underground,[27] and Portugal, where they changed their name to the Knights of Christ and continued for centuries.[28]

THE ACCUSATIONS

The list of accusations against the Templars is considerable and included:

1   The denial of Christ and defiling the cross
2   Adoration of an idol – Baphomet
3   Performing a perverted sacrament
4   Ritual murder
5   The wearing of a cord of heretical significance
6   A ritual kiss
7   Alteration in the ceremony of the Mass and an unorthodox form of absolution
8   Immorality
9   Treachery to other sections of the Christian forces[29]

The charge of treachery to other sections of the Christian forces in the Holy Land probably arose from their strategic incompetence rather than from any degree of truth. In view of the Templars' belief that Jesus came to reveal rather than to redeem, charges 3 and 7 are ridiculous. The charge of immorality was a common aberration in the minds of the inquisitors and was automatically brought into play against anyone they deemed heretical. The charge of the denial of Christ and defiling the cross undoubtedly had a certain degree of truth. The Knights Templar had no faith whatsoever in the so-called redemption that, according to Pauline theologians, flowed from the bloody ritual at Golgotha. For this reason, Chartres Cathedral, which was largely financed and designed by the Templar Order as a celebration of their beliefs, does not contain one carving or representation of the crucifixion dating from the first 200 years of its existence.[30]

The most credible charge made against the Knights Templar was that of the adoration of a bearded head or idol known as Baphomet. The existence of several internationally famous artefacts gives credence to this. The veneration of one head in particular, that of St John the Baptist, is proven beyond all doubt. The Cathedral at Amiens was designed and constructed by the Templars to fulfil two particular and important functions: the celebration of the Gnostic principle of Sophia or sacred wisdom and the housing of the reliquary containing the severed head of John the Baptist.[31]

Walter de Sarton brought the original reliquary and its contents to Amiens from Constantinople in 1206. According to Guy Jourdan, the Provençal Templar scholar, the head of John the Baptist was *La vrai tête Baphométique Templiér* – the true Baphometic head of the Templars – which, it is alleged, they consulted by means of necromancy. The Dead Sea Scrolls scholar, Hugh Schonfield, applied the Essene Atbash Cipher to the word Baphomet and translated it to mean Sophia or sacred wisdom.[32] One of the forms of carving which was held to be diagnostic of Templar influence was a representation of a bearded head, such as that found on the carving of the Veil of Veronica in Rosslyn Chapel,[33] in Scotland, or the painting of the bearded head at Templecombe in Somerset, in England. The most famous of all, one that has long been associated with the Templar Order, is the controversial Shroud of Turin. One noted English scholar, Noel Currer-Briggs, suggests that there is considerable evidence to indicate that the Shroud of Turin may be the original artefact on which the painted head at Templecombe is based. He is also of the belief that the Shroud was the Baphometic head used by the inner circle of the Templar Order. This theory is not as incredible as it sounds, as considerable doubts which have a sound scientific basis have been cast on the carbon dating techniques employed in examination of the Shroud of Turin.

Evidence confirming two further charges which have some degree of truth can be found in both the legends and the ritual of modern Freemasonry which, as we shall see, owes much to Templar influence. The charge of ritual murder could very easily derive from the masonic legend of Hiram Abif and the rituals that proceed from it. In this legend we find the ritual 'killing' of a candidate for initiation being struck on the temple with a mall or mallet prior to being 'resurrected' to a new life in a higher state of consciousness. This custom was quite probably deliberately misconstrued by the inquisitors and then used against their victims in order to 'prove' a charge of ritual murder. According to the Templar historian, Bothwell Gosse, and the masonic historians, Chris Knight and Robert Lomas, they were also certainly guilty of wearing a cord of heretical significance. Knight and Lomas relate this to the cable tow or noose that every masonic candidate has to wear at his initiation and which is again recorded in a carving at Rosslyn Chapel.[34]

THE TEMPLARS IN SCOTLAND

Rosslyn Chapel, which lies seven miles south of Edinburgh, was constructed as a memorial to the Knights Templar nearly 150 years after their suppression. To ascertain why this memorial is in Scotland, when their main centre of activity was in France, we need to re-examine the events that took place with the initial wave of arrests which occurred in France in 1307. The Templar treasure, much of which the king had seen at their headquarters immediately prior to the arrests, had vanished by the time his seneschals walked into the temple in Paris. Also missing from the port of La Rochelle was the fleet of 18 ships that had borne Jacques de Molay and his companions on their final journey to France, along with which had gone the entire Atlantic fleet of the Order. Individual Templar knights were in flight throughout Europe. The American historian, John Robinson, describes in his book *Born in Blood* how the lodges of Craftmasons assisted the fleeing knights in their escape until they reached safe havens. In Portugal, the refugees joined the Order of the Knights of Christ, which was soon to change the regulations for new entrants, restricting membership to nobles of Portuguese birth. In the Baltic states many fugitives joined the Teutonic Knights while those in Lombardy, aided by the Cathars who had preceded them, used their skills to strengthen the emergent banking system. The story in Scotland, however, was very different.

The Knights Templar who fled to Scotland did so for two very compelling reasons. The entire country of Scotland at that time was under papal interdict; the king, nobles and common people were all under an order of excommunication, making it the one place that the fugitives would be safe. Scotland was in a state of civil war and still subject to waves of invasion by the English, until the victorious new king, Robert the Bruce, vanquished his enemies at home and abroad. The final battle that secured the throne for Bruce took place at Bannockburn in 1314. According to HRH Prince Michael of Albany, a direct descendant of Robert the Bruce, 432 Templar knights, including Sir Henry St Clair, Baron of Roslin, and his sons William and Henry, took part in the charge which finally routed the English invader and preserved Scottish independence.[35] We mentioned that there were two reasons to seek refuge in the kingdom of Scotland: freedom from papal interference was one; the protection and guidance of the St Clairs of Roslin and other leading families of the Rex Deus group was the other. After Bannockburn, King Robert the Bruce became the sovereign grand master of the surviving Templars in his kingdom. However, he was above all a practical man and, knowing that he had to make peace with the Pope, warned the knights that it was time that they went underground. The property of the Knights Templar in Scotland passed into the hands of the Knights Hospitaller, with certain estates reverting to the traditional families of Rex Deus. The property that passed to the Hospitallers was never accounted for in their general inventory, it was always accounted for separately, almost as though it was being 'kept in trust' to facilitate its restoration to its rightful owners at some future time.

But what of the Templar treasure? According to French masonic ritual, when it vanished it was destined for Scotland. One thing beyond all doubt is the dramatic improvement of the fortunes of the St Clairs of Roslin, who were already extremely wealthy. A later St Clair, Earl William, the third and last St Clair 'Jarl' of Orkney, spent a small fortune and over 40 years of his life designing and building Rosslyn Chapel as a memorial to the beliefs of the 'heretical' Templar Order. In many respects, the chapel is the most superbly carved 'reliquary for the Holy Grail' in Europe.[36] Within its walls are carved symbolic references to every spiritual and initiatory path known to mankind at that time. Prominent among the carvings are the diagnostic signs of Templarism: the five-pointed star, the rosette, the dove bearing an olive branch in its beak, an indirect reference to the two brothers on one horse, the Templar seal known as the Agnus Dei, the floriated cross and finally, the seemingly innocuous symbolism which, to the initiated, clearly signifies the true heresy of the Templars – the Veil of Veronica.[37] This carving, like all its fellows throughout Europe, points us directly back to the heretical truth disclosed by the most controversial relic of them all – the Shroud of Turin.

PART
IV

~

Rex Deus Teaching
and its Preservation

14

The Controversial Shroud of Turin

The most controversial relic in Christendom, the Shroud of Turin, made its first documented appearance some years after the suppression of the Knights Templar. The dispute over the authenticity of this oddly stained cloth dates from its first public exposition when, in the 1350s, Henry, Bishop of Troyes, wrote:

> Many theologians and otherwise persons [have stated] that this could not be the real Shroud of Our Lord having the Saviour's likeness thus imprinted upon it, since the holy Gospel made no mention of such imprint, while, if it had been true, it was quite unlikely that the holy Evangelists would have omitted to record it, or that the fact should have remained hidden until the present time.[1]

The earliest reference to what could be the Shroud dates from 1203, when Robert de Clari, a French crusader, described an object that he had seen exhibited in the Church of My Lady Saint Mary of Blachernae at Constantinople '... where was kept the sydoine in which Our Lord had been wrapped, which stood up straight every Friday so that the *figure* of

Our Lord could be plainly seen there'. The translation of the key word
'figure' has caused considerable debate. Is it the modern French 'face' or
in the English sense, the 'full figure' or body? Provocatively de Clari
continued 'no one, either Greek or French, ever knew what became of
this sydoine after the city was taken'.[2]

There are historians who claim that folded and framed, the Shroud
may have been the object exhibited as the Mandylion, the imprint of the
face of Jesus on a cloth which, legend tells us, Jesus sent to King Abgar
of Edessa. Linking the Shroud of Turin and the Mandylion is the
consistent and powerful literary tradition that neither image was 'made
by the hand of man'.[3] Is it simply coincidence that the known and
provable history of the Mandylion completes, with one short gap, the
earlier missing history of the Turin Shroud? Were they one and the same?

SUCCESSIVE OWNERS OF THE SHROUD

The first known owner of the Shroud in France in the 1350s was
Geoffrey de Charney, who died in 1356; the name of Jacques de Molay's
fellow martyr was Geoffroi de Charney. If the Shroud had been brought
to France from Constantinople by the Knights Templar, who had so
recently been suppressed on charges of heresy, it is understandable why
the de Charneys were reluctant to declare its origins. In *The Shroud
and the Grail*, Noel Currer-Briggs, founder member of the Association
of Genealogists and Record Agents and a Fellow of the Society of
Genealogists, produces proof that Geoffrey de Charney was the nephew
of Jacques de Molay's companion in death, Geoffroi de Charney,[4] Templar
Master of Normandy. He also shows that this family are intimately linked
by ties of blood and marriage with the families of Brienne, de Joinville
and Burgundy. Could it be that Rex Deus ensured the preservation of the
Shroud in the certain knowledge that, sooner or later, it would play an
important part in disclosing that Jesus came to reveal the pathway to
initiation and not to make any form of redemptive sacrifice?

The last member of the de Charney line, the 72-year-old Marguerite de Charney, was childless when, in 1453, Duke Louis of Savoy ceded to her the Castle of Varanbon and the revenues of the estate of Miribel in return for certain 'valuable services', which included Marguerite's gift to the duke of the Shroud. Geoffrey II de Charney and Marguerite's second husband, Humbert de Villersexel, had both been created knights of the Order of the Collar of Savoy by earlier dukes.[5] Marguerite de Charney had found a noble and trusted family to ensure the preservation of this remarkable relic, as the House of Savoy were Rex Deus.

By the 15th century, Church authorities had begun to refer to the relic as Jesus' 'burial shroud'. The theologian Francesco della Rovere wrote, in 1464, 'This is now preserved with great devotion by the Dukes of Savoy, and it is coloured with the blood of Christ'.[6] Within five years della Rovere became Pope Sixtus IV. His treatise on *The Blood of Christ*, published in 1468, was the first time that the Shroud was recognized as genuine by the papacy and the relic was even given its own feast day, 4 May.[7]

Some time in the early 1500s, the Shroud suffered a degree of damage which appears to have been made by a red-hot poker being thrust through the folded cloth. Ian Wilson claims that 'it seems very likely that they are the scars of some primitive "trial by fire" ceremony…'. In 1532 the cloth was damaged still further by a fire in the building which caught one edge of it and scorched all 48 folds before it could be extinguished. Fourteen large triangular-shaped patches and eight smaller ones, made from altar cloth, were sewn over the worst of the damage, and it was backed with a simple piece of holland cloth.[8]

In 1578 the Duke of Savoy had the Shroud brought to Turin, where it has rested ever since. In the final decade of the 17th century a magnificent Baroque cathedral, dedicated to St John the Baptist, was commissioned from the architect Guarino Guarini.[9] The relic took up its new abode on 1 June 1694, being carried into the building and locked behind a grille in the place of honour above the high altar and only exposed publicly at very special events such as important weddings in the House of Savoy, papal visits or great Church occasions.[10]

THE RELIC ITSELF

The Shroud of Turin measures 14ft 3in (4.36m) long by 3ft 7in (1.1m) wide and consists of one single piece of cloth with the addition of a full length strip 3.5in (8.5cm) wide joined by a single seam on the left-hand side. Imprinted in an almost pure sepia monochrome, like a stained shadow on the cloth, is the faint outline of the front and back of a bearded, long-haired man laid out as if dead.[11] The image is subtle and, except when viewed from a distance, very difficult to discern. Despite the poor quality of the image there is sufficient detail in the blood-like stains to convince the devout for many centuries that this is the burial cloth of Jesus.

The Shroud was photographed during the 1898 exposition by an amateur photographer, Secondo Pia. In those early days of photography nothing was ever certain until the plates had been developed and Secondo admitted to considerable relief when he first saw the image appear. His relief soon turned to wonder, for he was not looking, as he had expected, at a negative version of the shadowy figure he had seen on the cloth, but at an unmistakable and highly detailed photographic likeness, the light and shade of which gave the figure an almost three-dimensional quality, with the blood flows from the head, hands, feet and side showing up with magical realism.[12] The overall impression was of a tall, impressively built man with a strikingly life-like face. The photographs caused a worldwide sensation and sparked in-depth investigations that have continued ever since. The Shroud was photographed professionally in 1931 and this time the results were even more remarkable, for considerable advances had been made in photographic techniques. Since then it has been photographed twice more, in 1969 and 1973.

SCIENTIFIC EXAMINATION

The first photographs stimulated the curiosity of the medical profession, particularly that of forensic pathologists and anatomists. Yves Delage, Professor of Comparative Anatomy at the Sorbonne in Paris, was the first to announce his findings publicly. On 21 April 1902 he gave a lecture entitled 'The image of Christ visible on the Holy Shroud of Turin'. Not surprisingly he had an unusually large and attentive audience. The professor explained that, from a medical point of view, the wounds and anatomical data recorded on the Shroud were so accurate that it seemed impossible that they could be the work of an artist. He continued by explaining how difficult and utterly pointless it would have been for an artist to depict such a figure in a negative manner and that, furthermore, as there was no trace of any known pigment on the cloth, he was convinced that the image found upon it must be that of Jesus, created by some physio-chemical process that had taken place in the tomb.[13]

Delage's lecture caused an uproar and Marcelin Berthelot, the secretary of the Academy, refused to publish the text of it in full. With the publication of the second set of photographs, the Shroud's authenticity began to gain far wider acceptance among the medical profession. Research by Dr Pierre Barbet of St Joseph's Hospital in Paris led to the conclusion that the wounds depicted on it were genuinely those of a crucified man.[14] These results were confirmed by the Cologne radiologist Professor Hermann Moedder[15] and Dr Judica-Cordiglia, the professor of forensic medicine of the University of Milan.[16] In the United States further study was made on the bloodstains by Dr Anthony Sava of Brooklyn. Most of the present-day medical opinion rests on research carried out by Dr Robert Bucklin of Michigan who now resides in California.

A life-size model of the head portrayed on the Shroud was made by the British photographer Leo Vala, who produced a three-dimensional image.[17] The distinguished ethnologist, Professor Carlton S. Coon of Harvard, who studied these photographs, described the face as that 'of a physical type found in modern times among Sephardic Jews and noble Arabs'.[18] The wounds depicted on the head, according to Dr David Willis, cannot be described except in the context of the crown or cap of thorns described in the Gospels.[19] Marks on the back and front of the body from the shoulders downwards, found in groups of three, have been described by doctors as being physiologically accurate representations of flogging. Bruising which is consistent with carrying the crossbeam of a cross has also been identified. Professor Judica-Cordiglia has classified the damage to the knees of the man in the image as being the result of repeated falls. [20]

THE EVIDENCE OF CRUCIFIXION

The wounds deriving from the crucifixion itself have naturally attracted considerable attention. The flow of blood originating from the wound in the left wrist indicates that at the time of bleeding the arm must have been raised at an angle between 55 and 65 degrees from the vertical.[21] This is consistent with crucifixion, as in order to maintain his breathing the victim would have flexed his elbows to raise his body and so bring relief to his labouring lungs. Contrary to many medieval depictions of the crucifixion, the nail wounds on the Shroud are on the wrist and not the hand. This above all is a further indication of authenticity, as nailing through the hands would not have supported the weight of the body. According to Dr Pierre Barbet, who studied the wounds in the 1930s, the soldiers who had nailed the victim to the cross were experienced men who knew their anatomy. Barbet had experimented in reproducing the wounds by nailing a recently amputated arm at the same point as that on the Shroud image. The nail passed through a gap in the bones of the wrist known as 'the space of destot'.[22]

The most unexpected proof that derived from Barbet's work was the contraction of the thumb as the nail was being driven through the wrist; the passage of the nail had stimulated the median nerve, causing the muscles of the thumb to contract. When he consulted the image on the Shroud he discovered that no thumbs were visible on either hand. He deduced that the nailing of the victim had produced exactly the same effect as his experiment. He then posed the question 'Could a forger have imagined this?' Barbet used the same techniques on amputated feet, again emulating the position shown on the Shroud. The nail passed easily between the second and third metatarsal bones, so that the body would have been supported by a single nail impaling the feet.[23] The nailing of the wrists and feet, with the dependant body weight, made the victims secure and incapable of freeing themselves.

A clear wound is visible on the left-hand side of the image between the fifth and sixth rib which, due to mirror image reversal, would have been on the right side of the victim. The blood flow from the wound, which must have been inflicted when the body was erect, is broken by some clear areas which are believed to show the mixture of a clear fluid with the blood[24] which, according to the German radiologist Professor Moedder, emanated from the pleural sac. Dr Anthony Sava noted that there is often an accumulation of fluid in the pleural cavity as a response to injury. He is of the opinion that the scourging which is indicated by the marks on the back, shoulders and front of the body were the most probable cause of the accumulation of fluid in the pleural cavity and this trauma-induced pleurisy was the principal cause of death, which was only exacerbated by the crucifixion.[25] The consensus that arises from the medical experts who have examined the photographic evidence of the Shroud is that the cloth was, beyond all reasonable doubt, in contact with a victim of crucifixion.

Jewish custom and the Gospels show that the body of Jesus would have been laid out full-length in the tomb prepared by Joseph of Arimathea. The position of the body with the hands crossed over the pelvic area is identical to that discovered by Father de Vaux of the Ecole

Biblique in his excavation of Essene burials at Qumran.[26] It is ironic that this connection of Jesus with Essene practices was inadvertently confirmed by de Vaux, whose principal aim in his handling of the Dead Sea Scrolls seems to have been to deny all contact between them and Jesus. Contrary to Jewish practice, it is plainly obvious from all the evidence on the Shroud that the body depicted on it was *not* washed according to custom and law, but had been anointed with copious quantities of expensive ointment and hurriedly wrapped in the burial cloth.

THE FORENSIC TESTS

In June 1969 a commission of specialists studied the Shroud so that they might recommend suitable tests in order to establish its nature and provenance. The commission was convened in secret, but the news leaked out and the cardinal and the custodians of the Shroud were accused of acting 'like thieves in the night'.[27] The commission reported on 17 June, noting that the Shroud was in an excellent state of preservation, and recommended tests which would require minimal samples of the cloth. The arrangement for taking samples was kept secret and was conducted on 24 November 1973, after a two-day exposition for the television cameras.

Seventeen samples of thread were removed from different areas on the Shroud, with great care being taken to avoid the slightest possibility of contamination. An expert from the Ghent Institute of Textile Technology, Professor Gilbert Raes, had joined the team and for his benefit, two samples, one of ½ x 1¾in (13 x 40mm) and the other of ⅓ x 1¾in (10 x 40mm), were taken from one side of the cloth. To add to these the professor had been given two individual threads to examine. One of 12 mm in length was taken from the weft and the second of 13 mm from the warp. The overall style of weave of the cloth was that of a three-to-one herringbone twill, which was used at the time of Jesus but was found more commonly in silk than linen. Examination of cloth fibres under polarized light satisfied him that it was linen. Microscopic examination disclosed unmistakable traces of cotton, which led Raes to conclude that the material had been woven on a loom that had also produced cotton fabric. Analysis of the cotton revealed that it was of a species known as *gossypium hebaceum* which is native to the eastern Mediterranean. This was extremely significant and, according to Raes, indicated that the fabric had been manufactured in the Middle East.[28]

The Swiss criminologist, Dr Max Frei, took samples of some of the particles adhering to the cloth and was able to identify small particles of mineral, fragments of hair and fibres deriving from plants, bacterial spores, spores from mosses and fungi, and pollen grains from flowering plants. Some of the pollens were halophytes from desert varieties of *tamarix*, *suaeda* and *artemisia*, which are to be found almost exclusively growing around the shores of the Dead Sea.[29] Frei stated simply:

> These plants are of great diagnostic value for our geo-graphical studies as identical desert plants are missing in all the other countries where the Shroud is believed to have been exposed in the open air. Consequently, a forgery, produced somewhere in France during the Middle Ages, in a country lacking these typical halophytes could not contain such characteristic pollen grains from the deserts of Palestine.[30]

Pollen from the surface of the Shroud includes six species of plant that are exclusively Palestinian in origin. He also states that there is pollen from a significant number of plants from the Anatolian Steppes of Turkey, as well as eight species of Mediterranean plants that are consistent with the Shroud's admitted exposure in France and Italy.

FURTHER SCIENTIFIC EXAMINATIONS

In March 1977 the United States hosted a scientific conference of research on the Turin Shroud which was attended by clergy from different denominations and a large number of scientists, including Dr Robert Bucklin, the pathologist, and Professor Joseph Gambescia.

The majority of the scientists were from a diverse range of backgrounds, which included the US Atomic Energy Commission, the Pasadena Jet Propulsion Laboratory, the Albuquerque Sandia Laboratory and the spectroscopy division of the Los Alamos Laboratory. Bishop John Robinson was deeply impressed not only with the calibre of the scientists involved but also with the seriousness with which they approached the question of the authenticity of the relic. He stated: 'There is no one in this thing who is being either gullible or just dismissive.'[31] The physicist Dr John Jackson and the aerodynamicist Dr Eric Jumper reported that the image had not been created by direct contact but by some form of emanation from the body and that there was a precise relationship between the intensity of the image and the degree of separation between the body and the cloth.[32]

Dr Jackson then used a 3 x 5in (7.5 x 12.5cm) transparency of the Shroud in a modern Interpretation Systems VP-8 Image Analyzer to display a figure in perfect three-dimensional relief. An ordinary photograph analysed by the same machine simply does not carry sufficient information regarding distance and proportion to create such an accurate image. However, there was one strange anomaly in this image; the eyes displayed a curious unnatural bulge as if something had been laid upon them. Jackson discovered that it was a long-standing Jewish custom to lay coins or a broken potsherd over the eyes of a corpse prior to burial. He realized that a coin laid over the eyes in this way would exactly match these unnatural bulges.[33]

As a result of the American experiments, the hardened sceptic, Dr John Robinson, was moved to claim that with the accumulated evidence already available, the burden of proof had shifted and it was now up to those who doubted the Shroud's authenticity to prove their case, rather than the reverse.[34] To the distress of those who supported its authenticity, this is apparently what happened.

THE CARBON DATING

After the death of ex-King Umberto of Italy in 1983, the Shroud of Turin passed into the hands of the Vatican, who gave permission for carbon dating as a result of intensive lobbying from a wide spectrum of interested parties. Three laboratories were involved, the University of Arizona in Tucson, the Swiss Federal Institute of Technology in Zurich, and the Oxford Research Laboratory.

The samples were taken in total secrecy, but the Church did allow representatives from all three laboratories to be present. One 2¾in (7cm) sample was cut from one corner and divided into three. Each piece was sealed in appropriate containers, one for each of the laboratories concerned. The whole process was videotaped. The results of the carbon dating were announced by Cardinal Anastasio Ballestrero in Turin on 13 October 1988 and later the same day by Dr Tite of the British Museum Research Laboratory, who had supervised the entire process. The results disclosed that it was 99.9 per cent certain that the Shroud of Turin had its origins in the period from 1000–1500 CE and 95 per cent certain that it dated from somewhere between 1260 and 1390.[35] The world reeled with shock from the announcement that the Shroud of Turin had been scientifically shown to be a fake. The papal hierarchy's attitude was oddly ambivalent. Professor Luigi Gonella, the scientific adviser to the Vatican, made a strange comment: 'The tests were not commissioned by the Church and we are not bound by the results.'

Journalists and fantasists had a field day; articles on the dating of the Shroud were soon replaced by multiple allegations of conspiracy concerning the tests. Brother Bruno Bonnet-Eymard, the extreme right-wing luminary of La Contre-Réforme Catholique au XXeme Siècle, accused Dr Michael Tite of switching samples taken from the Shroud with those from a 13th-century cope, and implied that Tite received a professorship for his pains. This eminent Christian claimed that the tests were a deliberate attempt by scientists to undermine Christianity.[36] Professor Werner Bulst denounced the scientific community on television, and fell back to a tried and trusted defence by claiming that it was all a masonic anti-Catholic plot.[37]

The German authors, Holger Kersten and Elmar Gruber, wrote that the carbon-dating results were rigged by the scientists acting in collusion with the Church.[38] For reasons that are completely unexplained, the video cameras had been switched off after the samples had been taken and were not switched on again until after they had been sealed into their containers. Thus there was ample opportunity for a deliberate breach of protocol and for Tite to have switched the samples as has been alleged by Brother Bonnet-Eymard. They also allege that there are serious discrepancies between the descriptions of the samples that were taken and those made by the scientists in respect of the samples that they had received. Viewed from the perspective of the hidden streams of spirituality, the motivation they ascribe to the Church to explain this alleged conspiracy is particularly interesting, for they assert that the Church wished to discredit the Shroud because it proves that Jesus was still alive when he was taken down from the cross.[39]

THE CONTROVERSY REOPENS

The validation of the carbon dating by three leading laboratories of international repute should have put an end to the argument over the authenticity of the Shroud once and for all. However, an American scientist made a discovery which appears to discredit the results. Carbon dating techniques are subject to massive distortion by extremely minute amounts of contamination, which is why the samples used for dating the Shroud were cleansed by the most reliable techniques then known. Yet despite all the precautions taken, one significant form of contamination that was unknown at the time arose from the very nature of the cloth that was being tested.[40]

Many commentators, including Ian Wilson, have described the holy relic as having 'a damask-like sheen'.[41] This shiny appearance has recently been discovered to arise from a natural growth of microbiological organisms which completely envelop each constituent thread of the cloth. The extent of this contamination, which has been proven to be completely resistant to the cleansing methods used by the three authorized laboratories, is such that what was in fact being tested was slightly less than 40 per cent Shroud material and more than 60 per cent living organism.[42] Recent tests have proved that the cleansing agents used by the laboratories doing the carbon dating were completely ineffective in respect of the microbiological organisms coating the Shroud, but do tend to dissolve part of the cellulose from the flax, thus increasing the distortion created by the microbiological coating.[43] The end result is that there is such a gross distortion of the results that the whole question of the age and authenticity of this controversial relic is still wide open.

The existence of a microbiological coating of living organisms has already been demonstrated on jade and stone carvings from the Mayan civilization in Mesoamerica and on mummy wrappings from ancient Egypt. The initial discoveries that led to this re-evaluation of carbon dating techniques were made by Dr Leoncio A Garza-Valdes from San Antonio, who held the chair of microbiology at the Health Sciences Centre of the University of Texas. He noticed that jade and stone carvings of the Mayans all had a particularly lustrous sheen. He found that the carvings had been coated by millions of bacteria which produce a pinkish pigment and also by some fungi which varied in colour from dark brown to black. This strange mixture combined to form a yellowish 'plastic coat' over the entire surface of the carving and the resultant lustrous gloss he called a 'bioplastic coating'.[44] One of the artefacts he examined was a pectoral formed of several pieces of carved jade held together by strong cotton filaments. Using an electron microscope he discovered that these cotton threads were also covered with fungi and bioplastic coating. A further examination of the coating by an industrial analysis laboratory in San Antonio confirmed his findings and proved that the lustre on the artefacts was organic and not man-made.

He then proceeded to study the textile wrappings on two very different Egyptian mummies, one of a 13-year-old girl which was found during excavations by Sir Flinders Petrie and which now rests in the Manchester Museum in England, the other of an ibis from his own private collection. Both the mummy and the wrappings of the girl were carbon dated by the University of Manchester with disturbing results. The bones were dated to 1510 BCE but the wrappings to 255 CE – a discrepancy of more than 1,700 years.[45] In January 1996 Dr Garza-Valdes discovered that the flax fibres making up the cloth all carried a thick bioplastic coating similar to those he had found on other ancient textiles. Similar tests were performed on the mummified ibis and the presence of a bioplastic coating on the fibres of the bird's wrapping was also clearly established. When both the ibis mummy and the wrappings were carbon dated the age discrepancy between the wrapping and the bone was 400–700 years.

The samples of the Shroud taken for radio carbon dating in 1988 were cut by Professor Giovanni Riggi Numana who showed small fragments of the original samples to Dr Garza-Valdes as well as pieces of Scotch tape with blood samples taken from the back of the head of the image. Riggi removed a thread from one of the original samples which Dr Garza-Valdes placed under the microscope and immediately discerned bioplastic coating completely covering the fibres.[46] He is of the opinion that if the carbon dating tests were to be repeated today, in exactly the same manner as they were conducted in 1988, the results would indicate an even later date because the bacteria have multiplied considerably in the last 12 years and will have skewed the date even further. He has been able to culture the bacteria from the Shroud and prove that they are still living and multiplying organisms, therefore the proportion of organism to thread is increasing. This American scientist has not restricted his investigations to the bioplastic coating alone, however, but has also rigorously examined the pieces of Scotch tape and the so-called 'blood' samples taken from the back of the head of the image.

There are already conflicting scientific reports in this respect. The Italian scientist Dr Bauma-Bollone reports that these stains were human blood of the AB group.[47] Drs Adler and Heller, examining the same tapes used by Dr McCrone, supported the statements of their Italian colleague, that these were indeed bloodstains.[48] Dr Garza-Valdes examined the sample given to him by Professor Riggi and proved that it contained human blood of the AB group, which has historically been the most common blood group found amongst Jewish people. He was able to state that the bloodstains were ancient because of the degree of degradation in the small amount of blood he had found on his sample.[49] He also examined everything else that could be found on the samples and Scotch tape provided by Riggi. In the sample taken from the occipital area of the image he found several microscopic tubules of wood which, if the Shroud is authentic, could only have come from the part of the cross that Jesus carried to Golgotha. These tubules proved to be of oak.[50]

Dr Garza-Valdes' research was published early in 1996 in an article which described his work on the Mayan artefacts and the Shroud of Turin, including the results of the DNA testing of the blood samples. The front cover of the journal carried the facial image of Jesus taken from the Shroud over the caption 'Secrets of the Shroud – Microbiologists discover how the Shroud of Turin hides its true age'. The article concluded that the Shroud of Turin is many centuries older than its carbon date would suggest. Even Dr Harry Gove of Rochester University in America, the prime inventor of the methodology used to carbon date the Shroud, was quoted as saying 'This is not a crazy idea'. Thanks to the immaculate research by the American microbiologist the validity of the 1988 carbon dating of the Shroud of Turin is now highly questionable.

THE HIDDEN MESSAGE OF THE SHROUD

If we first assess the scientific comment in chronological order we start by considering the words of Professor Yves Delage of Paris, who claimed in 1902 that the wounds and anatomical data recorded on the Shroud are so accurate that it seemed impossible to conceive that they could be the work of an artist. The research by Dr Pierre Barbet concluded that the wounds depicted on the relic were genuinely those of a crucified man and these results were confirmed by Professor Hermann Moedder of Cologne, Dr Judica-Cordiglia, professor of forensic medicine, Dr Anthony Sava of Brooklyn, and Dr Robert Bucklin of California. Then we have to include in our deliberations the views of the ethnologist Professor Coon of Harvard, who described the three-dimensional image derived from the face on the Shroud as 'of a physical type found in modern times among Sephardic Jews and noble Arabs'. The professional opinion of Dr David Willis and Professor Judica-Cordiglia in respect of the wounds depicted on the Shroud are given further credence by the work of Dr Pierre Barbet, whose experimentation on amputated limbs replicated many of the depicted details which could not possibly have been known by any artist of the medieval era.

The comparative studies of the weave of the cloth indicate that the cotton used derived from the Middle East, not Europe. Dr Max Frei's analysis of the small particles found on the Shroud indicate that the relic had been exposed to the air in the desert areas near the shores of the Dead Sea. The experiments in technological image processing conducted in 1976 moved Dr John Robinson to state unequivocally that the burden of proof had shifted and that it was now up to those who doubted the Shroud's authenticity to prove their case rather than the reverse. We believe that it is now almost certain that the Shroud of Turin is genuine, that it *is* the shroud or cloth in which Jesus was wrapped when he was taken down from the cross nearly 2,000 years ago. Its importance to the Knights Templar and the Rex Deus group lies in the hidden message contained within it; for the story told by the Shroud, if genuine, completely contradicts the teaching of the Church by proving that Jesus was still alive when taken down from the cross.

We mentioned earlier that the Shroud shows that, contrary to established Jewish custom and practice, the victim had not been washed before being wrapped in the cloth, but instead had been anointed with copious quantities of very expensive ointments. The reasons for this are plain. The ointments had been used to hasten the recovery from the terrible ordeal just endured. In victims of crucifixion, death occurs as a result of a massive increase in the secretion of fluids into the pleural sac, creating such pressure on the lungs that they cease to function and the victim suffocates. The spear thrust in the side of Jesus, in complete contradiction to the Gospel accounts, was not to prove that the Messiah was dead, but to relieve the pressure on his lungs and allow him to breathe.

Despite immense persecution, the legends that Jesus survived the crucifixion have endured for 2,000 years and now are made highly credible. We mentioned earlier, in connection with the Stations of the Cross at Rennes-le-Château, that *The Lost Gospel According to St Peter* indicates that Jesus was seen leaving the tomb supported by two white-clad Essene healers. The same message is enshrined within the Rex Deus tradition. Baigent, Leigh and Lincoln recount that an Anglican priest wrote to them stating that Jesus was alive as late as 45 CE. Other legends have linked him to appearances in Egypt and Kashmir long after the crucifixion.

Rex Deus teaching, long-standing esoteric traditions and the message preserved within the Shroud of Turin all point to a simple, rational and scientifically credible scenario that completely demolishes the central tenet of Christian belief. If Jesus survived the crucifixion and was nursed back to health, then he could not have died as a sacrifice on the cross to expiate our sins. St Paul, the originator of this heretical concept, far from being the great follower of the Messiah was correctly described by the Ebionites as the 'spouter of lies' and 'the distorter of the true teachings of Jesus'. After 2,000 years the truth is truly escaping the net. Jesus did come to reveal, *not* to redeem.

15

The Religious Beliefs of Rex Deus

ope Pius IX condemned the Knights Templar as being Gnostics from the beginning and followers of the Johannite Heresy.[1] Yet strangely, while it is easy to find descriptions of the majority of heresies – such as Gnosticism, Montanism, Arianism, Nestorianism, Manichaeism and Pelagianism – in Church documents, when it comes to the Johannite Heresy there is a deafening silence. The Church (as prosecutor of heretics) is hardly the most dispassionate of sources as to the true nature of heretical belief systems. It invariably used the accusations against heretics, and the definition of the heresies themselves, as a further opportunity to castigate its opponents. What is it about the nature and beliefs of the Johannite heretics that seems to frighten the Church into silence? Perhaps work earlier this century by the masonic scholar A E Waite and during the last century by Magnus Eliphas Levi may give us clues. Both authors came to the same conclusion which, if it were proved, would terrify the Church and utterly destroy the dogma about the divine nature of Jesus and the nature of his mission. They claimed that Jesus was an initiate of the Egyptian cult of Osiris and a follower of the goddess Isis,[2] which is largely confirmed by the well-documented

Templar veneration of Isis under the Christianized guise of the Black Madonna.[3]

The Rex Deus nobility showed consistent and remarkable tolerance towards persecuted groups such as the Jews and Cathars. Their overt arm, the Knights Templar, shared the benefits of their spiritual insight with the communities within which they moved. However, neither the actions of the Templars nor the accusations of heresy made against them do anything to explain the belief system that motivated them. Their written records disappeared with their treasure prior to their arrest, leaving no documentary evidence as to the differences in belief between them and the Christian Church, with the sole exception of their veneration of Isis in the acceptable guise of the Black Madonna. We have established that in the eyes of the members of Rex Deus, Jesus was an initiatory teacher who, supremely gifted as he was, was a man like any other; like the Jews of biblical Israel from which they sprang, they would have regarded his deification as outright blasphemy. As direct racial and religious descendants of Jesus and the High Priests of the Temple, they would have understood the truly blasphemous nature of the concept of drinking 'blood', even in allegorical form. One thing is certain, the religious beliefs of the Rex Deus group derived from the teaching of Jesus himself, and not from St Paul.

When we began our investigation, we could only speculate about the Judaic nature of the religion followed by members of Rex Deus, and were baffled by any attempt to assess their ultimate objectives. Several years after our first meeting with Michael, and after the publication of *The Second Messiah*, other members of Rex Deus made themselves known to us. As a result of these meetings and further in-depth interviews with Michael, we began to gain insights into the nature of their religious structure.

THE LITURGY AND GOSPEL
OF THE HOLY TWINS

The families of Rex Deus followed a form of 'New Covenant' Judaism that was proclaimed by Jesus the Messiah and preached after the crucifixion by his twin brother, Judas Thomas, and by James the Just. Judas Thomas became the Patriarch of Edessa, and James the Just is described in the Acts of the Apostles as the first Bishop of Jerusalem. This 'first bishop' and his followers seemed to behave rather oddly for people who were supposedly founding a new religion, for the Acts of the Apostles records 'And they, continuing daily with one accord in the temple ... '4 Their recorded actions are, however, entirely consistent with James' position as a High Priest and their desire to follow a new form of Judaism which became the foundation for Rex Deus belief.

The central beliefs and rituals of the Rex Deus religion were recorded in a document known as *The Liturgy and Gospel of the Holy Twins*, which incorporates several writings of disciples of Jesus, in particular those of John the Evangelist and Judas Thomas. The original Gospel of John, known to the Cathars as *The Gospel of Love*, was the major contributory source. Judas Thomas was the author of *The Gospel of Thomas*,5 which forms approximately 50 per cent of the contribution attributed to him in *The Liturgy and Gospel of the Holy Twins*. The *Gospel of Thomas* was buried with other documents at Nag Hammadi, for the Church had declared it heretical and ordered its destruction. As with other documents that were later placed on the Index of Proscribed Books by the Catholic Church, it is still regarded as heretical.

As there is no written copy of the liturgy available, we have had to rely on Michael, who told us that it begins with *The Proclamation of the Book* which is as follows:

The Book of the Old Covenant is sealed with seven seals
and is locked with seven keys.

The Angel of God holds the Book and it will be opened no more.

The Book of the New Covenant is opened at the first page and the Messiah has written:

- The Oath
- The Encryption
- The Prayer of the Abba Ra Heim
- The Proclamation of the Law
- The Proclamation concerning the Poor
- The Proclamation of Forgiveness
- The Commemoration

Some of this phrasing will be familiar to those who have read the Revelation of St John where the concept of the seven seals occurs repeatedly.[6] Symbolic representations of the seven seals are common in the Catholic world and particularly noteworthy examples can be found in those churches and cathedrals, such as St Sulpice in Paris, which are closely associated with the underground streams of spirituality.

After *The Proclamation of the Book* and preceding the statements of belief, law, commandments, prayers and ritual in the liturgy is the *Oath of the Messiah*, which reads as follows:

If the words that I spoke were not the words of God, but were my own words and if those who heard my words believed that they were the words of God and trusted in them [ie believed in the revised Law, the two first commandments – and relied upon the relaxing of the dietary laws, circumcision and travelling], then the sin of breaking the Law is not theirs, but mine – may the blood of their sin be upon my hands as I will answer for that sin when I stand before God at mine end. Therefore you can believe and trust in my words as being the words of God.

Jesus is in effect telling his flock that as Messiah he is taking sole responsibility for the massive change that he is enunciating in the Law, and for any sin committed due to actions arising from belief in his words.

The startling change in the Law preached by Jesus had its origins at the time of Moses, when we find a parallel in Judaism to the usurpation of power by the Popes within the Catholic Church. The beliefs of the prophet Abraham derived from an initiatory religion that he had largely learnt from his teacher or hierophant, Melchizedek.[7] The nature of this religion is what lies behind Abraham's ready acceptance by the pharaoh in Egypt – the Egyptian kingly initiate clearly recognized the enlightenment of the prophet.[8] Surprisingly this Gnostic form of early Judaism spoke of a far more loving and less demanding God than the vengeful legalistic Jehovah (Yahweh) preached by Moses. Moses' institution of the Law, described in considerable detail in the Books of Exodus and Leviticus, indicated a total transformation of Judaism from a loving and willing service of Almighty God (whose sacred gifts of gnosis were to be used for the benefit of the people of Abraham) into a strictly defined conformist and highly legalistic framework which placed demands upon its people that they could not reasonably be expected to meet. The Law was so complex and harsh that it made every man, however 'pious', a sinner. But even this religious burden had within it certain moderating influences. The High Priest acted as the spokesperson of his people before God, to make atonement for their sin and seek forgiveness.[9]

Following the oath we find *The Encryption*, which defines some of the aspects of God and the relationship of Jesus to Him. This insistence on the humanity of Jesus is a stark contradiction to the Christian doctrine that 'Jesus was divine'.

The Encryption

God is God.
God is the Great God of the Universe.

God is the Alpha and Omega.
God is the Creator.
God is the Destroyer.
God is Life.
God is the Lawgiver.
God is the Judge.
God is Mercy.
God is Love.
God is Knowledge.
God is Wisdom.

A Man was sent from God.
He was the Star.
He was the Teacher.
He was of the House of David.
He was of the Line of Aaron.
He is the Prince of Peace.
He is the Learned Lamb.
He is Our King.
He is Our High Priest.
He is the Prince of the West.
He is the Messiah.
His name is Jesus.

Any student of comparative religion reading this list would find little difficulty in accepting Baigent, Leigh and Lincoln's thesis that high on the hidden agenda of Templarism was the desire to reinstitute true monotheism by reuniting Judaism, Christianity and Islam.[10] No devout Muslim would have any problem with any of the statements in the Encryption. Few Jews of the time of Jesus would have had any cause to dispute the statements about God or the Messiah, although it must be admitted that modern Jews would have very great difficulty with the statement that it was Jesus who was the Messiah. However, it was neither the Muslims nor the Jews who persecuted the Knights Templar on religious grounds, it was the Christian Church who could not accept the monotheism of the Knights of the Holy Grail. Yet despite its fundamental monotheism there is at least one section in *The Liturgy and Gospel of the Holy Twins* which is almost guaranteed to upset adherents of all three major religions as it lays great emphasis on the polytheistic origins of early Judaism.

The majority of Old Testament teaching derives unequivocally from Egyptian and Mesopotamian initiatory roots. The Ten Commandments arise from the Judgements of the Soul before the court of Osiris in the Egyptian *Book of the Dead*,[11] and the Psalms of David bear an uncanny resemblance to certain hymns of Egyptian origin. The proverbs attributed to King Solomon are a verbatim translation into Hebrew from the work of a leading Egyptian sage, Amenemope. Many other Egyptian sources, including *The Pyramid Texts* and *The Coffin Texts*, were used as a basis for Old Testament writings, in which references to the sun god Ra were simply changed to relate to Jehovah. The definition of the Abba Ra Heim, which lies above the prayer attributed to him, is: 'The children who are the followers of their father the god Ra', a phrase which clearly displays the Egyptian initiatory roots of Judaism and thereby Christian spirituality. The distinction between the loving nature of this prayer and the demanding framework of the Law of later post-Mosaic Judaism is apparent. The teaching of Jesus and the creation of New Covenant Judaism was to revive the concepts taught by Abraham, based upon love and not upon fear or legalism.

The Prayer of the Abba Ra Heim

Our Heavenly Father
Allelujah
May Your Heavenly Kingdom come upon the earth

Allelujah
May Your Heavenly Laws be obeyed upon the earth
Allelujah
May you protect us from the chaos and grant us our needs
Allelujah
Amen.

The so-called Lord's Prayer of New Testament Christianity displays striking similarities to the prayer of the Abba Ra Heim. From this we can see not only the Egyptian roots of Jesus' teaching, but also considerable justification for the comments by A E Waite and Magnus Eliphas Levi that Jesus himself was an initiate of the Egyptian cult of Osiris.

THE NEW COVENANT

By the time of Jesus, the Law of Moses had become unwieldy and impossible to apply in everyday life. There were 613 binding strictures, complicated by a vast number of almost impenetrable commentaries which had been devised in order to interpret it in a meaningful manner. Jesus had been sent to create order out of this chaotic situation and make strict observance of the Law attainable by all men of goodwill. The entire structure of the Law of Moses, which governed every imaginable aspect of life, was swept away and replaced with two simple yet demanding precepts which, if followed, would transform the life of all true believers. The new law is recorded in full in *The Liturgy and Gospel of the Holy Twins* under *The Proclamation of the Law* which reads:

1
You will love God your Heavenly Father.
You will obey His Heavenly Commandments.
You will serve the Lord your God all the days of your life.

2
You will love your brother as you love yourself.
You will love all the peoples of the earth.
As you love your brother you will bring heaven upon earth.

The Proclamation of the Law is one of the true teachings of Jesus which escaped the attentions of those who followed St Paul and which crept into the doctrines of Christianity, although the second entreaty is preached more than it is practised. In St Matthew's Gospel we find the following passage:

> Master, which is the great commandment in the law?
> Jesus said unto him, Thou shalt love the Lord thy God with
> all thy heart, and with all thy soul, and with all thy mind.
> This is the first and great commandment.
> And the second is like unto it, Thou shalt **love thy**
> **neighbour as thyself.**
> On these two commandments hang all the law and the
> prophets. [our emphasis][12]

The responsibilities of all Jews to the poor who dwelt among them were detailed separately and clearly, so that there would be no excuse for anyone to be in any doubt as to their obligations to those less fortunate than themselves. This matter was considered so important that Jesus made it a central theme of a proclamation that he made from the steps of the Temple in Jerusalem after his triumphal entry into the city as the accepted heir to the throne of Judah. It was given in the early hours of the morning of the Tuesday before Passover, only three days before the crucifixion. As the accepted heir, Jesus was automatically regarded as a High Priest with all the privileges and obligations that went with it. Standing on the eastern steps of the portico of the temple, on the place reserved for the priest known as the Melchizedek, he spoke the following words:

You shall not eat
    If the poor do not eat.

You shall not have clothing
    If the poor do not have clothing.

You shall not have an habitation
    If the poor do not have an habitation.

You shall not have warmth or a fire in your grate
    If the poor do not have warmth or a fire in theirs.

You shall not be cured of your illness
    If the poor are not cured of theirs.

THE EBIONIM

The sect that Jesus led throughout his ministry were known as the Nazarenes or Nasoreans, who were part of the inner circle of the Essenes. At some point after the crucifixion, this sect began to be known as the Ebionim, or 'the poor'. By the time of the dispersal of the followers of James the Just, shortly before the destruction of Jerusalem and the Temple, the Ebionim had become the most common term for the followers of Jesus. The Ebionim continued with the concept of hereditary leadership for at least 100 years after the crucifixion, with the leaders always being drawn from among the descendants of the family of Jesus.[13] Saul of Tarsus, now known as Paul, joined the Nazarene sect after the crucifixion, before defecting and preaching a gospel which the Nazarenes considered to be heretical. The Catholic historian, Paul Johnson, admits that for many years the mission of St Paul was rapidly losing ground to that of the evangelists accredited by James the Just, the new leader of the Nazarenes.[14] But even Paul, who distorted the true teaching of Jesus with such disastrous consequences, seems to have got one thing more or less right when he talked of 'a priesthood of all believers'.

In Rex Deus, every male member is considered to be a priest from the moment of his conception. As part of his priestly duties he is entitled to officiate at a ceremony known as 'the Commemoration' and also give the 'Aaronic Blessing'. If, however, no male is present, the eldest female believer who is of the Rex Deus bloodline can officiate, as there were female priests and bishops in the early Church under the Patriarch Judas Thomas. It is the sacred duty of all believers to follow the teachings of Jesus the Messiah, to love and serve the Lord all the days of their life and by so doing bring about the creation of heaven upon earth.

The 'way' to bring about the creation of heaven upon earth is by strict adherence to the law of the New Covenant and the true teaching of Jesus. The medieval followers of the Way, the Knights Templar, were not, as it is popularly believed, sworn to vows of poverty. They were bound by solemn oath to hold all their property in common, so while the individual member might well be without wealth, the Order itself could amass riches[15] for the benefit of its members, the greater good of Rex Deus and the benefit of the communities within which they moved. The practice of Rex Deus belief by the Templars resulted, amongst other things, in the enrichment of ordinary people and the raising of the standard of living of the peasantry, the skilled craftsmen and the merchant classes. Thus their application of sacred knowledge upon the community at large clearly followed the precepts laid down in the *Proclamation of the Poor*. This proclamation, if followed with unswerving devotion, would bring about what we would now describe as social justice and nourish the qualities of compassion and mercy in a widespread and practical manner. However, these twin strands of action could rightly be claimed as being equally binding on all true Christians. So what are the real differences both in intent and effect between mainstream Christianity and the religion practised by the followers of Jesus within Rex Deus? The answer may well lie in the last two attributes of God described in the Encryption: **God is**

Knowledge and **God is Wisdom**. This concept was echoed many centuries later by Vincent de Beauvais who claimed that 'Man can encompass his salvation by means of knowledge.'[16]

CHURCH DOCTRINE

The members of Rex Deus, the inner circle of the Knights Templar and the Cathars had one major common strand uniting their religious beliefs – they were Gnostics. While there were certain minor differences of belief and practice that distinguished the Cathars from Rex Deus and the Knights Templar, all three were religious groups following an initiatory pathway, or 'Way', leading to higher levels of consciousness, knowledge and wisdom. This sacred knowledge, or gnosis, and the pursuit of 'Sophia', or wisdom, were the sacred responsibility of the initiates of the higher degrees. The gaining of this degree of enlightenment, however, while it was preserved secretly, was not for the benefit of the individual alone, nor was it to be solely used for the advancement of the group from which he sprang, it was to be treasured, enhanced and used for the benefit of society as a whole to bring about the creation of heaven on earth.

The Christian Church also claims to be following the true teaching of Jesus. However, the differences between the Church's view as to the nature of Jesus are markedly different from those held by Rex Deus, as are their views on the teaching of the Messiah. According to the Church, following firmly in the footsteps of St Paul, their version of the teaching of Jesus was crowned by the redemptive sacrifice at Golgotha, which was to atone for the sins of *all* mankind. Having stretched the bounds of credulity in this magical manner, the Church then lost the plot in a rather contradictory way. Despite the redemptive and all-embracing nature of the crucifixion of Jesus, every human being still had to atone personally for their sin or spend eternity in hellfire and damnation. The doctrine, ritual and practice of the Church was supposedly directed to encourage each individual member of the congregation to attain forgiveness for their sins and gain personal salvation. The comparison between the concepts of service to the community and the betterment of all mankind which are the central tenets of Rex Deus belief, compare rather oddly with the selfish aspirations for personal salvation encouraged by Holy Mother the Church. Yet the Church also called Jesus the Prince of Peace, and in his name persecuted, tortured and killed all who openly differed from them in matters of religious doctrine.

When St Augustine of Hippo formalized the principle of 'original sin', he gave the Church a superb justification for the creation of a guilt-inducing doctrine which it exploited ruthlessly in order to control the congregation it claimed to serve. Every man and woman who lived under the rule of the Christian Church was now held to be condemned, from birth, to everlasting hellfire and damnation because of the inherited guilt acquired through 'original sin'. There was only one route to salvation and that was under the ministrations of the Church. Confession and penance were the means used to keep a tight hold on the activities of the congregation. The Lord's Prayer, which asked our Heavenly Father to 'forgive us our trespasses as we forgive those who trespass against us', was considered insufficient by the Church hierarchy, despite its so-called 'divine' origin. If the words of our Lord and Saviour were deemed to be insufficient by the Pope, who are we to argue with His Holiness who is 'infallible' when speaking on matters of faith and doctrine.

THE PROCLAMATION OF FORGIVENESS

When it comes to the forgiveness of sin, the words of Jesus in the liturgy of Rex Deus are once again subtly different from the pronouncements of the Pope in Rome. Jesus' teaching on this important matter are to be found in *The Liturgy and Gospel of the Holy Twins* under the title of *The Proclamation of Forgiveness*, which he announced publicly after making the proclamation concerning the poor.

If a man sins against another, he shall seek forgiveness from that man.

If that man will not forgive the sinner, the sinner will turn to God, trusting in the words of the Messiah, and being sincere in his desire to be forgiven, ask God to forgive him his sins.

God has spoken through the Messiah and said that a man who sincerely desires to be forgiven will be forgiven.

If we study the history of Christianity we find that not only has the Church's doctrine of forgiveness empowered it at the expense of the people it serves, but that it has also had another damaging effect on society as a whole. The sinner, having gone through the ritual of confession and penance according to Church doctrine, is now quite literally at liberty to commit the same sin again and again. At no stage in this process is there any recognition in canon law or practice that the sinner has to seek the forgiveness of those he has sinned against or make amends to them. This is hardly in the spirit of the teaching of the Messiah and his attempts to make the Law attainable by all men of goodwill. The Rex Deus doctrine of forgiveness is far more credibly that of Jesus than the doctrine enunciated by the Church. In its insistence on the sinner first seeking forgiveness from those sinned against, *The Proclamation of Forgiveness* seems far more in accord with both natural justice and the law of God than any of the guilt-inducing doctrines originating from the Christian Church.

THE FOLLOWERS OF THE WAY

The Rex Deus group were instructed to outwardly conform with the prevailing religion of the time. One important ritual which they have always held, in secret, to commemorate the coronation meal of the Messiah, is the so-called 'Last Supper' described in the New Testament,

Figure 1 The church at Rennes-le-Château from the east.

Figure 2 An aerial view of Rennes-le-Château.

Figure 3 The entrance to the church at Rennes-le-Château.

Figure 4 Asmodeus holding the Holy Water Stoop in the entrance of the church at Rennes-le-Château.

Figure 5 Painting of Mary Magdalene on the front of the altar at the church at Rennes-le-Château.

Figure 6 The Tour Magdela in Rennes-le-Château.

Figure 7
The Villa Bethania in
Rennes-le-Château.

Figure 8 Aigues Mortes, a port in the Camargue used by the Templar.

Figure 9 *The fortified citadel of Carcassonne.*

Figure 10
The castle of
Gisors, home
of Jean de Gisors,
supposed
grandmaster of the
Priory of Sion.

Figures 11 and 12
Masonic
symbolism on a
St Clair grave
in Caithness.

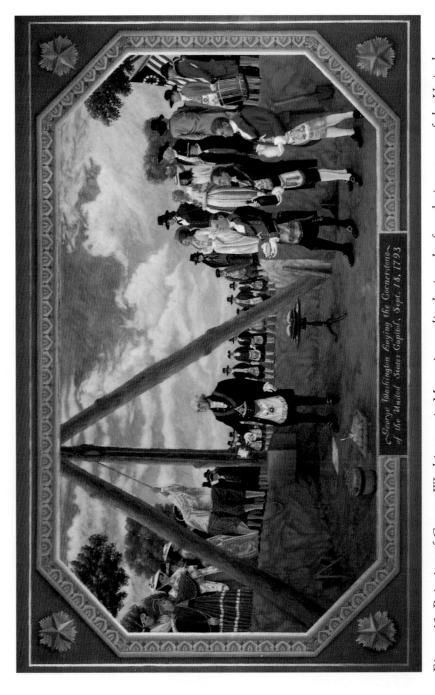

Figure 13 Painting of George Washington in Masonic regalia, laying the foundation stone of the United States Capitol; courtesy of the Supreme Council, 33rd Degree, Scottish Rite Freemasonry, USA.

which took place on the Thursday evening, the eve of the crucifixion. During the meal Jesus made a rather strange statement, which led into a parable: 'My royal priesthood I condemn: the disciples are like little children who have been orphaned and who have found a walled garden left unattended by the owners. They have climbed over the wall and dwelt in the garden eating and drinking the fruits therein. The owners return and the children stand naked before them and are sent away with nothing.'

He then recalled the first Passover and the liberation from Egypt, the crossing of the Red Sea and Moses standing before God on Mount Sinai. He asked that all those who believe that his words are the words of God should make this night a holy night and, at the family evening meal each Thursday, commemorate his coming as the Messiah and his teaching concerning the New Covenant. They were to remember his oath absolving the people from all sin that might be committed from following his teaching and that the blood for those sins was now on his hands. The bread of life was to represent him as bringing new life to the world and the duties of all who follow him to live according to his teaching and create heaven on earth.

The terms 'the Way', 'the Vineyard' and 'the Garden' had a very deep esoteric meaning to his followers. The followers of the Way and the labourers in the Vineyard or the Garden were interchangeable terms used to denote the disciples of Jesus and the members of Rex Deus. Of particular importance among those who followed the Way were the Knights Templar, who had already begun to transform the economic and political face of Europe. We would argue that the peace and prosperity that ensued from their activities indicates that the creation of heaven on earth was more than a theoretical possibility. However, with the brutal suppression of the Order, who was safe from persecution?

This dangerous situation posed particular problems for the members of the Rex Deus families. How were they now to preserve the knowledge of the Way for future labourers in the Garden? One obvious answer was to revert to the practices of earlier times. They would continue to practise their own beliefs in secret while outwardly conforming to those prevailing in their society; they would continue to intermarry with other Rex Deus families in order to preserve the bloodline, and they would exercise patience. They were well aware that the benefits brought to their cause by the Order of the Knights Templar had been enormous. They also realized that for the ultimate conversion of others, and to fulfil their sacred duty to bring about the institution of 'heaven upon earth', they had to create some other widespread, but clandestine, organization as a vehicle for promoting their aims and beliefs to a wider and more sympathetic audience. To keep control of such an organization, they relied on two basic principles: the first was the accepted principle of hereditary inheritance of power and responsibility; the second had proved its worth with the Knights Templar, that of reasonably open recruitment with truly sacred knowledge restricted to the select few, drawn from Rex Deus itself. The second option allowed for the possibility of slowly opening up the inner circle to selected outsiders who had proved their worth over the years by adherence to procedures encompassing several degrees of initiation. Thus, for example, in Scotland the Freemasons evolved from the Templars when Rex Deus families exercised their hereditary right of control over the craft guilds. The St Clair family of Roslin were the acknowledged hereditary grand masters of the craft guilds of Scotland[17] from medieval times until St Andrew's Day, 1736. On that day the hereditary grand master, yet another Sir William St Clair, resigned his 'Hereditary Patronage and Protectorship of the Masonic craft' to effect the creation of 'the Grand Lodge, of Ancient, Free and Accepted Masons of Scotland'. Needless to say, he became the first elected grand master of the Grand Lodge, in which position he is said to have served with distinction.[18]

It was not just the various Freemason organizations that were vehicles for the preservation of Rex Deus teaching, the families also used the creation of chivalric Orders to further their aims. In Portugal, the Knights Templar had not been suppressed but had simply changed its name to the Knights of Christ and sworn allegiance to the King.[19] Within a short time they restricted entry to the Order to the nobility of Portugal but continued in all other respects as before. In the centuries that followed the suppression of the Templars, a variety of chivalric Orders and organizations were created which spanned the face of Europe, and which were either originated by members of Rex Deus, such as René d'Anjou, the Duke of Savoy and the Duke of Burgundy, or largely dominated by them. In the next chapter we will give a brief overview of some of the principal organizations created, infiltrated or used by Rex Deus to further its own aims and objectives.

16

The Shadowy World of Early Freemasonry

The Knights Templar maintained close links with certain lodges of the Craftmasons throughout their history, especially the branch of the Compagnonage known as the Children of Solomon. The Templars and the Children of Solomon were so closely associated that the knights gave them their rule.[1] It was not only the building of the Gothic cathedrals that encouraged relations between them, the Templars also used the masons to build their farms, commanderies, chateaux and chapels all over Europe. After the suppression of the Templars, the Children of Solomon forfeited many of their legal privileges and exemptions.[2]

The American historian, John Robinson, made an in-depth study of those Knights Templar who fled after the first wave of arrests in France and England. His book, *Born in Blood*, describes the help given to them by the lodges of Craftmasons. While links between the suppressed Order and various of the Craftmasons' guilds can be established in many countries, the most obvious ones are discernible in Scotland, for it was there that the guilds eventually developed into the fraternal brotherhood known as Freemasonry.

At the trial of the Templars in Scotland, the judge, Bishop

Lamberton, brought in the Scottish equivocal verdict of 'not proven'.[3] Nonetheless, as King Robert the Bruce ultimately had to make his peace with the Pope, the Order was advised by their sovereign grand master to go underground.[4] Much of their property then passed into the hands of the Knights Hospitaller or reverted to the original donors, and it is in the history of the family of one of these, the St Clairs of Roslin, that we can detect the clearest linkages between the Templars, Craft-masons and Freemasons.

THE ST CLAIRS

The lordly line of the high St Clairs were not only a Rex Deus family, but also the hereditary grand masters of all the guilds in Scotland.[5] They acted not only as leaders but also as respected judges of all disputes within the activities of the guilds at courts held at Kilwinning. The St Clairs were also the most likely guardians of the vanished treasure of the Templar Order. The political power and influence of this aristocratic dynasty is demonstrable from the time of William the Seemly St Clair, cupbearer to King Malcolm Canmore, right up to the present, for it is only a few years since the last true Sinclair (St Clair eventually became Sinclair) member of the House of Lords resigned his post as a Government minister.[6] The family's influence on emerging Freemasonry and its antecedents is equally impressive.

Under the guidance of the St Clairs, the hidden members of the Templar Order selected suitable candidates from the operative craft guilds for instruction in various branches of sacred knowledge. The subjects covered included science, geometry, history, philosophy and the contents of the manuscripts recovered by the Templars during their excavations in Jerusalem.[7] As a result, Scotland in general and Midlothian in particular became a beacon of enlightenment. The new brotherhood of speculative 'free' masons created charitable institutions to support the poorer members of society and their respective guilds also set money aside for the benefit of their less fortunate neighbours. According to Prince Michael of Albany, these were the first charitable institutions to be established in Britain which were outside the direct control or instigation of the Church.[8]

EARLY SCOTTISH FREEMASONRY

King James VI of Scotland was initiated as a speculative Freemason in 1601 at the lodge of Perth and Scone.[9] When James acceded to the throne of England two years later he needed political allies to counterbalance the self-serving British aristocracy. He found good allies in certain of the trade and craft guilds in England and introduced these, on an informal basis, to the concept of Freemasonry.[10] The first inductions into English Freemasonry are recorded in 1640, during the reign of his son Charles I. In an era of repression, the movement that grew into Freemasonry had to be secretive from the beginning. Even today it is still regarded by many, incorrectly according to its members, as a 'secret society'; modern Freemasons prefer to describe themselves as members of an 'organization with secrets'.

The absolute secrecy that shrouded the first three centuries of Freemasonry makes it extremely difficult to assess the full spectrum of esoteric influences that formed the Order. We have no doubt that, while circumstances undoubtedly differed from country to country, the Knights Templar were the prime movers behind the transformation of the guilds of operative masons into the speculative and fraternal society of Freemasonry. It developed along very different lines in each country where it took root; in Scotland it was particularly democratic and continued to admit ordinary working people into its ranks in large numbers. There the tradition of preserving secret and sacred knowledge through teaching rituals leading to the higher degrees was preserved almost intact, and developed a high degree of sophistication and complexity. This led ultimately to the development of Scottish Rite Freemasonry and the Royal Arch degrees.

Scottish Rite Freemasonry was founded upon the fundamental principles enunciated in 1320, in the Declaration of Arbroath, which was the written constitution of Scotland established at the time of King Robert the Bruce.[11] These principles were later incorporated into a formal constitution for Scottish Rite Freemasonry.

FREEMASONRY IN ENGLAND, EUROPE AND ELSEWHERE

In continental Europe, Freemasonry developed with an innate anti-clerical and anti-Catholic foundation and kept particularly close ties with its brothers in Scotland. This long-term close and intimate association is recorded in the rite of 'Strict Observance'. Within this rite it is recorded that speculative masons from operative lodges of the Compannonage in France visited the lodge at Aberdeen as early as 1361, thereby cementing a relationship which continued for centuries. Like their Scottish counterparts, French lodges took particular pains to preserve the original esoteric teaching as much as possible. By contrast, in England where the Church was itself part of the political and hierarchical establishment, the anticlerical bias was not as pronounced and, as a result, English Freemasonry became an integral part of the Church/State establishment.

The Scottish masonic traditions that were the foundation of the Royal Arch and Rosicrucian degrees of American Freemasonry may explain the high quality of the attainments of their members, who were supremely gifted with great spiritual insight and moral force. These perceptive and powerful men left a lasting imprint on the emerging American nation. The Constitution of the United States of America, which has become the legal foundation for all the Western values of freedom, democracy and the rights of man, is the lasting spiritual legacy that we have all received from this branch of Freemasonry.[12] The majority of those who signed the American Constitution were either Rosicrucians or Freemasons,[13] such as George Washington, Benjamin

Franklin, Thomas Jefferson, John Adams and Charles Thompson. It was through these men that alchemical symbolism became part of the American way of life. The eagle, olive branch, arrows, pentagrams, truncated pyramid and the 'all-seeing eye' which decorate American banknotes, buildings and monuments are all evidence of the fact that the roots of American life lie deeply embedded in the mystical past of Freemasonry.

Freemasonry in all its forms, for good or ill, became an indispensable key to high office. For instance, nearly every Prime Minister in England from Walpole in the 18th century to Ramsay MacDonald in the 20th was a member of the Freemasons, a pattern of power that was repeated throughout Europe. The same situation existed in America, where a substantial majority of presidents until the election of John F. Kennedy were Freemasons of a high degree. The influence of Freemasonry permeated the entire power structures of the judiciary, the police, the armed services and civil administration of the Western world.

REX DEUS, TEMPLAR AND MASONIC LINKS

Due to the secretive nature of the Freemasons and the modern Templar Order, the information we can obtain either from personal contact or from research into published works is circumscribed by the vows of secrecy taken by the members of these Orders. Therefore the limited information at our disposal is presented in the full knowledge that it only represents the tip of an iceberg. However, the correspondence between masonic ritual and Rex Deus tradition that we have been able to discover is extremely interesting. For example, the Rex Deus oath of secrecy 'lest my throat be cut or my tongue cut out' has a direct correspondence in the first craft degree of Freemasonry:

> These several points I solemnly swear to observe, without
> evasion, equivocation, or mental reservation of any kind

under no less a penalty than to have my throat cut across, my tongue torn out by the root and my body buried in the rough sands of the sea at low water mark or a cable's length from the shore where the tide regularly ebbs and flows twice in the course of a natural day.

The second part of the penalty mentioned in the Rex Deus oath 'lest my heart be torn or cut out of my chest' is directly quoted in the masonic craft second degree:

> ... under no less a penalty than to have my left breast cut open, my heart torn therefrom, and given to the ravenous birds of the air, or the devouring beasts of the field as prey.

The Rex Deus oath also mentions the threat of emasculation by having testicles cut off or crushed and also having the ears sliced off, but our informants could not find either of these threats in masonic ritual. However, there are at least two further occasions where threats in the Rex Deus oath are used in Freemasonry. That of 'lest my eyes be plucked out' is to be found in the ritual of the degree of 'the Knight of the White Eagle' or 'Pelican' in the form of '... under the penalty of forever remaining in perpetual darkness'. The use of a knife as a threat in the oath has again a direct parallel in the use of the knife in the penalties mentioned for the 'Past Master' degree.

> ... having my hands lopped off at the wrist and my arms struck from my body and both hung at my breast suspended at the neck as a sign of infamy till time and putridity consume the same.

The charge of idolatry that was levelled at the Templars at the time of their trial also has parallels within Freemasonry and modern Templarism.

According to the masonic historians Christopher Knight and Robert Lomas, 'Freemasonry around the world probably possesses a total of some 50,000 skulls!' They concluded that the third degree in Freemasonry was a replication of earlier Templar practice, for which a supply of skulls and long white burial shrouds would be needed: a similar situation exists in modern Templarism. Tim and Marilyn were present at a modern Templar investiture of new candidates which took place in Rosslyn Chapel in 1995. Throughout this impressive ceremony various items of regalia and symbolic significance were used to decorate the chapel, including a skull. The Templars were quite open about their ritual, but when questioned about the significance of the skull they simply muttered *memento mori*, and when pressed became rather evasive. Tim was permitted to take photographs throughout the investiture, but when he was seen photographing the skull was politely but firmly asked not to use that one for any publication and, conscious that he had inadvertently upset his hosts, he offered to send them the negative. Ultimately this request was not fulfilled, as that was the only photograph taken in the entire ceremony that did not come out. The use of human skulls in the initiatory practices of the Freemasons and the modern Templar Order simply forms one of a miriad of fascinating parallels between their traditions and those of the medieval Knights Templar.

The direct linkage between the Knights Templar and the Craftmasons of Scotland that led to the foundation of Freemasonry there is clearly established.[14] The Order came to England when James VI of Scotland travelled south to become James I of England. It is not surprising that the beliefs of Freemasonry travelled south with him when we consider that it was the primary repository of Rex Deus tradition and Stewart history; the strands of Freemasonry, Rex Deus tradition and the Stewart cause were so seamlessly entwined as to be inseparable. When Charles II was in exile in Holland, the masonic lodges in England acted as his intelligence service and kept him abreast of political developments in his one-time kingdom. After his restoration in 1660, he became the patron of the Royal Society, which was formed to promote the cause of science by members of the lodges who had actively worked to secure his restoration.[15] The Stewarts were ultimately deposed and replaced by William of Orange, which ultimately led to the present Hanoverian dynasty becoming the royal house of Great Britain. When the Grand Lodge of London was established in 1717 the new organization promptly disowned its Scottish origins because these and the rituals that celebrated them were too intimately linked with the Stewart cause to survive under the Hanoverians.[16] Nearly 100 years later, when English Freemasonry had developed to the point that it spawned the United Grand Lodge of England, the rites, ceremonies and rituals of the 33 initiatory degrees of the ancient Scottish Rite were deemed dangerous and outrageous and were abolished by the Duke of Sussex, who was grand master.[17]

REX DEUS IN RITE AND RITUAL

Knight and Lomas were not the first to discover that, even to this day, the United Grand Lodge of England actively discourages any form of investigation into the true origins of Freemasonry. The purging of Scottish rituals from English masonic practice was extremely thorough, but although the censors were familiar with masonic symbolism they were unfamiliar with its deeper associations, and so left traces of Rex Deus. In *The Second Messiah* Knight and Lomas reveal how they discovered the library of the masonic scholar Dimitrije Mitrinovic who worked in London in the early years of this century. From his library they were able to ascertain the nature of significant points of ritual from the purged higher degrees of Freemasonry. In one book from this library, *Freemasonry and the Ancient Gods* by J S M Ward, they found that the fourth degree, that of the 'Secret Master', is concerned with mourning someone who remains anonymous.[18] In this ceremony the lodge is hung with black and illuminated by the light of 81 candles. The jewel of the degree is inscribed with the letter 'Z' and is said to refer to Zadok.[19]

The ritual of the 'Secret Master' commemorates a time when construction work on the Temple was brought to a halt due to a tragedy. The lessons contained within it are to remind the candidate of the supreme importance of *Duty and Secrecy*. Knight and Lomas believe that the Zadok referred to in this ritual contains a double meaning, relating first to Zadok, the High Priest at the time of Solomon, and second, and perhaps more important, to James the Just who had succeeded his brother Jesus in the position of the Zadok or Teacher of Righteousness. In the Dead Sea Scrolls we learn that at this time an esoteric group known as the Sons of Zadok arose and played a major part in the collection of these documents. The Sons of Zadok were the descendants of the High Priests of the Temple, and were also known as 'the Righteous Seed' and 'the Sons of Dawn'. These honorific titles stress the ancient Jewish conception of the hereditary transmission of holiness on the one hand and the fact that, in biblical Israel as well as in the Egyptian esoteric tradition that preceded it, the ceremony of resurrection to a new spiritual life always took place at dawn under the light of the morning star. One of the many descriptions of Jesus that occurs in devotional literature is 'the morning star'. Even today in Freemasonic ritual candidates are solemnly resurrected or 'raised extended' under the light of the morning star.

The tradition that Freemasonry arose from the time of Hiram Abif, who was killed by a blow to his head rather than betray a secret, has inescapable parallels with the death of James the Just. Hiram Abif was murdered just before the completion of Solomon's Temple. Almost 1,000 years later, James was thrown down from a pinnacle of the Temple in Jerusalem, stoned and given the *coup de grâce* by being struck on his temple by a fuller's club. Work on the Herodian Temple that was near completion came to a temporary standstill as a mark of respect. Knight and Lomas suggest quite plausibly that the tradition concerning the death of Hiram Abif is an allegory for the death of James the Just, the brother of Jesus and one of the hereditary High Priests of the Temple in Jerusalem. Therefore, when Freemasons worldwide celebrate the fact that the origins of their fraternity arise from the actions of Hiram Abif they are in fact commemorating the source of Rex Deus.[20]

Among the lost or suppressed degrees which Knight and Lomas rediscovered was that of the 'Perfect Master', which commemorates the discovery and reburial of the corpse of Hiram Abif. In the rituals for this degree, the lodge room is hung in green and illuminated by groups of four candles placed at each cardinal point, 16 candles in all. In the ritual, the story is that Solomon ordered Adoniram to build a tomb for Hiram Abif as a mark of respect for his friend. The tomb was completed within nine days as an obelisk of black and white marble. Here the parallels between the death of Hiram Abif and James the Just are explicit. The entrance to the tomb is set between two pillars that support a square lintel engraved with the letter 'J'.

Before Knight and Lomas began their trawl through the purged masonic rituals, they rang and asked us to enquire of our contacts what symbolic keys they needed to be aware of in searching for traces of Rex Deus. Michael's first response was to mention that certain colours were of immense importance and could sometimes be found in the armorial bearings of some of the leading families of the group. These colours were green and gold, heraldic indications of the Royal House of David at the time of biblical Israel. Thus the green hangings used in masonic lodges for the ritual of the 'Perfect Master', commemorating in allegorical form the murder of the brother of Jesus and a High Priest of the Temple in Jerusalem, is a double reinforcement of the Rex Deus origin of this particular ritual.

The 15th degree, 'the Knight of the Sword and the Knight of the East', is commemorated at Rosslyn Chapel, which was erected by Earl William St Clair as a memorial to Templar beliefs, in 1446.[21] On one lintel within it is a quotation from the Book of Esdras, 'Wine is strong, a king is stronger, women are even stronger but truth will conquer all', which commemorates the rebuilding of the Temple at Jerusalem by Zerubbabel after the Babylonian exile.[22] We have always felt it strange that this superbly carved chapel, which is of such importance to the worldwide movement of Freemasonry, makes no symbolic reference whatsoever to the Temple of Solomon, but in this instance refers to Zerubbabel's Temple. The 15th degree celebrates the rebuilding of Zerubbabel's Temple and during the ritual the lodge is illuminated by 70 candles, one for each year of the Babylonian captivity. In it we find once again a symbolic reference to the Royal House of David, for the colour of the sash worn in this degree is green fringed with gold.[23]

THE RITUAL CELEBRATING THE FOUNDATION OF THE TEMPLARS

In the suppressed degree of the 'Knight of the East and West', the ritual states that it was first promulgated during the crusades in the year 1118, when 11 knights took vows of secrecy, friendship and discretion under the supervision of the Patriarch of Jerusalem. When Knight and Lomas discovered this degree, they were puzzled to find 11 knights mentioned, not the nine recorded as founding the Templar Order. The eleven knights concerned are the nine founding knights we listed earlier – Hugh de Payen, Geoffroi de St Omer, André de Montbard, Payen de Montdidier, Achambaud de St-Amand, Gondemar, Rossal, Godfroi and Geoffroi Bisol – with the addition of Count Fulk d'Anjou and Hughes I of Champagne. The presiding officer for this rite is described as the 'Most Equitable Sovereign Prince Master' who is supported by the High Priest. Knight and Lomas speculated accurately that the Most Equitable Sovereign Prince Master was originally King Baudoin I of Jerusalem and subsequently his successors. They also concluded that the High Priest might have been the grand master of the Templar Order and, while this may be so, we suggest that it could just as easily have been the Patriarch of Jerusalem. During the ritual for this degree a large bible with seven seals suspended from it is placed on a pedestal of the lodge with a floor display consisting of a heptagon within a circle. In each of the angles of the heptagon are certain letters; depicted in the centre is the figure of a white-bearded, white-cloaked man with a golden girdle encircling his waist. In his extended hand are seven stars, representing the qualities of friendship, union, submission, discretion, fidelity, prudence and temperance. This odd figure has a halo around its head, a two-edged sword issuing from its mouth and is surrounded by seven candlesticks.[24] The principle of sevenfoldedness that underpins the coded symbolism of the Revelation of St John and the Templar Order abounds.

THE REX DEUS DIASPORA

If, as we suggest, Freemasonry was deliberately created or taken over and modified as the repository for the Rex Deus story, then we would expect to find something far more explicit than just these references to the Knights Templar in the Royal House of David. Fascinating though they are, the rites that link Freemasonry to the Templars are only reinforcements of facts that can be established from the historical record. However, when we study another of the suppressed degrees, the 20th known as 'Grand Master', we find that the evidence of Rex Deus involvement is overwhelming. This degree describes the appalling destruction of the Third Temple by the Romans in 70 CE. It recounts the grief felt by 'the Brethren' who were in Palestine at that time and how they had to disperse from their homeland with the avowed intention of erecting a Fourth Temple which, in contrast to its predecessors, would be a spiritual edifice which would be created by them as part of their sacred duty. The story then recalls how the Brethren who escaped the mass slaughter in Jerusalem divided themselves into a number of lodges before scattering throughout the length and breadth of Europe. It tells how, eventually, one of these came to Scotland and established a lodge at Kilwinning, which was entrusted with the records of their Order. These were to be stored in an abbey that was constructed in 1140.[25] Here in masonic ritual are the bare bones of the Rex Deus story. Not only does one degree describe the foundation of the Knights Templar, the military arm of Rex Deus, but here is another describing the diaspora of Rex Deus. The building of the Abbey of Kilwinning in 1140 was obviously to store the documents discovered by the Knights Templar in their excavations under the Temple Mount in Jerusalem.

The hiding of the main Rex Deus secrets in one degree of the multi-faceted and complex symbolism of Freemasonry is akin to a man on the run seeking refuge in a large and crowded city. A similar ruse was employed by Earl William St Clair in hiding Templar and Rex Deus symbolism in the crowded and apparently confused carvings in Rosslyn Chapel. There, heretical symbolism is explicitly displayed for all to see, yet can only be understood by those initiates who can discern its importance in the plethora of carvings that surround it.[26] In Scottish Rite Freemasonry, with its large number of complex ascending degrees, there lies concealed a number of degrees which tell the hidden story of the Knights Templar, the Rex Deus families and the sacred bloodline. Despite the attempts of the Hanoverian censors, we have no doubt that these degrees, rites and rituals are still used in Scotland, France and America. We are also convinced that access to these degrees and their true meaning is restricted to the privileged few, those already in the know by virtue of their birth, and those who have earned the highest levels of trust by their previous actions. Are these the only repositories of Rex Deus tradition outside the families? Or are there other aspects of the historical record that we can consult which may disclose other facets of the same story?

17

The Chivalric Orders

The Rex Deus tradition of having a military organization within their movement did not die with the suppression of the Knights Templar. The advantage of having a disciplined executive arm close to the seat of political power was one that they strove to retain. The new chivalric Orders used by Rex Deus were smaller than the Templars and posed far less of a political threat to the Church/State establishment which they appeared to support. As a matter of policy, these new organizations owned no land or property and derived no income from their own resources. Ostensibly they lacked autonomy and were outwardly attached to one sovereign or another, from whom they drew their income. Many appeared to be Orders of prestige rather than military organizations of real power; vehicles of royal patronage apparently staffed by courtiers rather than military officers. Yet they looked to the Knights Templar as a role model in their rites and rituals and in the mystique they deliberately created. While the most notable of these Orders operated in France, it was undeniably Scottish in origin and personnel.

In Scotland a tightly bonded nucleus of powerful dynasties linked by marriage and alliance acted as a repository of Rex Deus tradition and sacred knowledge and also as a conduit for its transmission. They spawned a military organization which Michael Baigent and Richard Leigh describe as '… perhaps the most genuinely neo-Templar institution of all'.[1] This regiment slotted neatly into a long-standing Franco-Scottish military sphere of co-operation that grew naturally out of the 'auld alliance', which was initiated by a treaty signed by Robert the Bruce and Charles IV of France in 1326. This led to military co-operation between Scotland and France which continued throughout the Hundred Years War and for centuries afterwards. Scottish troops played a highly significant role in the campaigns led by Joan of Arc and particularly distinguished themselves at the siege of Orléans, where the commanders included three notable Scots, Sir John Stewart and two of the Douglas brothers. Scottish influence in France at that time was such that John Kirkmichael was the Bishop of Orléans and even the celebrated white banner which was the rallying point for the French army was painted by a Scot.[2]

France, though triumphant in this campaign, was left in a state of civil turmoil with the countryside under threat of ravishment by bands of demobilized soldiers. To restore social order, the new king, Charles VII, created a standing army, the first of its kind to be established in Europe since the dissolution of the Templars and the first national one since the decline of the Roman Empire.[3] The army was formed of 15 *compagnies d'ordonnance* of 600 men each; the élite regiment was the *Compagnie des Gendarmes Ecossais*. This supreme honour marked more than 100 years of distinguished service rendered by Scottish soldiers to the French Crown. Their bravery, self-sacrifice and loyalty had reached its peak in 1424 at the bloody Battle of Verneuil, where the Scottish contingent, led by John Stewart, the Earl of Buchan, assisted by Alexander Lindsay, Sir William Seton and the Earls of Douglas, Murray and Mar, was virtually annihilated.[4]

THE SCOTS GUARD

As a result of this collective act of gallantry and in recognition of the special nature of the auld alliance, a special unit of Scottish troops was established to render personal service to the King of France, consisting of a company of 13 knights at arms supported by 20 archers. This unique formation had two parts, the *Garde du Roi* – the King's Guard – and the *Garde du Corps du Roi* – the King's Bodyguard – with the collective title of the Scots Guard[5]. The term 'personal bodyguard' meant that members of this company were in constant attendance upon the king, with some even sleeping in his bedchamber. In 1445, with the creation of the new standing army, the Scots Guard was increased to 67 men and their commander in the King's Guard, and to 25 men and their commander in the King's Bodyguard. All the officers and commanders were also honoured by induction into the Order of St Michael, one branch of which was later created in Scotland.[6]

Unlike purely chivalric Orders of greater renown such as the Knights of the Garter, the Knights of the Bath or the Knights of the Golden Fleece, the Scots Guard were a truly military Order that fulfilled important roles in the political and diplomatic fields as well as the military. Its members were offered military training, an opportunity to 'blood oneself in battle' and all the rights and privileges of professional soldiers. Like the Templars before them and the élite military formations of today, such as the SAS or the Brigade of Guards in England, the Scots Guard were a highly skilled and professional force.[7] Despite the fact that they were fewer in number than the Templars, they were still large enough to play a decisive role in the wars of the time. They professed no particular religious beliefs; their allegiance was to the French king and not to the Pope but, like the Templars, they often pursued policies that belied this. All knights who joined the Templar Order had to be of proven noble birth and knightly rank; similarly the Scots Guard recruited its officers from the leading families in Scotland, such as the Setons, St Clairs, Stewarts, Montgomeries and Hamiltons – all families intimately connected with the Templar Order and Rex Deus. The Guard became '… a special vehicle whereby they [the young Scottish nobles] were initiated into martial skills, politics, court affairs, foreign manners and mores and, it would appear, some species of ritualistic rite as well'.[8] Baigent and Leigh tell of one present-day member of the Montgomery family who spoke to them of the pride that his family took in their ancestors' long association with the Scots Guard. He also informed them that there exists in the family a neo-masonic, chivalric restricted Order called the Order of the Temple, to which all men of the Montgomery line had absolute right of entry. Here we find a clear verification of basic Rex Deus tradition that slipped almost unnoticed into the public record.

The Scots Guard enjoyed a unique status in France for more than 150 years. Their functions were not restricted to the battlefield but extended into the political and diplomatic arenas, where they were used as emissaries and couriers in matters of importance and delicacy. Those who attained the rank of commander usually held a number of other posts, some honorary but most practical. Almost invariably the commander discharged the dual function of the Royal Chamberlain. Commissions in the Guard were not honorary sinecures but demanding and extremely well-rewarded positions. It has been estimated that in 1461 a captain received a salary of over 2,000 *livres tournois* a year,[9] approximately £128,000[10] in modern terms, enabling the Scottish officers, who often possessed considerable means of their own, to maintain extremely comfortable lifestyles.

DIVIDED LOYALTIES?

Ostensibly the Scots Guard had sworn allegiance to the Valois dynasty,[11] who were the kings of France, but their right to rule was under threat from the House of Lorraine in general and the House of Guise, a branch of Lorraine, in particular.[12] The feuding between these rival dynasties was murderous; five French monarchs are alleged to have died by violence or poisoning, with the families of Guise and Lorraine themselves subject to assassination. As official bodyguards to the king, the Scots Guard were placed in an extremely ambivalent position, for the family of Guise was Rex Deus and, in 1538, Mary of Guise, Princess of Lorraine,[13] married James V of Scotland,[14] thereby uniting two supremely important families within the hidden group. Henry II, the Valois King of France, substantially increased the status and privileges of the Scots Guard in 1547; nonetheless, they often acted on behalf of his rivals from the House of Guise. Gabriel Montgomery, the captain of the Scots Guard, inadvertently caused the death of Henry II during a jousting tournament in June 1559, during which the lances splintered and Montgomery 'neglected to throw away the broken shaft' which burst open the king's visor and pierced the skull above the right eye.[15] Henry died of his wounds 11 days later. It has been argued, by Baigent and Leigh amongst others, that this event was not an accident, but part of a plot.[16] The death of the king certainly seemed to benefit the Guise dynasty, who continued to jockey for power for the next ten years.

The Scots Guard's role throughout this troubled era became obviously allied with the Stewart-Guise interests, which caused consternation among the supporters of the crown. Henry III was so incensed by their partisan activities that he refused to provide maintainance for them and, although they were later brought back into favour, they soon faded into relative oblivion. By 1610 they had lost most of their privileges and were seen as just one regiment among others in the French army, although their tattered reputation retained some shreds of their former prestige. In 1612 they were commanded by the Duke of York, a Stewart who later became King Charles I of England.[17] Despite their troubled history this military arm of Rex Deus became a major conduit for their tradition and proved to be the vehicle by which it was renewed, refreshed and re-implanted on French soil, to bear fruit as the Freemasons. This also enabled many of the French traditions of Rex Deus to flow in the reverse direction and refresh the Scottish branches with insights deriving from the families of Lorraine, Guise, Savoy and the House of Burgundy.

ROSSLYN CHAPEL AND THE ST CLAIRS

After the suppression of the Templar Order, Rex Deus were rightly suspicious of any attempt to 'put all their eggs in one basket' and went to considerable lengths to safeguard their traditions. Their use of the military Order of the Scots Guard was only one means among many. Earl William St Clair poured his knowledge, insight and resources into the creation of another. This insightful and gifted man who was described as 'one of the illuminati'[18] resolved to erect a permanent and lasting memorial in the form of an arcane library in stone of esoteric and Rex Deus tradition – Rosslyn Chapel. Ostensibly created as a Christian church and, at another level, as a memorial to the Knights Templar, this superbly carved reliquary of the Grail contains overt and hidden symbolic references to every valid spiritual pathway to Almighty God known to the initiates at the time of its construction.[19] Today it is a centre of pilgrimage for the worldwide brotherhood of Freemasonry, members of the modern Templar Orders, esoteric scholars and all who seek spiritual enlightenment. Also recorded within the chapel are obvious clues to the activities of an earlier member of this Rex Deus family who sought to establish a new commonwealth, far from the repressive reach of Holy Mother the Church. Carvings at Rosslyn which date from 50 years before Columbus' reputed 'discovery' of America record the voyage to North America in 1398 by Earl William's grandfather, Prince Henry St Clair, the first St Clair Jarl of Orkney. Stylized carvings of maize and aloe cactus are dotted among the coral-like profusion of the sculptors' craft that decorate this half-hidden memorial to the dynasty of Jesus.[20]

One indication of both the importance of Earl William and of Rosslyn Chapel to the Rex Deus tradition can be found in a quotation from the Rosslyn Hay manuscript, a historical treatise on the St Clairs of Roslin which now reposes in the National Library at Edinburgh:

About this time [1447] there was a fire in the square keep by occasion of which the occupants were forced to flee the building. The Prince's chaplain seeing this, and remembering all of his masters writings, passed to the head of the dungeon where they all were, and threw out four great trunks where they were. The news of the fire coming to the Prince through the lamentable cries of the ladies and gentlewomen, and the sight thereof coming to his view in the place where he stood upon Colledge Hill, he was sorry for nothing but the loss of his Charters and other writings; but when the chaplain who had saved himself by coming down the bell rope tied to a beam, declared how his Charters and Writts were all saved, he became cheerful and went to recomfort his Princess and the Ladys.[21]

Tim quoted this passage in *An Illustrated Guidebook to Rosslyn Chapel*, and Chris Knight and Robert Lomas then used it in their first work, *The Hiram Key*. They had discovered a chain of evidence which pointed to Rosslyn Chapel as the ultimate repository for certain scrolls and artefacts discovered by the Templars in their excavations at Jerusalem. They were curious as to why Earl William, a man of noted courtesy, seemed more concerned with the safety of his writs and charters than he was with the wellbeing of his ladies. They came to the conclusion that this may have been because the documents referred to were those from the Jerusalem excavations,[22] and so were of huge significance.

This hypothesis is supported by another document from a later period which is also housed in the National Library at Edinburgh. There is a letter from Mary of Guise, the Queen Regent of Scotland, to Lord William St Clair of Roslin, dated 1546, in which her attitude is a complete reversal of what one would expect. She swears to be a 'true mistress' to him and protect him and his servants for the rest of her life in gratitude for being shown *a great secret within Rosslyn*, the nature of which is not disclosed.[23] The general tone of the letter is more like that of someone subservient to a superior lord than that of a sovereign to her vassal. This is simply due to the deference shown by a senior representative of a senior branch of the Rex Deus dynasty, namely Mary of Guise, to the leading member of the principal dynasty of the group, Lord William of Roslin. The St Clairs had for some time been the titular 'Fisher Kings' of the Rex Deus dynasty, the true heirs to the hereditary kingship of Jerusalem.

At all times in Rex Deus history in Europe there had been a defined Fisher King and an heir-in-waiting. The symbolism denoting these ranks was outwardly orthodox and in keeping with ecclesiastical practice. In this way the symbols were unnoticed by the Inquisition, their true meaning known only to the initiated. The symbols denoting this rank, when used in normal church practice, would have occupied a central position. In Rex Deus usage they were always tucked away, or marginalized, so as not to be confused with orthodox interpretation. The symbol denoting the rank of Fisher King is the classical 'Sun in Splendour' with 32 flames rising from its rim. In Rosslyn this can be found tucked away behind a balustrade in the north-west corner of the stone vaulted roof in the section decorated with five-pointed stars. The symbol for the heir apparent to the Fisher King, when this position was not held in the direct biological line by a son, is again the Sun in Splendour, but this time with 24 flames surrounding it. A beautiful example of this can be seen on the west front of Exeter Cathedral in Devon, where it celebrates the importance to Rex Deus of a senior churchman, Bishop Grandison.

CHIVALRIC ORDERS

Earl William St Clair is not only the bridge between Templarism and the chapel; he also forms a human link in several chains of transmission of the Rex Deus story. Among his many claims to fame, apart from his hereditary grand mastership of the hard and soft guilds of Scotland, was his membership of two distinguished chivalric Orders of international renown. The first of these was the Order of the Coquille, better known as the Knights of Santiago.[24] This military Order, which proved such a haven of refuge for fleeing Templar knights in Spain, carried on Templar traditions and practice throughout the Spanish-speaking world for centuries. Over time it developed a 'chivalric' nature and welcomed into its ranks, on an honorary basis, leading luminaries drawn from Rex Deus nobility throughout the length and breadth of Europe.

The Knights of Santiago proved to be an incredibly useful covert means of transmission as it was validated by its allegiance to the Spanish crown and the role it played in the Reconquista – the expulsion of the Moorish invaders from Spain. Learning from their experience with the Knights Templar, Rex Deus readily used the Knights of the Coquille as a vehicle for their activities. The difference between the two Orders was simple; the Templars, being wholly Rex Deus, were ultimately identifiable and thereby vulnerable; the Knights of Santiago, on the other hand, were respectable with its membership drawn from a variety of impeccable sources of which Rex Deus was merely one. Thus the members of this secretive dynasty exerted a degree of control while their activities were hidden behind the membership drawn from the Church/State establishment.

The second Order to which Earl William belonged was a highly exclusive one, which we suspect drew its membership solely from senior members of Rex Deus. This was the Order of the Golden Fleece founded by Philip the Good, the Duke of Burgundy, in 1430.[25] The Order was restricted to 24 carefully selected knightly initiates who were described, paradoxically yet tellingly, by Pope Eugenius IV as 'Maccabeans resurrected',[26] which seems to reflect the true dynastic origins of the initiates. The status of this Order was such that expulsion, or any deviation from its high sense of purpose, were held to shame a family name for ever;

in a church at Bruges a black shield carved above the seat of the Count of Nevers proclaims to the world the infamy attendant upon his expulsion from the Order.[27]

In 1408 Sigismund von Luxembourg, the King of Hungary and a leading member of Rex Deus, founded another chivalric Order that was again restricted to a membership of 24. The noble members of this new Order pledged themselves to practise 'true and pure fraternity' and were granted the right to wear armorial bearings emblazoned with a dragon encurved into a circle and decorated with a red cross. The founding document of this Order carries a revealing title – *Sigismundis dei rex Hungaraie*. Shortly after the Order was founded, King Sigismund attained the rank of Holy Roman Emperor and the Order achieved a new importance as the 'Imperial and Royal Court of the Dragon'.[28] Its members were not merely noble but in many cases royal and included the Duke of Lithuania, the King of Poland and the King of Aragon. Within 200 years autonomous branches could be found in Bulgaria, Bosnia, Arcadia, Italy and France.

No account of Rex Deus and the chivalric Orders during the early 15th century would be complete without mentioning the role played by René d'Anjou who, as a young man, showed his absolute faith in the mystical nature of spiritual insight by marching on Paris under the leadership of Joan of Arc. This pivotal figure in late medieval chivalry was known as 'Good King René', the titular King of Jerusalem and also the King of the two Sicilies, Aragon, Valencia, Majorca, Sardinia and Corsica. His list of titles seems almost endless, being at the same time the Count of Provence, Forcalquier and Piedmont and also the Prince of Gerona, Duke of Calabria, Lord of Genoa and the Count of Guise.[29] Several strands of the Rex Deus lineage were united within his family, for his mother was Yolande of Aragon and he was married to Isobel of Lorraine. Yolande was the eldest daughter of Robert I, the Duke of Bar, and Princess Marie of France. His wife, Isobel of Lorraine, was the daughter of Charles II, Duke of Lorraine, and Margaret, the daughter of the Emperor Robert III of Bavaria. Cardinal Louis de Bar, who arranged René's marriage was his grand-uncle.

This creative genius composed many *motets* that are still sung in village churches in Provence and also many *caroles*, songs for dance that are performed at village fêtes. Like his distant relative Earl William St Clair he was a scholar of international repute who collected original works in Hebrew, Greek, Arabic, Turkish and Latin. These consisted of scripture, philosophy, history, geography, natural history and physics. In 1448 René d'Anjou established a new restricted chivalric Order, the 'Ordre du Croissant', at Angers. The emblem of the Order was two fishes inscribed with the Greek letters spelling ICTUS, standing on a crescent which gave the Order its name. Only knights of noble birth and unblemished reputation were deemed eligible to enter. The lifestyle of the membership was dictated by the precepts of religion, courtesy and charity operating together in harmony; they were expected to be living examples of the principles of fraternal love. Neither an impious oath nor an indecent jest were supposed to pass their lips, and their chivalric standards were such that women and children could safely be committed to their care. They were especially enjoined to use their best offices in aiding the poor. The parallels between these principles and the beliefs of Rex Deus are obvious.

Rex Deus undoubtedly infiltrated other military and chivalric Orders, such as the Order of the Collar of Savoy, which awarded its honours to several members of the de Charney family.[30] We mentioned earlier that Bernard of Clairvaux, one of the leading Rex Deus churchmen of the 12th century, played a mysterious role in the foundation of two other Spanish Orders, the Knights of Calatrava and the Knights of Alcantara.[31] We suggest therefore that it is likely that both of these were used not just as places of refuge for fleeing Templars, but as an ongoing means of transmission of Templar and therefore Rex Deus belief. Michael claims that a high proportion of the original members of one of Britain's leading chivalric Orders were also drawn from the families descended from the 24 High Priests of the Temple in Jerusalem. He asserts that the Order of the Bath provided a legitimate 'cover' for Rex Deus activity in England at a time of repression. If Michael's ideas about the Order of the Bath and our view of the Order of the Golden Fleece have any degree of validity, a comparative study of the membership of certain chivalric and military Orders, on the one hand, and the leading members of the Freemasons and Rosicrucians on the other, will give sufficiently accurate cross-references that can identify the Rex Deus families in this formative period of European history. Where else can we look for clues that will identify people who were past masters at camouflage and subterfuge?

THE HIDDEN HAND OF HISTORY

Society is not simply founded on the principals of self-preservation sustained by the prevailing belief system of the time, it is largely moulded and formed by a complex series of conflicts of ideas, philosophies and ideologies. History is simply the self-serving record of the victors of such conflicts and debates and, as such, records the deeds of the 'great and the good'; largely ignoring the experience of ordinary people. For some years there has been a growing awareness that this incomplete and unsatisfactory story needs to be fleshed out from the often opposing viewpoint of the vanquished and the repressed. Behind the official record there lies 'the hidden hand of history' which records the experience of the underdogs, the beliefs of the hidden schools of philosophy and spirituality, and the hidden tensions within society that have formed and moulded it.[32] The imprint of the hidden hand of history is recorded in the stories, song, dance, drama and ritual of the folklore tradition. In many cases the disguise that surrounds this subversive story was effective, for the rituals were accepted as an everyday part of normal life. For example, the carvings of the green man that decorate so many medieval church buildings and the dances celebrating the rites of

Mayday, were deemed harmless; yet both of these are visual expressions of a 'spiritual resurrection' that plays a central role in the heretical religious beliefs of Rex Deus and its offshoots, Freemasonry and Rosicrucianism. In other cases the true import of the celebration was seen for what it was, a means of transmission of heresy and subversion, and was thereby condemned.

When Tim first went to Rosslyn Chapel and began to delve into the history of the St Clairs, certain aspects of the story that he heard were extremely puzzling. He learnt that Earl William St Clair was most hospitable to those medieval outcasts, the Gypsies, and entertained them in the grounds of Roslin Castle on an annual basis. He heard many stories of the protection offered by the lords of Roslin against acts of harassment to individual members of this persecuted tribe. At the annual gathering, held in a part of the Roslin lands known as 'the Stanks', the Gypsies were encouraged to break the law and perform a drama that was forbidden by statute – the Robin Hood play. One of the towers of Roslin Castle itself was known as the Robin Hood Tower. Why was this seemingly innocuous play banned? Why did the St Clair family develop such a long association with the persecuted minority of the Gypsy people? What significance was there, if any, in the performance of this banned drama?

Earlier we mentioned that certain Cathars fleeing from the Inquisition had sought refuge near Roslin and had started a paper-making business with the support of the St Clairs. Earl William used the paper they produced in the scriptorium at Roslin Castle so that the craftsmen he employed could increase and preserve his collection of priceless manuscripts. There is a chain of belief linking the Cathar refugees, the Gypsies and Rex Deus which found vivid expression in the Robin Hood plays, and which completely contradicted the distorted theology and downright lies upon which the Church/State establishment were founded, so leading to the banning of public performances of these seemingly innocuous dramas. The Church preached the redemptive nature of the resurrection after Golgotha; it feared the resurrection of the truth about the dynasty of Jesus. It was this truth that lay at the heart of the Robin Hood plays, the Cathar beliefs, the Rex Deus tradition and Gypsy celebrations that continue to this day at the southern French village of Les Saintes-Maries-de-la-Mer.

The fact that Mary Magdalene, the wife of Jesus the Nazarene, bore children and took them to Europe lies at the heart of the Robin Hood story. We remember it as Robin Hood and his merry men, the men of the greenwood, the green men. Robin Hood, the subversive fighter against usurped authority represented, in real life, Rex Deus who carried the beacon of truth despite persecution by the false prophets of Holy Mother the Church. His 'merry men' is a corruption of 'Mary's men', those who knew the truth about the children of Jesus and the true nature and importance of Mary Magdalene. Roslin, under the suzerainty of the St Clairs, had become a sanctuary for truth and a repository for Rex Deus and Templar tradition. Rosslyn Chapel is also a signpost carved in stone to the various routes one might take in search of the Holy Grail, and a three-dimensional teaching board of late medieval initiation. The body of sacred knowledge passed down through the centuries by the initiates of the Rex Deus tradition was neither a sterile collection of abstruse intellectual theory nor an arcane collection of 'other worldly' spiritual abstraction, but was the basis for tangible action in the real world of Europe.

18

Action is the Magic Word

The secretive nature of the guilds and fraternities that were transformed into Freemasonry poses great difficulties for any historian. Documentary evidence charting the transformation of the medieval guilds in Scotland into Freemasonry is virtually non-existent, so we have to rely on oral tradition. The officials at masonic archives in Scotland and London do make their resources available to any serious researcher, so that details about the foundations of early lodges of Freemasons are easily accessible. What these generous archivists cannot so readily share is the necessary understanding of how the fraternity really evolved. Later political differences between English and Scottish Grand Lodge Freemasonry further complicate the issue. How then are we to evaluate the full worth of the traditions enshrined within this worldwide fraternal movement? The words of Jesus give us the answer: 'By their fruits shall ye know them'.

Profound political and social change, influenced by various masonic groups, took place in the 17th and 18th centuries. The causes of democracy, freedom and science all benefited from the touch of spiritually-gifted men who derived their insights from the Rex Deus tradition operating through the brotherhood of Freemasonry.[1] For example, certain initiates combined in a loose network with scholars in the tradition of Erasmus to form the 'Third Force', a movement of moderation which campaigned against the excesses of both Catholics and Protestants in the decades that followed the Reformation. This was influenced in its turn by a group of loving and ecumenical evangelists who, in concert with the Dutch esoteric movement known as 'the Family of Love', formed a trans-European 'Invisible College' of spiritually inspired scholars who remained in constant correspondence with one another. This movement eventually came into the open in England with the founding of the Royal Society.[2]

Founded in 1645 under the reign of the Stewart king, Charles I, the Royal Society was granted its royal charter by Charles II in 1662 after the restoration of the monarchy. It was formed by a group of scientists of profound spiritual commitment who were mainly drawn from the Freemasonic tradition. These included Robert Boyle (1627–91) and Isaac Newton (1642–1727) who, like the Templars, were endowed with knowledge that went far beyond the boundaries of what we would now describe as science.[3] Robert Boyle was not only one of the founding fathers of physics, but also a natural philosopher, a noted alchemist, a student of the prophet Nostradamus (1503–66) and a well-known authority on the mythology of the Holy Grail.[4] Isaac Newton, one of the founding fathers of modern science who is famous for discovering the law of gravity, was also an alchemist who claimed that the Judaic heritage deriving from Old Testament times was a divinely blessed archive of sacred knowledge and numerology. While he is known to have studied early religion, he was not a 'religious' man in the accepted sense of the word, but a spiritual one who rejected the theological concepts of the Holy Trinity and the deification of Jesus. He is one of the first public figures of note in England who had the courage to state that the New Testament had been distorted by the Church.[5]

Freemasonry played an equally dramatic role in the political field in the 18th century, which has had lasting and beneficial consequences. We have already mentioned the formative influence on the concept of democracy and freedom played by those remarkable products of Scottish Rite Freemasonry, the signatories to the American Constitution.[6] This supreme gift was not the only political consequence of Freemasonic thought; a development of the Invisible College, known as the Correspondence Societies, played an important role in shaping the democratic ideals of *Liberté, Egalité, Fraternité* that inspired the French Revolution.

Charting the progress and development of Freemasonry in its many forms in Scotland, England and Europe during the 17th and 18th centuries is fraught with problems. Considerable conflict and a power struggle that ranged far beyond the British Isles and extended into France and Germany, arose between English Grand Lodge Freemasonry and its Scottish predecessors. On the continent of Europe various lodges were formed which were accused of being illegitimate and which were alleged to rely on rites of disputed provenance and dubious validity. And if that were not enough, the whole concept of esoteric transmission of Templar thought is given a further twist by a variety of 'Templar' Orders which only surfaced centuries after the original Order's suppression, all claiming one form or another of 'legitimate' descent. To gain some sense of order out of chaos we need to look at the point when Freemasonry began to operate as an open society, when English Grand Lodge Freemasonry claims, with more force than conviction, that it actually began.

EARLY FREEMASONRY

English official historians of Freemasonry would have us believe that the brotherhood sprang fully formed from some intellectual and spiritual vacuum in the early years of the 17th century.[7] This so-called 'new society' immediately became intimately entwined with Rosicrucianism. It would also appear that the fraternal brotherhood had come into the open rather prematurely in the naïve belief that, in England at least, some degree of religious toleration had been achieved. If that were so, they had a rather rude awakening, for the Thirty Years War in continental Europe threatened mainland Protestants with extinction, with England and the Low Countries becoming a haven of refuge for German Protestant refugees. Civil war then struck England and religious repression once more reared its ugly head under the rule of Oliver Cromwell and the Puritans. Despite the fact that many in Cromwell's army were Freemasons, the brotherhood as a whole kept a low profile. Many commentators claim that this era of repression, and the Hanoverian succession which followed some decades later, explain why English Freemasonry claims today to be apolitical. This belies the fact that for the first 150 years of its open existence the movement was very political indeed, for its roots sprang from ancient guilds and families bound together by two particularly strong ties, a common descent and their sworn allegiance to the House of Stewart.[8] This tradition was started centuries earlier, when the St Clair charters for the Guilds of Scotland acknowledged the patronage and protection afforded to the hard and soft guilds of Scotland by the crown. During the civil war and the protectorate that followed, this situation changed dramatically, for the brotherhood of Freemasonry would have been committing collective suicide if they had openly acknowledged their Stewart allegiance at that time. With the restoration of the Stewart monarchy in 1660, such inhibitions were no longer necessary. This loyalty to the crown, however, was neither blind nor absolute, for the lodges were not slow to protest against abuses of royal power which they believed were against the common good.

An indication of the loyalty of 17th-century Freemasons to their Templar forebears occurs in a curious episode in 1651, when Heinrich Cornelius Agrippa von Nettesheim's *Of Occult Philosophy* was published in English for the first time.[9] This work had originally been composed in Latin and contained one phrase pertaining to the Templar Order, which translates as 'the detestable heresy of the Templars'. In the English edition, this phrase appears to have been magically transformed into one that is far more in keeping with Rex Deus tradition, for it no longer maligned the Grail knights of the Templar Order but referred to 'the detestable heresy of old churchmen'.

Freemasonry eventually began to spread across the Channel into France with the ambassadors and plenipotentiaries of the British crown. When the Stewart monarch was exiled in 1691, he fled to France accompanied by a large entourage.[10] Any masonic movements there, deriving from the Compannonage, now received a massive injection of Freemasons who derived their knowledge, rites and rituals from Scotland, not from England. This influx of many thousands of Jacobite supporters into mainland Europe resulted in the spread of masonic ideals all over the continent.[11] Their principles of fraternity, loyalty and public service led to the formation of the Lodges of the Carbonari in Italy, which ultimately became the roots from which Italian nationalism sprang.[12] The reunification of Italy as a nation, therefore, owes an immense debt to the fraternal brotherhood originating from the Rex Deus families. The early intimate association between Freemasonry and Rosicrucianism found further expression in Germany, where members of the early lodges strengthened and perpetuated the Order of the Rose Cross. In Spain, the Order known as the Alumbrados Illuminati again sprang from early Stewart lodges of Freemasons. At first Freemasonry in France seemed to be restricted to the exiles from Scotland and to the lodges implanted under the authority of the Grand Lodge in London, for the French people took very little interest in a society that claimed descent from medieval masons. This situation changed dramatically, largely due to the controversial actions of one mysterious man.

THE RAMSAY ORATION

A graduate of the University of Edinburgh, Andrew Michael Ramsay (1681–1743), became involved in the religious disputes which almost tore Scotland apart towards the end of the first decade of the 18th century. In 1710 he fled to France where he converted to Catholicism and took a variety of posts, first under the Duc de Chateau-Thierry and eventually under the Prince de Turenne.[13] For his services to these nobles he was made a Knight of the Order of St Lazarus, thereby gaining the title by which he is remembered by all masonic historians, Chevalier Ramsay. His first loyalty was not to the nobility of his host country, but to his own Stewart king who was at that time a king without a country, 'the king over the water'. In 1724 Ramsay went to Rome to act as tutor to Prince Charles Edward Stewart and assisted in efforts to restore him to his rightful inheritance. On his return to France, he took an active role in French Freemasonry and began to transform the movement. Ramsay had not one shred of documentation or tangible evidence that might indicate the true origins of the masonic movement, but as a tutor to the royal prince, a Chevalier of the Order of St Lazarus, a one-time member of the Royal Society and now grand chancellor of the Grand Paris Lodge of Freemasonry, he had what really mattered – credibility and authority. He proclaimed that Freemasonry had its true origins not among the unlettered masonic craftsmen of the medieval era, but among the kings, princes, knights and nobility of the crusades.

This verbal bombshell burst upon the masonic world in a speech that Ramsay delivered at the Masonic Lodge of St Thomas in Paris on 21 March 1737. He began with the words:

> Our ancestors the Crusaders, gathered together from all parts of Christendom in the Holy Land, desired thus to reunite into one sole Fraternity the individuals of all nations ... [14]

He was explicit about the role of the feminine and its connections with the Order, mentioning the goddesses Isis and Minerva by name. He further claimed that the original knightly masons of the crusades were not in fact workers in stone but men who had vowed to rebuild the Temple of God on earth in the Holy Land. He asserted that lodges were established by the crusaders on their return to Europe, in France, Italy, Spain, Germany and Scotland where the Lord Steward of Scotland was grand master of the Lodge at Kilwinning in 1286.[15] It is far from clear whether he knew or cared if his audience were already aware that the hereditary Lord Stewards of Scotland ultimately became the family of Stewart, the legitimate kings of Scotland and England. According to Ramsay the early lodges founded in Europe were neglected in every country except his own. In his eyes, therefore, Scotland was the fount of Freemasonry and the only country where it had continued in an unbroken line from the time of the crusades.[16] He called upon his brothers in France to join the fraternity and 'become the centre of the Order'.

The Oration by Chevalier Ramsay gained wide public notice when it was published in 1741 in the *Almanac des Cocus*. The idea that Freemasonry was the spiritual heir of medieval chivalric Orders immediately touched a chord with his snobbish French audience; an Order founded by illiterate stonemasons had little appeal, but one founded by kings, princes and crusaders was another matter entirely. A tidal wave of masonic activity swept across France, immersing all who had any pretensions to chivalry and fraternity. This new populism gave the Rex Deus families the opportunity they had been waiting for and they began to direct operations without fear of discovery. A host of masonic degrees and rites appeared and were exported to other countries where they were further embellished. This new swathe of ceremonies and rituals were named after Old Testament characters and events and contained cross-references to every known Order of chivalry.

Ramsay's acknowledgement of Freemasonry's Scottish roots resulted in one French system, heavily influenced by supporters of the Stewart cause, gaining its rightful title as Scottish Rite Freemasonry.[17] This 'new' form of Freemasonry had 33 degrees of initiation, each attended by the complex rituals and teaching that sprang from the spiritual insights of the Rex Deus families. In 1738 Pope Clement XII responded predictably to this new manifestation of the teaching of the hidden succession. He issued the papal Bull *In Eminenti Apostolatus Specula*, the first of a continuing series of denunciations against Freemasonry which once again provoked the office of the Holy Roman Inquisition into action. The Pope prohibited any Catholic from joining the fraternity of Freemasons under pain of excommunication, and those in Catholic countries were harried, imprisoned, tortured and deported. Two years later these prohibitions were taken to their logical conclusion when membership in a Freemasons' lodge by any citizen of the papal states became an offence punishable by death.[18]

One bizarre episode took place in Paris in 1743, when a German nobleman, Baron von Hund, was initiated into a form of Freemasonry known as 'Strict Observance', which required his absolute obedience to certain unspecified and unknown superiors. Von Hund's diary reveals that he was received into this Masonic Order of the Temple by an unknown official with the title of the 'Knight of the Red Feather'. This ceremony was attended by Lord Kilmarnock, a leading Jacobite, and Lord Clifford, a Catholic nobleman from Chudleigh in Devon, England. Von Hund claimed that he was later presented to Prince Charles Edward Stewart who was introduced to him as 'a distinguished brother'.[19] His story then took a familiar turn, when he recounts the 'true history' of Freemasonry that was disclosed to him at his initiation. According to this tale, a group of Templar knights had sought refuge in Scotland after the suppression and had kept their Order in being by joining a guild of working masons. From among their number they chose a grand master to succeed Jacques de Molay, and ever since the Order had continued and had been governed by an unbroken succession of grand masters. Learning from the past, the secret Order never revealed the identity of a grand master during his lifetime, so that his name was known only to those who had elected him. This was the justification for the strange oath of absolute obedience to an unknown superior. Von Hund was given a list of the alleged grand masters of the Templar Order, which most scholars dismissed, along with the rest of his story, as nonsense.[20] Bizarre though it may seem, the list given to him is identical to that in the so-called Secret Dossiers, which we now know to be a clever piece of intellectual fraud perpetrated by people with a profound knowledge of both exoteric and esoteric history. Did von Hund's list form the basis upon which the authors of the Secret Dossiers constructed their fantasy?

The baron was instructed to return to Germany and set up lodges of the Rite of Strict Observance and then await further orders. Von Hund took his obligations and instructions from his vanished masters seriously. The lodges he founded spread not only throughout Germany and the rest of Europe but also took root and spread widely in North America. He had been true to his oath and obeyed his instructions to the letter despite the fact that he never had any further contact with either his unknown superiors or those present at his induction, a desertion that was more apparent than real. What happened to Lord Kilmarnock and the Knight of the Red Feather? Why did they 'desert' their loyal German brother? After the disaster of Bonny Prince Charlie's campaign in 1745, which ended at the blood bath of Culloden, the Earl of Kilmarnock was executed for high treason. In the archives of the 'Stella Templum', a Scottish Order claiming some form of descent from the Templars, is a document attesting that the so-called Knight of the Red Feather was Alexander Seton, otherwise known as Alexander Montgomery, who was known to be active in the Jacobite cause in France at that time.[21] There is an Order of the Temple still extant among the Montgomery family to this day.

THE CHARTER OF LARMENIUS

Scotland was not the only country where people claimed to belong to Orders which derived from the medieval Knights Templar. Portugal still supported the Order of the Knights of Christ, which derived directly from the Knights Templar. Documents that came to light in France in 1804 were used to support the claim of direct and continuous Templar survival. An Order created by Bernard-Raymond Fabré-Palaprat in that year relied upon a document known as the Charter of Larmenius to substantiate the legitimacy of its claim.[22] This charter is dated 1324, over ten years after the execution of the last Templar grand master, Jaques de Molay, yet it claims that shortly before his execution de Molay nominated one of the Templars in Cyprus, Jean-Marc Larmenius, as his successor and that the Order continued in secret after the suppression. On this basis Fabré-Palaprat claimed that a non-masonic neo-chivalric Order still existed, which was the direct heir of the medieval Templars. This Order, 'the Ancient and Sovereign Military Order of the Temple of Jerusalem', is still extant. There is one bizarre statement within the so-called Charter of Larmenius which deserves further study: 'I, lastly ... will say and order that the Scot-Templars deserters of the Order, be blasted by an anathema.'[23] This statement apparently confirms the flight of Templar fugitives to Scotland and their survival there.

The authenticity of the Charter of Larmenius has been a constant source of dispute among historians from the time of its publication, and unless further evidence comes to light this argument seems set to continue. Whether the charter is true or false, however, the quotation above indicates that at the time it was composed, whether 1324, 1705 or 1804 – and all three dates have been suggested – the authors were prepared to admit the fact of Templar survival in Scotland. There is no other evidence suggesting Templar survival in France and, until the provenance of the Charter of Larmenius is settled beyond all doubt, this question must remain open. The one country which can justly claim a history of secret unbroken Templar tradition is Scotland. Templarism survived there in a manner that can legitimately claim continuity with the medieval Order, the Templar degrees in Scottish Rite Freemasonry.

THE ORDER OF ST GERMAIN

There is an organization still operative today which legitimately combines both aspects of Scottish Templar survival in one chivalric Order devoted to the Stewart cause. This is 'the Most Noble and Ancient and Jacobite Order of St Germain'. This Order of chivalry was founded by King James VII on 18 June 1692, and at its inception comprised two categories, knights and companions. It was modelled on the Stewart Order of the Thistle and the first knights admitted to its ranks included exiled Thistle knights, loyal Templars, members of the Order of Lorraine and several knights of the Orders of St Louis and St Michael.[24] Among the primary duties of the members of this Order of chivalry was the safety and security of the royal family in exile and the promotion of the Stewart cause. The present grand master is the Stewart heir, HRH Prince Michael of Albany, who still retains under international law the legal right of *Jus Majestatis* which, amongst other things, confirms his right to grant knighthoods in the chivalric Orders created by his exiled ancestors.[25] It has been suggested that this body possesses the sole rights of leadership in Scottish Rite Freemasonry. If this is so, then it would be in full accord with the traditions of Rex Deus.

The massive expansion of Freemasonic activity and the surfacing of previously secret neo-chivalric Orders which claimed Templar antecedents survived the creation of the republic in France and the founding of the United States of America. Both of these great republics have modelled themselves upon the ideals of freedom of the individual, equality of opportunity and democratic rule. The very ideals of brotherhood, service and mutual respect which had pervaded the Rex Deus tradition for centuries had now found their embodiment in political structures that arose in the 18th century in France and America. The fraternal brotherhoods and chivalric Orders continued to spread and flourish, and their growing membership was to play a significant role in the esoteric revival of the 19th century.

PART

V

By Their Fruits
Shall Ye Know Them

19

Rex Deus and the Esoteric Revival

The involvement of Freemasons in the French Revolution and the American War of Independence and after was part of a pattern of behaviour that was replicated many times. Freemasonry contributed to the campaign for the reunification of Italy through the Carbonari; both leaders of this revolutionary movement, Garibaldi and Mazzini, were active Freemasons. It also played a revolutionary role in Russia and elsewhere in Europe where exiled Russian revolutionaries sought refuge, replicating the role it had played in events in France prior to the revolution. Lafayette, who had attained high rank within Freemasonry during his time in America, was eager to see the ideals he had seen enshrined in law in the New World exported to France. Other revolutionaries, including Danton, the Abbé Sieyès and Camille Desmoulin were all active in the brotherhood.[1] Indeed, Freemasonry had proved to be the ideal vehicle for revolution as by its very nature it was capable of being used as a secret network for intelligence, communication and organization. This provoked one lasting reaction which is very much alive today.

The publication by a royalist and right-wing priest, the Abbé Augustin de Barruel, of *Memoirs pour Servir a l'Histoire du Jacobinisme* in 1797, described the French Revolution as the bloody aftermath of a plot by Freemasons to overthrow both royal and ecclesiastical authority.[2] This paranoid work promulgated a vision of the brotherhood as a sinister international revolutionary conspiracy that is anti-religious and dedicated to revolution to bring about 'a new world order'. Thanks largely to the paranoia of this priest the concept of a conspiracy by Freemasons and Jews still spreads its malign influence among the delusional right-wing organizations of Europe and America. Reality, however, indicates the contrary, for just as Rex Deus had adopted a mechanism of survival that obliged its followers to practise the prevailing religion of its time, its offshoot, Freemasonry, employed a similar stratagem in political terms.

Freemasons were undoubtedly active in revolutionary movements, but it is equally demonstrable, though not so well known, that they were also heavily engaged in supporting conservative and right-wing regimes in Austria, Prussia and, of course, in Britain. Even in France and Switzerland there were as many conservative and royalist Freemasons and lodges as revolutionary ones. Thus a list of 19th-century leading Freemasons is, in political terms, remarkably inconsistent and contradictory. On the revolutionary side it mentions Mazzini and Garibaldi in Italy, Bakunin and Kerensky in Russia, and Daniel O'Connell and Henry Grattan in Ireland.[3] The other extreme within the worldwide fraternity would include the political arch turncoat Talleyrand in France, three French presidents, two 19th-century kings of Prussia, the right-wing administrator and poet Goethe and, of course, various kings of England, members of the English nobility and many Anglican clergy.[4] A similar situation obtained in South America where most of the later freedom fighters were Freemasons, but then so too were the Spanish viceroys and the aristocrats and landowners against whom they fought. This situation was replicated at the Alamo, where the Texan leaders were all Freemasons, as was their opponent General Santa Anna. To complicate the issue still further, there were the internal differences that became manifest when English Grand Lodge Freemasonry seemed to have become a social club for the business community and the establishment, in stark contrast to the esoteric tradition that was the driving force in the Grand Orient Lodge in France and in Scottish Rite Freemasonry.

THE ESOTERIC REVIVAL

The rising tide of Freemasonry in France, allied to increasing intellectual freedom and speculation, provided the foundation for a deepening interest in the occult throughout the 19th century, which led ultimately to the massive esoteric revival which took place in the final decades. This revival spread throughout Europe, to Britain and to the Americas. Its study was not restricted to Christian esoterics or to Templarism, but embraced a wide-ranging interest in alternative belief systems and forms of spirituality from ancient times from all over the globe. The Theosophical Society founded by Helena Petrovna Blavatsky (1831–91) became popular throughout the English-speaking world, as well as in Germany and Spain.[5] In this manner, knowledge of Eastern spiritual systems began to gain widespread acceptance in Europe and the States. Europe's own prehistory also became a source of inspiration, and renewed interest was taken in its many neolithic sites.

One particular esoteric Order that provoked renewed interest in France was the Compagnie du St-Sacrement. Founded in the early years of the 17th century under the guidance of Jean-Jacques Olier, it has been compared by many to the medieval Templars or as a precursor of certain forms of Freemasonry. Centred on the Church of St Sulpice in Paris, it created a complex web of provincial branches and chapters that had much in common with the 20th-century organization of the communist party, in that only a chosen few knew the senior leaders' identities. Strange references in contemporary accounts at the time of its foundation refer to a mysterious secret which is at the centre of its power.

Outwardly devoted to charitable works, its real motivation was to seek political power. One of its directors, Vincent de Paul, became confessor to King Louis XIII. It has been alleged that the Compagnie played some mysterious role in the foundation of the Canadian city of Montreal, and to confuse the issue still further it has been described variously as ultra right-wing and piously Catholic on the one hand, and heretical on the other. In its final years certain familiar names, which include the Duke de Guise and the Viscount of Turin, were openly associated with the Compagnie. Suppressed in 1665, it allegedly recalled all its documents which were concealed in secret in an unnamed Paris depository, possibly the Church of St Sulpice.[6]

SAUNIÈRE, THE HABSBURGS AND REX DEUS

Most recent books on the mystery of Rennes-le-Château and the life of Saunière accept without question that he was involved with leading figures in the esoteric revival in Paris, such as Emil Hoffet, Claude Debussy and Emma Calvé. The relationship described as existing between Saunière and members of the Habsburg family is similarly accepted as an absolute fact. Yet not one documentary source of any repute can provide proof of any link whatsoever between this parish priest from a remote village in Southwest France and the ruling dynasty of the Austro-Hungarian Empire.

Nonetheless, there is lasting and visible proof that the Habsburg dynasty are an integral part of Rex Deus. The mausoleum of the Emperor Maximilian I at Innsbruck was designed by the emperor himself, who died in 1519. To represent his ancestors, 40 superb larger than life-size bronze statues were made. They included the Merovingian King Clovis, King Theoderic, Godfroi de Bouillon, Queen Elizabeth of Hungary, King Ferdinand of Aragon, Philip 'the Good' Duke of Burgundy, Archduke Sigismund and the Duchess Mary of Burgundy. This collection of statues is a three-dimensional ancestral list of the great and the good of Rex Deus throughout the ages. So while we do not find the claim that Saunière had close contact with members of the Habsburg family surprising, there is, as yet, not one shred of documentary evidence that has come to light to substantiate these allegations.

LES BERGERS D'ARCADIE

Various claims have been made that Poussin's painting *Les Bergers d'Arcadie* is constructed on a geometrical framework which has some mysterious relevance to the landscape surrounding Rennes-le-Château. In the course of certain television documentaries separated by many years, two professors of art history have argued vehemently both for and against this concept. Books and television programmes have proposed, rather unconvincingly to all except the converted, that this painting holds the key to some gigantic masterpiece of sacred geometry encompassing a vast swathe of this mountainous district.[7] So far no corroborative evidence whatsoever has come to light in support of these theories. As to the inscription on the tomb in the painting, *Et In Arcadia Ego*, the standard explanation is the most likely; in view of the incorporation of a skull in the design of the painting, the whole work is a *memento mori* and a reminder that death also resides in Arcadia. There is, however, another intriguing explanation which has been put forward by the medievalist Stella Pates[8] that has some credibility in the light of our own investigations. This explanation is based on an anagram of *Et In Arcadia Ego – Et In Arca Dei Ago*, a Latin phrase which translates as 'And I act on behalf of the Ark of God'. If the Poussin painting does prove relevant to the Saunière story, then this may well have considerable validity.

RENNES-LE-CHÂTEAU AND REX DEUS

The small church at Rennes-le-Château, restored so garishly and at such cost by the Abbé Saunière, stands almost unaltered to this day. For nearly

1,000 years this tiny country church has been dedicated to Mary Magdalene, the bride of Jesus. An examination of the symbolism of certain statues near the altar gives rise to two different yet not mutually exclusive explanations that tie in with possible actions on behalf of the 'Ark of God'. If we equate the Ark of God with divinely blessed truth, the truly heretical nature of the message within the church may yet reveal itself. Remember that symbolism can be interpreted at many levels according to the insight of the initiate.

Flanking the altar are a pair of statues which, at first glance and taken separately, seem part and parcel of standard church decoration. On one side is a stylized statue of a Madonna with child; on the other the bearded figure of her husband, also holding a child. In the eyes of the Church perhaps it is the same child represented in both statues with its holy parents. Or are there two further, less obvious, explanations? Is it Mary and Joseph and the Holy Twins, Jesus and his brother Judas Thomas Didymus? Or, as the church is dedicated to Mary Magdalene, is it Jesus and his bride with their two children, the founders of the bloodline?

Elsewhere in the church is a painting of the Magdalene with a trephined skull, a symbol that is repeated in Templar iconography and the paintings of Teniers and Poussin, and in Freemasonic and modern Templar ritual. Is the decoration and symbolism in this church dedicated to the wife of Jesus related to the strange motto on the exterior above the porch? Carved above the entrance to the church is the Latin inscription that Henry Lincoln found so bizarre – *Terribilis Est Locus Iste* – which he translated as *This Place Is Terrible*. An alternative translation exists which is possibly more accurate: *This Place Is Awesome*. In view of the possibly heretical nature of the message enshrined within the church regarding the Magdalene and her children, this translation is perhaps more meaningful.

The television documentaries presented by Henry Lincoln, and *The Holy Blood and the Holy Grail* that followed, have not been the only works centred on Rennes-le-Château which described the existence of a bloodline descended from the marriage of Jesus and Mary Magdalene. Gérard de Sède's earlier work had also spoken obliquely of the same theme. The sequel to Baigent, Leigh and Lincoln's best-seller was *The Messianic Legacy*, which focused almost exclusively on the bloodline. Another work, *The Dreamer and the Vine*, whose author at least had the honesty to classify it as fiction, was published three years prior to *The Holy Blood and the Holy Grail* and dealt with closely related themes. This fictional reconstruction of the life of Nostradamus touches on many of the mysteries, political intrigues and conflicts that we have described.

Rex Deus, the heirs to the bloodline, were not the only initiatory sect who had successfully transmitted the secret teachings of Jesus from master to pupil for 2,000 years. In the remote mountain range of the Jebel Asariya, that runs from northern Lebanon to the Turkish border, live the sect of the Nosairi. In order to discourage the inquisitive, this hereditary group of secret initiates practise Islam, the prevailing religion of the region, as a 'garment to conceal the true faith!'. The presence of a considerable number of both Christian and pagan elements – the use of incense, the observation of the feasts of Christmas, Epiphany and Whitsun, and the veneration of Sts George and Matthew – in the belief system of this supposedly Islamic sect has led to some scholarly comment. One French scholar, Massignon, suggests that at heart the sect is Christian.[9] Another French scholar, René Dussaud, goes even further and claims that the sect grew from the same group to which Jesus belonged, namely the Nazarenes, and that the Nosairi religion is more ancient than either Pauline Christianity or Islam.

One Englishman, Walter N Birks, who served as an intelligence officer among the Nosairi for more than two years during the Second World War, grew to be trusted by their leaders. They disclosed certain secret aspects of their belief system to him. He learnt that, in order to survive, they practised dissimulation and disguise as a mask for their true beliefs, which were revealed only to high adepts under oaths of secrecy promising death to those who revealed these sacred truths to the profane. The two most important symbols in their liturgy are the light and the chalice, both of which are encompassed in one central prayer which says 'I drink to the light'. When Birks discussed the Holy Grail with the Nosairi initiates their response disclosed a startling similarity to Rex Deus liturgy: 'The Grail you speak of is a symbol and it stands for the doctrine that Jesus taught to John the Beloved alone. We have it still!' Birks' comment to this response was: 'Here preserved in the remote mountains is a precious relic, a living fragment of the *alternative tradition*.'[10]

Within the sect itself, in a strange parallel to Catharism, there are divisions between the hearers and the initiated who are known as the 'elect'. This division is given visible symbolic form by the wearing of a girdle to mark the initiate; this was also the practice with the Essenes, the Templars and the Cathars. The Nosairi believe that Jesus, although only a man and not a god, became the perfect vessel for 'the Light'. According to this sect 'the Word' as used in the Gospel of St John 'is *not* the expression of a transcendent person, but *is* the expression of a transcendent quality in the universe which is ultimately attainable by *all* men.' Jesus was regarded by the sect as a forerunner and an exemplar, a human being who had achieved enlightenment and union with the divine in a manner that all men could follow. The nature of his mission was to teach the way to enlightenment and not for redemption. The only salvation that the supreme teacher brought about was from ignorance and not from sin. Thus here with the Nosairi we find confirmation of the fact of secret spiritual transmission of the teaching of Jesus down through the ages from master to initiate under the cover of outwardly practising the prevailing religion of the time.[11] It is ironic that this replicates almost in its entirety the beliefs and the traditions of Rex Deus, but this time in the context of an Islamic society rather than a Christian one.

In 1993 Michael made his first contact with Tim and gave the outlines of his intriguing story which replicated the Nosairi tradition in a

European context. Working from a completely different perspective but focusing on exactly the same theme, Laurence Gardner's best-selling work, *The Bloodline of the Holy Grail*, reached the public in 1996.[12] This traced not the complete Rex Deus story, but one intriguing aspect of it, the descent of the Royal House of Stewart from the biblical Royal House of David. Hot on the heels of this came *The Forgotten Monarchy of Scotland*,[13] this time from an author who claimed to be a direct descendant of Jesus, HRH Prince Michael of Albany, the last living descendant of Prince Charles Edward Stewart, Bonnie Prince Charlie himself. Is it a coincidence that all these separate streams of information welled up from various sources in different parts of the world and converged to form such a massive 'heretical stream'? Furthermore, what significance can we attach to the timing of these revelations as we approach the final hours of the second millennium? Two millennia from the birth of the obscure Jewish rabbi, Jesus the Nazarene, and after 2,000 years of dogmatism, theological disputes, distortion, lies and repression, are we finally to celebrate the validity of the age-old aphorism 'truth will out'?

20

Rex Deus – the Evidence

The starting point for our investigation of the Rex Deus tradition was to research, study and analyse the major points related by our principal informant. Using this as a tool, we checked the accepted historical record to see if the families of Rex Deus repeatedly acted in concert with one another in order to achieve common objectives. At the outset we believed that it would be impossible to establish the existence of residential schools at the Temple in Jerusalem, much less link Mary the mother of Jesus to them, and we also felt that it might prove impossible to find evidence that would convince committed Christians that Jesus was married.

We mentioned that the task of tracing genealogical descent over a 2,000-year period posed certain insuperable problems, due to the vast gaps in the record. This, of course, was not the only hurdle to be overcome. History as we have been taught it is simply a selective account of past events written by the victors in any conflict, be it military, intellectual, ideological or religious. The general thrust of European history is firmly rooted in Latin sources deriving from the Roman Empire or its successor, the Roman Catholic Church. It carries with it the explicit message that we owe all progress, freedom and comfort to the

Church/State establishment, a view reinforced by leading academics of every discipline who are, of course, employees of the Church/State establishment whose views they so staunchly defend. Our investigations were further hampered by the oath-bound secrecy of Rex Deus itself. Both witnesses and evidence for the existence of this underground stream were physically destroyed by the priests and politicians who used any means, however immoral, to retain their grip on the reins of power.

Tracing lines of family descent was complicated by gaps in the record and the fact that many families of noble descent were known by several names, such as those derived from their estates or from the area they ruled. An example is the name of Blanchefort, which was used by several families which were rarely if ever related by blood. Further confusion ensued as families named after their estates began to intermittently use 'surnames' which did not necessarily appear in public records with any degree of consistency.

If direct and unbroken descent was beyond proof, what was the point of the exercise? Assuming that we have found sufficient evidence or indication that concerted co-operation between members of Rex Deus occurred repeatedly throughout European history, does this validate the truth of Rex Deus descent? The answer must be no. What then does it indicate?

Concerted action is not an indication of either the truth or falsehood of the belief system from which it arises, but reflects the depth of sincerity or the fanaticism of the believer. Hitler and Stalin used ideologies to inspire highly effective action, yet this does not validate the belief systems they espoused. Collective action indicates that, at the heart of the community performing it, there is a common belief system or communal objective which, to one degree or another, inspires them all. Therefore, by examining Western European history, including the crusades, in the light of our knowledge of Rex Deus, we have clearly established that there *was* a group of families which transcended national boundaries who did, repeatedly, act together in attempting to achieve certain common goals. Furthermore, there is enough evidence to demonstrate the belief held by certain individuals of probity that the families they represent are lineal descendants of important figures of the New Testament era.

We did find documents contemporaneous with the Gospels which stated unequivocally that Mary was a pupil at the Temple School in Jerusalem[1] and the attendance of Jesus at such a school can be reasonably inferred from the Gospels. The ranking and naming of the High Priests of the Temple as the Melchizedek, the Michael and the Gabriel is confirmed by the Book of Enoch, the work of Barbara Thiering the Dead Sea Scrolls' scholar, and is referred to in *The Bloodline of the Holy Grail* by Laurence Gardner.[2] Perceived difficulties in finding sufficient evidence for the marriage of Jesus vanished when we realized that the sceptical Catholic theologian Margaret Starbird had now accepted this matter as being proven fact. Her work was also useful in discerning the thread of truth that lies at the heart of the legends concerning Mary Magdalene, which have been current in the south of France among the Gypsy community for the last 2,000 years.[3]

We have stressed the pivotal role played by a closely linked network of Rex Deus families who were resident in the north of France and the Low Countries who, acting in collusion with others in Scotland and the Languedoc, formed the central active core of the First Crusade. The capture of Jerusalem and the election of Godfroi de Bouillon, the accepted Fisher King of Rex Deus at the time, as the elected Protector of the Holy Sepulchre or King of Jerusalem, was the first major example of successful collective action by the group that we were able to establish. The second important example, mounted by families originating from the County of Champagne, actually took place in the heart of Jerusalem. This was the founding of the Order of the Knights Templar at the behest of Bernard of Clairvaux, Hughes I of Champagne, André de Montbard and, above all, the ancestor of our informant and the Templars' first grand master, Hughes de Payen.[4]

TEMPLAR INFLUENCE ON EUROPE

The Knights Templar, who are remembered as the knights of the Holy Grail and as warriors of extreme bravery, acted as the overt arm of Rex Deus in European affairs for the 200 years of their existence. Why such an Order had such a profound effect on European architecture, trade, banking and culture remains, for many scholars, a mystery to this day. There are many accounts which relate the transformative activities of the Templars, yet signally fail to make any comparison, other than in the military field, with the actions of other religious Orders throughout Europe. People have rarely compared the significant impact of the Templars on European culture with the minimal impression made by the Knights Hospitaller, Benedictines, Franciscans or other monastic Orders. We described in considerable detail the transformative effect they had on the peace and stability of 12th-century Europe, their role in the accumulation of capital, and the part they played in setting the scene for the rise of capitalism.[5] Yet no one has ever asked why it was the Templars and not others who brought about such profound change. What made this Order so different? What was it about their beliefs that gave them the insight and the motivation to use them in this manner?

The Templars, like the Egyptian initiates of old, were secret followers of a spiritual pathway that led to the attainment of ascending levels of sacred knowledge. This knowledge was to be used for the benefit of the communities within which they moved.[6] It is a sad reflection on modern academic scholarship that it shies away from any realistic investigation of Templar beliefs. There seems to be an unwritten conspiracy to avoid all mention of gnosis in respect of the Templars; Gnosticism pervaded them from their very inception until their untimely demise.[7] Brought into the public arena by the accusations of heresy that heralded the suppression of the Order, it had been there from the beginning in the traditions that sustained Hughes de Payen, André de Montbard and the *éminence grise* of European Christianity, Bernard of Clairvaux.

Bernard's instruction to the Knights Templar to swear 'allegiance to the House of Bethany and that of Mary and Martha' is strange to say the least. According to Church belief, Mary of Bethany, better known as Mary Magdalene, died childless. So how could she have founded a dynasty? We suggest that Bernard's comments indicate that he knew that she had children and that the bloodline was still extant. Further indications of the existence of Rex Deus belief at this time exist in a variety of modern works on the era, wherein the authors float the theory that the Gothic cathedrals of the 12th and 13th centuries were not dedicated to Our Lady, Mary the mother of Jesus, but Our Lady Mary Magdalene,[8] the wife of Jesus.

One of the families of Rex Deus was that of Anjou, and the son of Mary of Anjou, King Louis XI of France, claimed repeatedly that he was in the direct dynastic line of descent from Mary Magdalene.[9] The first wife of Louis XI was Margaret Stewart, the daughter of King James I of Scotland, and when she died nine years later Louis married the daughter of another leading family within the group, Charlotte, the daughter of Duke Ludovico of Savoy. During prolonged disputes with his father, King Charles, and in fear of his life, Louis fled to Flanders to the court of Philip the Good, Duke of Burgundy and founder of the Order of the Golden Fleece.[10] On 16 August 1461 Louis was anointed and crowned King of France at Reims.

THE UNDERGROUND WAY

Constantly irrigating the roots of the Rex Deus tradition was an underground stream of spirituality which derived directly from the Gnostic and initiatory 'Way' preached originally by Jesus. This step-by-step progress towards spiritual enlightenment first came to public notice in the late 12th century with the Grail romance written by yet another resident of the county of Champagne, Chrétien de Troyes.[11] Working firstly under the patronage of the Count of Champagne, Chrétien dedicated *Le Conte del Graal* to a later patron, the Count of Flanders, who sprang from the same stem as Godfroi de Bouillon. Inseparably linked in the public mind with the Grail romances of Chrétien de Troyes and Wolfram von Eschenbach were the Arthurian legends which gained popularity in England somewhat earlier. As we have demonstrated, these were used to legitimize the claims of leading Rex Deus families to the English throne and to unify the country under the Plantagenet kings.[12]

Another manifestation of the Way preached by Jesus developed throughout Lombardy, the Languedoc and many other parts of France under the protection of noble families of the Rex Deus tradition. The nobility of the Languedoc had joined with their noble kinfolk of Normandy, Flanders and Scotland in the First Crusade and played their part in establishing the true Rex Deus family on the throne of Jerusalem. In the 12th and 13th centuries this same group of nobles protected the Cathars of the Languedoc who established a flourishing religion that began to rival Roman Christianity in its appeal to the local population. The Cathar perfecti led lives of humility and service and claimed to follow the true teachings of Jesus. They too acknowledged the fact that Jesus was married to Mary Magdalene and had fathered a family. Perhaps the only significant difference between their beliefs and those of Rex Deus is that they acknowledged that Jesus had died on the cross, while the hidden families knew that their teacher had survived that ordeal. More importantly they were completely in accord with Rex Deus tradition in the central tenet of their religion and they made explicit reference to the fact that Jesus came to reveal the pathway to sacred knowledge and not to redeem. They publicly practised an initiatory tradition so that they might gain gnosis or sacred knowledge and eventual enlightenment prior to their spiritual union with Almighty God.

THE WAY COMES INTO THE OPEN

The role played by the noble families of Rex Deus in preserving Templar traditions in Scotland has been widely recognized in other works.[13] We have shown the various ways they used to ensure that the inspirational truth of the teachings of Jesus were preserved within the family group and progressively spread beyond it by means of the craft guilds, emergent Freemasonry, Rosicrucianism and the private survival of the Templar Order within the ranks of certain families. Here again we found compelling examples of concerted Rex Deus activity over a long period of time, using the Scots Guard as the overt and legitimate vehicle for their actions.[14] These were not restricted to issues that were of direct benefit to the families concerned, but were specifically targeted at promoting the cause of two important Rex Deus dynasties, the family of Guise and the Royal House of Stewart.[15] Freemasonry made its real impact on European society after the expulsion of the Stewarts from Britain and it spread like wildfire throughout the upper reaches of European society following the Oration of Chevalier Ramsay.

The fraternal brotherhoods that were used to ensure the survival of Templar tradition, the Grail romances, the chivalric Orders, the Arthurian mythology, the Robin Hood legends and the enduring spiritual beliefs of the Gypsies, all ensured that the core beliefs of Rex Deus began to spread beyond the confines of dynastic alliance. The concepts of brotherhood, loyalty, integrity and service to others, that were fundamental to Freemasonry and Rosicrucianism, played a pivotal role in the formation of modern European society. The varying strands of Rex Deus belief permeated all walks of life and ensured that the teachings would be transmitted irrespective of the fate of any Order, organization or family within Rex Deus. The principle of toleration for the Jews which had so distinguished the county of Champagne and the Languedoc were reflected in the protection granted so freely by the St Clair family of Roslin to the Gypsies performing the banned Robin Hood plays at Roslin Castle. The concept of democratic responsibility and service to others that flowered as the principles of *Liberté, Egalité, Fraternité* at the time of the French Revolution ultimately led to the *Declaration of the Rights of Man* and the Constitution of the United States of America. This struggling new republic was not the only state to benefit from the ideals that had been preserved in secret for nearly 2,000 years; many of the new political states of Central and Southern America were also led to freedom by men imbued with masonic beliefs and traditions. The leading figures in the campaign that unified Italy and finally freed it from the repressive rule of the papacy were cast from the same mould.

Rex Deus beliefs operating throughout the secret initiatory Orders exerted a formative influence on the great artists of Europe, biblical scholars and the fathers of modern science.[16] Throughout the Renaissance and the Reformation, the initiation cults exerted their influence upon individuals who might, at first glance, seem unlikely candidates for their attention. Botticelli was a hermeticist and a pupil of Verrocchio, a hierophant who also instructed Leonardo da Vinci. Leonardo's historical reputation as an esotericist is well attested; he is described by some as a Rosicrucian and by contemporary Catholics as 'of an heretical cast of mind'. The great scholar Robert Fludd, of England, was one of Europe's leading exponents of esoteric thought and the author of one of the most comprehensive compilations of ancient hermetic philosophy ever written. He was one of the principal scholars responsible for the translation of *The Authorized Version of the Bible* – the King James Version. It is interesting to note that this translation was conducted by a Rex Deus scholar under the patronage of the reigning king of the Royal House of Stewart.

The priest, alchemist and author Johann Valentin Andrea was certainly the principal author of the so-called 'Rosicrucian Manifestos' which gained wide circulation in Europe in the mid-17th century. The scientists of the new era included several leading members of the hidden stream of initiates, including Isaac Newton and Robert Boyle. We have mentioned those initiates who combined in a network known as the Third Force, who acted as a force for moderation in the troubled religious disputes of the Reformation and after. The Dutch esoteric movement, the Family of Love, combined with the Third Force to form the Invisible College, which later manifested in England as the Royal Society.

We have given many examples of the benefits in the Templar era which resulted from the application of Rex Deus ideals and Gnostic beliefs and delineated many of the roots of transmission that the group used to ensure the survival of their philosophy. More importantly we have been able to show for the first time some of the rituals and underlying belief system that have sustained the secret bloodline for two millennia. Like all Gnostic groups, Rex Deus followed a pathway that led inevitably to the transmission of sacred knowledge. The benefits of the application of this form of knowledge are clearly manifest in the history of the Knights Templar, the work of the Renaissance giants we have already listed and in the political advances that have flowed from Freemasonry. Is there any evidence that demonstrates that this sacred knowledge is still being passed on in an effective manner?

MODERN FRUITS OF ANCIENT GNOSIS

The sacred knowledge and oral traditions of Rex Deus led ultimately to the Knights Templars' highly successful excavations under the Temple Mount. Over five centuries later, a leading Scottish Freemason used his spiritual knowledge and insight to make an equally startling discovery in a far-off land. James Bruce of Kinnaird, a renowned classical scholar, travelled extensively in North Africa and the Holy Land, returning occasionally to Scotland to attend to his family affairs. In 1768 he began a five-year exploration of Ethiopia, with the ostensible motive of searching for the source of the Nile. However, we have reason to believe that this was simply a cover for his true purpose; with his scholarly background Bruce was well aware that the source of the Blue Nile had been located in the early 1600s by two Portuguese priests, Pedro Paez and Jeronimo Lobo.[17]

In Volume I of his *Travels* Bruce wrote at considerable length about the close cultural and commercial links that had existed between Ethiopia and the Holy Land in Old Testament times. He was a biblical scholar of considerable skill and experience who was fluent in ancient

Hebrew, Aramaic and Syriac. His knowledge of the Old Testament has been described by other scriptural scholars as outstanding. He made a profound study into the culture and traditions of the Falashas, the black Jews of Ethiopia. The present-day author Graham Hancock, enquired from the Ethiopian historian, Belai Gedai, as to what were Bruce's true motives for the expedition. He received the following reply:

> As a matter of fact what we Ethiopians say is that Mr James Bruce did not come to our country to discover the source of the Nile. We say he was just pretending that. We say that he had another reason … The real reason … was to steal our treasures, our cultural treasures. He took many precious manuscripts back to Europe.[18]

Prior to Bruce's explorations one of the most important pieces of Jewish mystical literature was believed to be irretrievably lost. This work was only known from fragments and by references to it in other texts, yet surprisingly, it was constantly referred to in the rituals of Freemasonry and was therefore of great significance to the fraternal Orders. Was the retrieval of this manuscript the true reason for Bruce's prolonged and dangerous expedition? He was not the first to discover the source of the Blue Nile but he was the man who brought back the first complete copy of *The Book of Enoch* that was ever seen in Europe.[19] According to masonic legend Enoch was the inventor of writing, and it was believed:

> … that he taught men the art of building … he feared that the real secrets would be lost – to prevent which he concealed the Grand Secret, engraved on a white oriental porphyry stone in the bowels of the earth … *The Book of Enoch* was known to exist from very ancient times, and is continually alluded to by the fathers of the Church.[20]

Bruce returned from Ethiopia with three copies of *The Book of Enoch* and two copies of *The Kebra Nagast,* an ancient Ethiopian manuscript which is believed to tell 'the truth, the whole truth and nothing but the truth' about the Ethiopian origins of the Queen of Sheba and her association with King Solomon of Israel. Bruce donated copies of both manuscripts to the Bodleian Library for the benefit of posterity.[21] How did he know of the exact location of either of these manuscripts if it were not by means of initiatory tradition passed down from teacher to pupil throughout the generations? It has been established that Freemasonry was one of the most important aspects of Bruce's life, but that is not all; James Bruce the explorer was a direct descendant of Robert the Bruce, King of Scotland.[22] His discovery demonstrates that in the late 18th century the insights and gnosis passed down within the Rex Deus tradition was still valid. The ongoing transmission of this insight resulted in further discoveries over 100 years later. The re-excavation in the 19th century of the original Templar dig in Jerusalem did not occur by accident. Rex Deus insight operating through the fraternal brother-hoods was the major impetus that lay behind this vital piece of archaeological detective work. It is no coincidence that in this instance it was again the Scottish roots of transmission of the traditions which stimulated this expedition.

ROSSLYN CHAPEL

There was a wave of church restoration in Britain during the late 19th century that was funded by the Freemasons. In many cases this simply took the form of redecoration and restoration of existing art work, carvings and stained glass. However, in certain instances there were significant exceptions and original work was installed in sites of masonic significance. Rosslyn Chapel is an outstanding example. Originally the windows at Rosslyn had been unglazed and simply covered by shutters during inclement weather. The ground floor windows were now filled with stained glass in the medieval style, portraying standard church iconography. The four windows in the clerestory were glazed at a far higher level of quality, with designs specially commissioned to reflect the spiritual insight and knowledge of the donors. On the south wall in solitary splendour stands St Michael, the patron saint of the Knights Templar. Facing him on the north wall are three oddly assorted saints of profound esoteric significance. On one side of the central figure is St Longinus, the Roman centurion whose spear pierced the side of Jesus at the crucifixion. He is shown holding 'the Spear of Destiny', a vivid reminder to the initiated that the family of the Grail who own the spear hold the destiny of the entire world in their hands, for good or ill, while they possess it.[23] On the other side is St Mauritius, another Roman soldier who once held the Spear of Destiny and who was martyred for his beliefs. But it is the central figure that is most intriguing and revealing.

The central window is a vivid full-length portrait of St George. Why is there a window dedicated to the patron saint of England in a Scottish chapel? If we study the history of the mythical personage we call St George, we find that he was reputed to be an Armenian. According to Pope Gelasius (494 CE), St George 'was a Saint, venerated by man, but whose acts were known only to God.' The earliest known mythological personage on whom St George is held to be based is Tammuz, whose origins are much earlier. Most modern authorities now believe that el Khidir, the patron of the Sufis, Tammuz and St George are simply one and the same person portrayed in different guises. Tammuz is variously described as the spouse, son or brother of the goddess Ishtar, and is known as 'the Lord of Life and Death', a title which has deep masonic overtones but yet pre-dates the reputed history of the masonic movement by several millennia. It is interesting to note that St George is depicted as standing upon a rose-coloured board decorated with roses or rosettes, making an explicit link with the Babylonian goddess Ishtar – for her temples were traditionally decorated with rosettes.[24] The other windows show Longinus and Mauritius standing on chess boards, the so-called 'Checkerboard of Joy' which represents both the Templar battle flag, 'the Beauseante', and the mystical hopscotch symbol of the 'Pilgrimage of Initiation'. Here it is depicted in the exact manner in which it is used in masonic lodges, as part of the floor design upon which people stand for ceremonies and rituals.

The superbly carved stone vaulted roof of Rosslyn is divided into sections, each decorated differently. The western section is adorned with five-pointed stars and, almost hidden among them, the Templar symbol of the dove bearing an olive branch in its beak, a cornucopia and, tucked away almost out of sight, the symbolic mark of the Fisher King, the Sun in Splendour with its 32 points. Another section contains carvings of lilies which orthodox historians of church art claim to be representations of purity, but to the initiated they convey the descending bloodline of the Royal House of Israel.[25] The section decorated with superbly carved rosettes is a direct symbolic reference to the goddess Ishtar and her resurrecting son Tammuz, who is probably the earliest deity embodying the principal of resurrection to a new life, which was held to take place in springtime and is celebrated today in the folk festivals of May Day. To the Freemasons, Tammuz is a figure of immense significance as he is the embodiment of spiritual resurrection to a heightened state of consciousness and gnosis. Thus in this 15th-century chapel we have explicit reminders of far earlier deities and concepts of spirituality than we have any logical reason to expect. Our modern knowledge of the early worship of Ishtar and Tammuz is based on archaeological evidence which has only become available over the last century. How did the founder of Rosslyn Chapel know of these things? The only answer that makes any rational sense is that he learnt of them through the sacred traditions of Rex Deus.

It is significant to note that one of the central features at Rosslyn is the Apprentice Pillar, a superbly carved stylized representation of the cabbalistic Tree of Life. Yet this particular symbol pre-dates the Cabbala by nearly 3,000 years, and the earliest representation of it that we have seen is to be found on a Sumerian cylinder seal dated at circa 2500 BCE, which depicts Tammuz and the goddess Ishtar sitting on either side of the Tree of Life. We believe that the Freemasons who installed the clerestory windows at Rosslyn during the 19th century designed them so that we might learn something of the true nature of the spiritual insight that inspired the founder of the chapel. From the evidence provided by the windows themselves it is apparent that the same line of spiritual knowledge that inspired Earl William continued well into the 19th century. Recent publications by the authors Laurence Gardner and HRH Prince Michael of Albany demonstrate quite clearly that the Rex Deus tradition was alive and well in the final decade of the 20th century.[26] The question we now have to answer is what relevance does the Rex Deus tradition have in the new millennium?

21

At the Dawn of the New Millennium

The end of the first millennium in the Christian era was approached with a strange mixture of faith, fear and expectation, for it was widely believed that the 1,000th anniversary of the birth of Jesus heralded the end of the world. Prophecies abounded which forecast disaster, the coming of the anti-Christ, Armageddon and a series of cataclysms that would culminate with the glorious second coming of Jesus. Many of these fears were revived at the end of the second millennium. In Israel, early 1999 saw the arrest and deportation of groups of militant Christians who had openly declared their intention of blowing up the mosque known as the Dome of the Rock. These devout disciples were prepared to sacrifice themselves and others in order to provoke the final cosmic showdown on the Plains of Megiddo by acting as instruments of Almighty God in triggering Armageddon, the 'last times' and the second coming of Christ. Prophecies of world disaster proliferated, some justified by faith, while others claimed a scientific basis citing very real threats, such as the greenhouse effect. But the militant fundamentalist Christians and doom merchants were a vociferous, but nonetheless dangerous, minority in comparison to a growing majority who believed in a completely different and far more uplifting scenario – the prophets of the new Aquarian age.

At the end of the 9th century the underground streams of spirituality were hidden from sight and the knowledge that they preserved rarely, if ever, entered the public domain, for Western Europe was dominated by the repressive thinking of Holy Mother the Church. The 19th-century esoteric revival, which brought Gnosticism and the occult to the attention of many articulate and creative groups at the turn of the century, laid the foundations for a very different way of thinking which continued to grow and flourish. The work of Helena Petrovna Blavatsky had brought knowledge of Eastern mystical thought to a wide European and American audience[1] and throughout the early decades of the 20th century these two spiritual streams combined and spawned a host of offshoots which amalgamated and resynthesized the thinking of both. Interest in the occult inspired poets such as W B Yeats as well as figures of far more dubious repute such as Aleister Crowley. Adolf Hitler and his henchman Himmler misused the occult and the tradition of the knightly Orders to found the SS and during the Second World War Prime Minister Winston Churchill of Great Britain employed Dr Walter Johannes Stein as his adviser on the occult aspects of the Nazi party.[2] Recent American presidents, such as Ronald Reagan, were publicly known to rely to a certain extent on the age-old art of astrology. President Charles de Gaulle, the man who saved France from disaster on two separate occasions, was a devout Christian who used the services of an astrologer who was 'officially' employed as a press attaché at the Ministry of Defence.[3]

By the mid-1950s esoteric thinking and its offshoots, alternative therapies and New Age thinking, had established a firm base among the middle classes in Britain and America. The rebellious wave of psychedelic culture that swept across the developed world in the 1960s helped to popularize 'alternative' thinking. The publication of *The Spear of Destiny* by Trevor Ravenscroft in 1971, *The Occult* by Colin Wilson and *The Morning of the Magicians* by Pauwels and Bergier fuelled this burgeoning interest. By the 1980s, a period when the churches of all Christian denominations were suffering from declining congregations and an increasing lack of credibility, the concept of alternative lifestyles, holistic thinking and 'new-age' spirituality had taken root among the educated middle classes throughout the Western world. More and more people began to re-examine the relevance of the Church to modern-day society; dogma, ritual and articles of belief came into question in a manner never seen before. This was, as often as not, led by leading churchmen and bishops who began to publicly dispute previously sacrosanct beliefs such as the divinity of Jesus, the virgin birth, New Testament miracles and, above all, the resurrection – the central tenet of Christian belief.[4]

This rising tide of dissatisfaction did not focus its attention on the Church alone, but began to examine the entire Church/State establishment and the dubious philosophy that underpinned 20th-century materialism. A growing sense of alienation from society, religion and modern values left the comfortable middle classes with a dilemma. They, above all, were the achievers in modern society who had attained undreamt of levels of success and material comfort and yet inwardly and spiritually they experienced an aching void that could neither be filled by Church dogma, political ideology or the material benefits of the modern age. In London in 1978 nearly 90,000 people attended an event celebrating the rising tide of New Age beliefs – the Festival of Mind and Body. Describing the throngs flocking into the festival, one commentator remarked:

> Countries like ours are full of people who have all the material comforts they desire, yet lead lives of quiet (and at some times noisy) desperation, understanding nothing but the fact that there is a hole inside them and however much food and drink they pour into it, however many motor cars and television sets they stuff it with, however many well-balanced children and loyal friends they parade around the edges of it … it aches.

> Those who attend the festival are seeking something –
> not certainty, but understanding: understanding of them-
> selves. Almost every path on view starts in the same place,
> inside the seeker.[5]

Millions of individuals from every class in modern society had received an awakening call which had inspired them to begin an inner spiritual journey in search of understanding and self-knowledge. They set out on this quest for spiritual enlightenment by a variety of routes, for their new vision ranged beyond family, nation, colour, creed, race and gender. In many cases they took their first steps along this path without necessarily being aware of its truly spiritual nature. The entry points ranged from the religious, the political and the rebellious to the therapeutic and, therefore, often masked the true nature of the chosen way. A subtle, cumulative and irreversible change of consciousness was demonstrably underway. This ever-changing state of perception and understanding led inevitably to the rediscovery of the 'old way of knowing',[6] the gnosis that had been preserved at such cost by Rex Deus, the medieval mystics and the hidden streams of spirituality. A widespread belief began to arise that the application of treasured sacred knowledge to the human condition in the complex and often threatening final decades of the 20th century was capable of reshaping society into a more caring, compassionate and ecologically aware culture. Gnosis, that old way of knowing that had its roots in Babylonia and ancient Egypt, had been refined by the Jewish mystics and treasured and preserved by the medieval initiates so that it could find its ultimate expression at the dawn of the new age.

It was once claimed that 'all roads lead to Rome', a saying which reflected the political importance of the eternal city at the time of the Roman Empire as well as its spiritual importance throughout the Christian era. In the new millennium all roads lead to gnosis which, in its modern synthesis, has become 'a new way of knowing' which leads inevitably to a lifestyle founded on spiritual values of mutual respect, compassion and natural justice. Contributory factors to the paradigm shift that is underway include concern for the environment, worries about pollution, a marked decline in social cohesion, and a growing loss of faith in both the established political and religious systems.

The Church's response to this was predictable and encompassed a range of options including intellectual repression, excommunication of dissidents, a frenetic last-ditch stand of evangelical activity as church attendance declined ever more rapidly and a frantic, vociferous reiteration of outworn dogma. The modern questioning middle class, however, are a growing army of men and women drawn from all races, creeds and cultures who are united in their collective refusal to be told 'what to think'. They defend their right to question and think for themselves, questioning which has already led them far beyond the limits of materialism and political or religious ideologies. They are supremely conscious that the material values of the modern world simply highlight the spiritual vacuum that lies at the heart of Western society.

In the Middle Ages the cult of relics spawned the development of mass pilgrimage. The Christian Church, which had forcibly taken over many ancient sacred sites, little knew that its own pilgrimage routes replicated in many instances those of pagan times. In *Rosslyn – Guardian of the Secrets of the Holy Grail* the authors recount the story of the limping pilgrim who was met by Elyn Aviva, a fellow pilgrim *en route* to the Cathedral of St James at Compostela. This disabled elderly gentleman described his pilgrimage not as travel upon the Camiño St Jacques (the Way of St James), but on the Camiño des Estrellas (the Way of the Stars), a far more ancient and revered form of pilgrimage made by the initiates of old, which passed through churches adorned with esoteric symbolism. His description of his pilgrimage was 'the milky way is the true and ancient path of spiritual death and rebirth'. In response, Elyn made the following perceptive comment: 'I do not know what road I travel, except that there are many hidden beneath the one – and, perhaps beneath the many is the One'.[7] At the dawn of the new Aquarian age the complex proliferation of starting points and motivating impulses that inspire our New Age spiritual pilgrims replicate Elyn's perceptive and all-pervading truth. Beneath the many modern spiritual paths, there lies *the One.*

Mass revulsion at the savagery, torture and genocide that seems endemic in certain parts of the world is shared among the thinking people of every creed. But man's inhumanity to man is as old as the history of mankind itself, so what is really changing? Fuelled by a strange and complex mixture of outrage, compassion and practicality, the spiritually gifted people of the New Age are no longer prepared to sit idly by and do nothing in the face of natural disaster, human intolerance and brutality. The harrowing vision of suffering humanity is brought into every living room in the developed world by means of television. People of every race, creed and culture then unite in their efforts to provide immediate compassionate relief, to the extent that relief agencies, such as Oxfam, Médecins Sans Frontières, Action Aid and the United Nations programmes for refugees, are now phrases that are common in every language of the Western world.

Many people believe that some form of democratic process takes place in the world of ideas, but nothing could be further from the truth. Rarely does one ruling paradigm evolve peacefully from its predecessor as the result of overwhelming conscious support among the people it purports to serve. Each age looks back at the dominant ideas of its ancestors with a certain degree of contempt, for it is as if they cannot understand the delusions that dominated the previous age. The paradigms that are used to support a given society have neither evolved nor been given the imprimatur of democratic consent, but arose on the rebellious fringes of society and have forcibly displaced their predecessors. It is necessary, therefore, that in these turbulent times we examine the conditions within which this brutal displacement occurs.

The conditions necessary for a paradigm shift to take place are threefold. Firstly, a growing dissatisfaction with the ruling paradigm of the present; secondly, the existence of an articulate and influential minority committed to change and, lastly, a climate of socio-economic turbulence and intellectual ferment or threat which underpins the urgent need for change. To use modern therapeutic parlance, 'there is no gain without pain'.

We have already provided graphic evidence of the rising tide of dissatisfaction that has become manifest among the middle classes throughout the developed world. Dissatisfaction, a growing alienation from the norms that underpin our empty materialist society, allied to an ever-increasing recognition of the futile nature of the preaching promulgated by the Church, has already spawned a worldwide quest for alternative answers that work. The well-established precepts of New Age philosophy and spirituality are being taught by an ever-increasing army of committed individualists throughout the Americas, Europe and the many lands that encircle the Pacific ring. The power of the concerted minority who seek fundamental change is already well-established. No one who has lived through the last 30 years and whose thoughts range beyond the problems of subsistence or the anodyne of sport, can fail to be aware that we live in an age of growing perturbation. All the necessary conditions for a paradigm shift are now firmly in place. But are there, among all the varied religious cultures of our planet, any older and more respected roots that will sustain this shift?

If we examine briefly the treasured truths that lie at the spiritual centre of our innate human desire to live in peace with our fellow beings, we will see the similarities and not the differences between the various religious traditions. In the Talmud, the scriptural basis of Judaic belief, we find the simple instruction, 'What is hateful to you, do not to your fellow men. That is the entire law, all the rest is commentary'; central to the Buddhist way of life is this precept of peace from the Udana-Varqa, 'Hurt not others with that which pains yourself'; in the earlier scriptures of the Zoroastrian religion, the Dadistan-i-Dink, we find, 'That nature only is good when it shall not do unto another whatever is not good for its own self.' It is hardly surprising that in the Gospel of St Matthew this theme is echoed strongly once again, 'Therefore all things whatsoever ye would that men should do to you, do ye even so to them: for this is the law and the prophets.' Islam, the religion of obedience to God, teaches simply, 'No one of you is a believer until he desires for his brother that which he desires for himself'; and in the Hindu Mahabharat it is written, 'This is the sum of duty: do naught to others which if done to thee would cause thee pain.' Yet the sad commentary by Aristotle on the condition of humanity, 'It is more difficult to organize peace than to win a war', which was written more than 2,000 years ago, seems just as true today and reinforces the urgency with which we need to learn to live by spiritual principles.

Rex Deus have preserved the true teachings of Jesus for nearly 2,000 years, patiently and courageously keeping the faith despite persecution and torture. The Church, by the simple and devastating act of the deification of Jesus, placed the teachings of the Messiah beyond the reach of ordinary people. They then proceeded to complete this task by burying the simple and direct teachings of the master under a mountain of dogma and papal pronouncement. Now, at the dawn of the new Aquarian age, it is apparent that the hidden streams of Rex Deus are bubbling to the surface. *The Holy Blood and the Holy Grail*, *The Bloodline of the Holy Grail* and *The Forgotten Monarchy of Scotland* have forewarned the public that the priestly tradition of biblical Israel has been carried down through the ages through the families of Rex Deus.

In the Rex Deus liturgy and *Gospel of the Holy Twins* we recounted the *Proclamation of the Law* which reads:

You will love God your Heavenly Father.
You will obey His Heavenly Commandments.
You will serve the Lord your God all the days of your life.

You will love your brother as you love yourself.
You will love all the peoples of the earth.
As you love your brother you will bring heaven upon earth.

When we compare the simple all-embracing commands embedded in the *Proclamation of the Law*, there is nothing within it which conflicts with the unifying precepts from all the great religions that we quoted above. The commandments laid upon the dynasty of Rex Deus are to bring about heaven upon *all* the earth, not just the 'Christianized' segment of it. Would any devotee of the great religions, Buddhism, Christianity, Judaism, Islam or the Hindu faith have any difficulty with the content of the Rex Deus *Encryption*?

God is God.
God is the Great God of the Universe.
God is the Alpha and Omega.
God is the Creator.
God is the Destroyer.
God is Life.
God is the Lawgiver.
God is the Judge.
God is Mercy.
God is Love.
God is Knowledge.
God is Wisdom.

A Man was sent from God.
He was the Star.
He was the Teacher.
He was of the House of David.
He was of the Line of Aaron.
He is the Prince of Peace.
He is the Learned Lamb.
He is Our King.
He is Our High Priest.
He is the Prince of the West.

He is the Messiah.
His name is Jesus.

In a time characterized by an apparently endless succession of natural and man-made disasters, when our television screens are filled on a nightly basis by the heart-wrenching pictures of human misery arising from flood, famine, earthquake and war, what compassionate, caring people can fail to rise to the challenge posed by Jesus and preserved by Rex Deus in the *Proclamation of the Poor*?

You shall not eat
If the poor do not eat.

You shall not have clothing
If the poor do not have clothing.

You shall not have an habitation
If the poor do not have an habitation.

You shall not have warmth or a fire in your grate
If the poor do not have warmth or a fire in theirs.

You shall not be cured of your illness
If the poor are not cured of theirs.

The European members of Rex Deus preserved the true teachings of Jesus for our benefit in these troubled times which mark the beginning of the third millennium and the dawn of the new Aquarian age. We do not believe that it is a coincidence that the same teaching has been preserved in remarkably similar circumstances among the people of Islam, the Nosairi.[8] Almighty God in His infinite wisdom has ensured that the message of the true teachings of Jesus as given to John, the beloved disciple, have come through to us in a pure and unadulterated form. Stripped of Paul's deification of Jesus, the Master's teaching is now becoming available to all who seek it. The obligation lies upon us to use it for the benefit of the worldwide community of which we are such a small and insignificant part. If we can apply this teaching for the benefit of others in a true sense of humility and service, then and only then will we do justice to those who have preserved the message, and to Almighty God and the Messiah He used to teach it. One modern member of the Rex Deus dynasty, HRH Prince Michael of Albany, has returned to Scotland and has begun the long struggle to reintroduce Celtic Christianity. This ancient spiritual pathway whose teaching had served all the Celtic peoples in the British Isles and brought them the blessings of tolerance, love and scholarship for over 1,400 years, was based on the sure knowledge that Jesus came to reveal and not to redeem. To the Celtic Christians of old, Jesus was a man as they were, an initiatory teacher whose true worth was enshrined in the words of St Colomba, 'Jesus is my Druid'. In reviving Celtic Christianity under circumstances of incredible difficulty, Prince Michael is being true to his spiritual and dynastic roots.

According to the majority of astrologers, the new Aquarian age is to be an age under which science will be used not for its own sake but in the true service of humanity; an age of growing international co-operation that will allow mankind to apply warm-hearted generosity to practical humanitarian ends. It is also predicted that there will be a reconciliation between science and the ageless stream of truths that run through man's unconscious. The Age of Aquarius is expected to be exciting, stimulating, even dangerous from time to time, but above all an age of compassion and spirituality. It will also be the time when the rituals and liturgy of Rex Deus will play their part in bringing about 'heaven upon earth' and where the principal prayer in the liturgy will be answered in full.

The Prayer of the Abba Ra Heim
Our Heavenly Father
Allelujah
May Your Heavenly Kingdom come upon the earth
Allelujah
May Your Heavenly Laws be obeyed upon the earth
Allelujah
May you protect us from the chaos and grant us our needs
Allelujah
Amen.

Chapter Notes and Sources

INTRODUCTION

1 *The Lost Treasure of Jerusalem*, broadcast in the 'Chronicle' series by the BBC in Feb 1972.

2 *The Priest, the Painter and the Devil*, a 'Chronicle' film broadcast by the BBC in 1974, and T*he Shadow of the Templars* broadcast in 1979.

3 First published by Jonathan Cape in 1982.

4 Anthony Powell, *The Daily Telegraph*.

5 Miron Grindea, *The Sunday Telegraph*.

6 Gérard de Sède, *Le Trésor Maudit*.

7 John M. Saul and Janice A Glaholm, London 1985.

8 First published by Jonathan Cape in 1986.

9 The 'Timewatch' programme, *The History of a Mystery*, broadcast by the BBC.

10 *The Tomb of God* by Richard Andrews and Paul Schellenberger.

1 THE TURBULENT HISTORY OF A HILLTOP VILLAGE

1 Gérard de Sède, *Rennes-le-Château, Les Impostures, Les Phantasmes, Les Hypothèses,* p 11.

2 *Ibid.*, p 12.

3 *Ibid.*, p 85.

4 Baigent, Leigh and Lincoln, *The Holy Blood and the Holy Grail*, p 12, and Gérard de Sède, *op. cit.*, p 85.

5 *Ibid.*

6 Baigent, Leigh and Lincoln, *The Holy Blood ...*, p 12.

7 Gérard de Sède, *op. cit.*, p 87.

8 *The Cambridge Illustrated History of the Middle Ages*, Vol I, 350–950, Robert Fossier, ed. p 63 and Baigent, Leigh and Lincoln, *The Holy Blood ...*, p 12.

9 Baigent, Leigh and Lincoln, *op. cit.*, p 12.

10 Louis Fédié, *Le Comte de Razés et le Diocese d'Alet.*

11 Wallace-Murphy and Hopkins, *Rosslyn – Guardian of the Secrets of the Holy Grail*, p 123.

12 Georges Serrus, *The Land of the Cathars*, pp 3 and 16.

13 Michèle Aué (Alison Hebborn, trans.), *The Cathars*.

14 Georges Serrus, *op. cit.*, p 50.

15 Raimonde Reznikov, *Cathares et Templières*, p 7.

16 *Ibid.*, pp 7–8.

17 Picknett and Prince, *The Templar Revelation*, p 87.

18 Information supplied by the *Centre des Etudes Recherches Templières*, based upon the research of the founder, Georges Kiess.

19 Baigent, Leigh and Lincoln, *op. cit.*, p 5.

20 Tim Wallace-Murphy, *The Templar Legacy and the Masonic Inheritance within Rosslyn Chapel*, p 19, and Wallace-Murphy and Hopkins, *Rosslyn ...*, pp 99–100.

21 Gérard de Sède, *op. cit.*, p 91.

22 Georges Serrus, *op. cit.*, p 33.

23 Gérard de Sède, *op. cit.*, p 19.

24 *Ibid.*, p 17.

25 Baigent, Leigh and Lincoln, *op. cit.*, p 4, and Gérard de Sède, *op. cit.*, p 19.

26 Gérard de Sède, *op. cit.*, p 20.

27 Baigent, Leigh and Lincoln, *op. cit.*, p 4.

28 Gérard de Sède, *op. cit.*, p 20.

29 Baigent, Leigh and Lincoln, *op. cit.*, p 4.

30 *Ibid.*, p 5.

31 Gérard de Sède, *op. cit.*, p 19.

32 Baigent, Leigh and Lincoln, *op. cit.*, p 5.

33 Gérard de Sède, *op. cit.*, p 27.

34 Confirmed in Hoffet's archives in Paris at the Villa Mozart, also cited in Gérard de Sède, *op. cit.*, p 27.

35 Gérard de Sède, *op. cit.*, p 29.

36 *Ibid.*, p 29 and Baigent, Leigh and Lincoln, *op. cit.*, p 7.

37 Baigent, Leigh and Lincoln, *op. cit.*, p 7.

38 Gérard de Sède, *op. cit.*, pp 34–5.

39 Baigent, Leigh and Lincoln, *op. cit.*, p 8.

40 *Ibid.*

41 *Ibid.*

42 *Ibid.*

43 *Ibid.*, pp 8–9.

44 The Lost Gospel according to St Peter, v. 10.

45 Gérard de Sède, *op. cit.*, p 41.

46 *Ibid.*

47 Baigent, Leigh and Lincoln, *op. cit.*, p 9.

48 Gérard de Sède, *op. cit.*, p 46.

49 *Ibid.*, p 66.

50 *Ibid.*, p 47.

51 Baigent, Leigh and Lincoln, *op. cit.*, p 9.

52 *Ibid.*, p 10.

53 *Ibid.*

54 Gérard de Sède, *op. cit.*, p 77.

55 Baigent, Leigh and Lincoln, *op. cit.*, p 10.

2 THE STORY BREAKS

1 Baigent, Leigh and Lincoln, *The Holy Blood and the Holy Grail*, p xiii.

2 *Ibid.*, p xiv.

3 *Ibid.*, p 6.

4 *Ibid.*

5 *Ibid.*, p xiv.

6 *Ibid.*, pp xv–xvi.

7 *Ibid.*, p 16.

8 *Ibid.*, pp 36–7.

9 Ravenscroft and Wallace-Murphy, *The Mark of the Beast*, p 52.

10 Wallace-Murphy and Hopkins, *Rosslyn – Guardian of the Secrets of the Holy Grail*, p 97.

11 *Ibid.*, p 98.

12 Baigent, Leigh and Lincoln, *op. cit.*, pp 76–7.

13 Ravenscroft and Wallace-Murphy, *op. cit.*, p 52.

14 Baigent, Leigh and Lincoln, *op. cit.*, pp 66ff.

15 *Ibid.*, pp 69–70.

16 *Ibid.*, Chapter 4.

17 *Ibid.*, p 71.

18 *Ibid.*, p 72.

19 *Ibid.*, pp 76–7.

20 *Ibid.*, p 85.

21 *Ibid.*, p 92.

22 *Ibid.*, p 93.

23 *Ibid.*, pp 97–9.

24 *Ibid.*, p 100.

25 *Ibid.*, pp 101–2.

26 Tim Wallace-Murphy, *The Templar Legacy and the Masonic Inheritance within Rosslyn Chapel*, p 18.

27 Baigent, Leigh and Lincoln, *op. cit.*, p 110.

28 *Ibid.*, p 267.

29 *Ibid.*, pp 368–9.

3 ACTION AND REACTION

1 Richard Andrews and Paul Schellenberger, *The Tomb of God.*

4 OUR FIRST GLIMPSE OF THE REX DEUS TRADITION

This chapter is based upon a series of conversations with our principal Rex Deus informant. In order to fulfil our promise to protect his anonymity, we give no details about him other than those in the text.

1 Wallace-Murphy and Hopkins, *op. cit.*, p 7.

2 A strange cross-reference to this place of burial occurs in *The Tomb of God,* but sadly we have been unable to establish the original source used for this. As far as we are aware, there are no documents extant which allege that Jesus was buried anywhere in Palestine.

3 Wallace-Murphy and Hopkins, *op. cit.*, pp 67–9.

5 BIBLICAL ISRAEL AT THE TIME OF JESUS

1   Wallace-Murphy and Hopkins, *Rosslyn – Guardian of the Secrets of the Holy Grail*, p 68.

2   Paul Johnson, *A History of Christianity*, p 36.

3   See the Kerygmata Petrou, an ancient document which pre-dates the Gospels, in which Paul is described as 'the spouter of lies' and 'the distorter of the true teachings of Jesus'.

4   *The Lost Books of the Bible*, p 17 ff, attributed to Matthew, mentioned by the early theologians, Jerome, Epiphanius and Austin.

5   *Ibid.*, p 24.

6   *Ibid.*, p 60.

7   *Ibid.*, p 38.

8   Paul Johnson, *op. cit.*, p19.

9   Laurence Gardner, *Bloodline of the Holy Grail*, p 38.

10 The *Book of Enoch* was discovered in Ethiopia in the late 18th century by leading Freemason, James Bruce.

11 The Gospel of the Birth of Mary (from *The Lost Books of the Bible*), ch 1 v 1.

12 *Ibid.* ch 5 v 3.

13 *Ibid.* ch 6 v 6.

14 The Protoevangelion of James (from *The Lost Books of the Bible*), ch 10 v 1.

15 The Gospel according to Matthew, ch 2 vs 1–2.

16 *Ibid.*, ch 2 v 16.

17 The Gospel according to Luke, ch 2 v 4, and Matthew ch 2 vs 1–5.

18 The Gospel according to John, ch 7 v 42.

19 Hugh Schonfield, *The Essene Odyssey*, p 59.

20 Hugh Schonfield, *The Pentecost Revolution*, p 290.

21 The Gospel according to Matthew, ch 1 v 23, and Luke ch 1 v 27.

22 Laurence Gardner, *Bloodline of the Holy Grail*, p 162.

23 The Book of Genesis, ch 17 v 19.

24 *Ibid.*, ch 29 v 12.

25 The Book of Judges, ch 13 v 24.

26 The Gospel according to Luke, ch 1 v 13.

27   Laurence Gardner, *op. cit.*, p 162.
28   Uta Ranke-Heinemann, *Putting Away Childish Things*, pp 40ff.
29   The Gospel according to Luke, ch 2 vs 42–50.
30   The Gospel of Thomas (from the Nag Hammadi Library), cited by Professor Joseph Campbell and Bill Moyers in *The Power of Myth*, p 200.
31   A N Wilson, *Jesus*, p xvi.
32   *Ibid.*, p 21.
33   See *The Concise Encyclopedia of Judaism* under 'marriage'; also The Book of Genesis, ch 1 v 22.
34   The Gospel according to Matthew, ch 23 vs 7–8, and John ch 1 vs 38–40, ch 3 vs 2 and 26, ch 6 v 25.
35   The Gospel according to Luke, ch 1 v 27 and ch 2 v 4.

6 JESUS, THE ESSENE TEACHER OF RIGHTEOUSNESS
AND ST PAUL, THE FIRST CHRISTIAN HERETIC

1   Josephus, *The Antiquities of the Jews*, book xiii, ch v, v ix, and Hugh Schonfield, *The Essene Odyssey*, pp 6–7.
2   Hugh Schonfield, *The Essene Odyssey*, p 25.
3   Paul Johnson, *A History of Christianity*, pp 15–16.
4   Josephus, *The Antiquities of the Jews*, book xv, ch x, v v.
5   Hugh Schonfield, *op. cit.*, pp 4–5.
6   Norman Golb, *Who Wrote the Dead Sea Scrolls?*
7   Andrew Welburn, *The Beginnings of Christianity*, p 76.
8   *Ibid.*, pp 79–80.
9   Douglas Lockhart, *Jesus the Heretic*, pp 229–30.
10   *Ibid.*
11   Hugh Schonfield, *op. cit.*, pp 18–19.
12   Andrew Welburn, *The Beginnings of Christianity*, p 243.
13   *Ibid.*
14   Dr John Robinson, *The Priority of John*.
15   Andrew Welburn, *op. cit.*, p 244.
16   *Ibid.*, p 55.
17   Paul's Epistle to the Galatians, ch 2 v 9.

18 The Gospel according to St Matthew, ch 16 v 18.
19 Claim based upon the passage in *The Acts of the Apostles*, ch 2 vs 41–7.
20 Hugh Schonfield, *op. cit.*, p 24.
21 Uta Ranke-Heinemann, *Putting away Childish Things*, p 173.
22 Andrew Welburn, *op. cit.*, p 87.
23 Laurence Gardner, *Bloodline of the Holy Grail*, p 154.
24 Wallace-Murphy and Hopkins, *Rosslyn …* , p 64.
25 The Acts of the Apostles, ch 7 v 59, ch 8 vs 1–3 and ch 9 vs 1–2.
26 Paul's Epistle to the Galatians, ch 1 v 17.
27 The Acts of the Apostles, ch 24 v 14.
28 Paul Johnson, *op. cit.*, p 41.
29 Uta Ranke-Heinemann, *Putting Away Childish Things*, p 215.
30 Andrew Welburn, *op. cit.*
31 The Gospel according to St Matthew, ch 28 v 19.
32 *Ibid.*, ch 10 vs 5–6.
33 *Ibid.*, ch. 15 vs 22–5.
34 A N Wilson, *Jesus*, p x.
35 Paul Johnson, *op. cit.*, p 30.
36 A N Wilson, *op. cit.*, p 210.
37 Paul Johnson, *op. cit.*, p 36.
38 Wallace-Murphy and Hopkins, *op. cit.*, p 57.
39 *Epiphanus-Haeres*, lxxxviii.
40 A N Wilson, *op. cit.*, pp 124–6.
41 The Acts of the Apostles, ch 9 vs 1–2.
42 Paul's Epistle to the Romans, ch 16 v 10, and Robert Eisenman, *James the Brother of Jesus*, pp 349–50.
43 See the account in the Pseudoclementine *Recognitions*, and also the chapter entitled 'The Attack by Paul on James and the Attack on Stephen' in Eisenman, *op. cit.*
44 Paul's Epistle to Titus, ch 2 v 13.
45 Paul's Epistle to the Romans, ch 5 vs 6 and 8, ch 14 v 9, and Paul's First Epistle to the Corinthians, ch 15 v 3.
46 The *Kerygmata Petrou*.

47 Paul's First Epistle to the Corinthians, ch 9 v 6.
48 *Ibid.*, ch 7 v 8.
49 Paul's Epistle to the Philippians, ch 3 v 5.

7 THE MARRIAGE AND DYNASTY OF JESUS

1 A N Wilson, Jesus, p 101.
2 The Gospel according to John, ch 2 vs 1–5.
3 Fida Hassnain, *A Search for the Historical Jesus*, p 84.
4 The Gospel according to John, ch 11 vs 20 and 28–9.
5 The Gospel according to Luke, ch 10 v 39.
6 Laurence Gardner, *Bloodline of the Holy Grail*, p 116.
7 Margaret Starbird, *The Woman with the Alabaster Jar*, p 121.
8 The end result of Margaret Starbird's research, originally begun to refute the 'heresy' of *The Holy Blood and the Holy Grail*, was the confirmation of its most 'blasphemous' theme. She then wrote *The Woman with the Alabaster Jar* to confirm that Jesus was married and had founded a dynasty.
9 Margaret Starbird, *op. cit.*, p 36.
10 Barbara Thiering, *Jesus the Man*, p 118.
11 Fida Hassnain, *op. cit.*, p 84.
12 Jewish men of all trades and professions were expected to marry and produce children by their early to mid-teens. Above all, teachers, rabbis and royal heirs had a particular sacred duty to do so.
13 The Gospel according to Matthew, ch 26 v 7, and Mark, ch 14 v 3.
14 Margaret Starbird, *op. cit.*, p 36.
15 *Ibid.*, p 31.
16 *Ibid.*, pp 53–4.
17 After the description of Thomas in the Gospel according to John, ch 20 v 25.
18 A N Wilson, *op. cit.*, p xi.
19 Margaret Starbird, *op. cit.*, p 57.
20 *Ibid.*, p 58.
21 *Ibid.*, pp 55–60.
22 Fida Hassnain, *op. cit.*, p 85.

23 Guidebook to Les Stes-Maries-de-la-Mer, p 3.
24 Margaret Starbird, *op. cit.*, pp 61–2.
25 See the work of Barbara Thiering on peshers in *Jesus the Man*.
26 Hugh Schonfield, *The Essene Odyssey*, p 7.
27 Margaret Starbird, *op. cit.*, pp 61–2.
28 The Book of Lamentations, ch 4 v 7–8.
29 Fr. Philippe Devcouvoux du Buysson, *The Sainte Baume*, p 5, and Fida Hassnain, *op. cit.*, p 85.
30 Fr. Philippe Devcouvoux du Buysson, *The Sainte Baume*, p 5.
31 *Ibid.*, p 6.
32 *Ibid.*, p 8; see also *Les Cahiers de Ste Baume*, vol. 9, *Vie de Ste Marie Madeleine*, text attributed to Raban Maur.
33 See the various guidebooks to the cathedral of Santiago of Compostela.
34 L S Lewis, *St Joseph of Arimathea at Glastonbury*, 1922, and E C Dobson, *Did Our Lord Visit Britain?*, 1860.
35 Paul Johnson, *A History of Christianity*, pp 40–1.
36 Laurence Gardner, *op. cit.*, p 1.

8 THE COUNCIL OF NICEA

1 Paul Johnson, *op. cit.*, pp 43–4 and 50.
2 Hubert Jedin (ed.), *History of the Church*, vol. I – From the Apostolic Community to Constantine, p 356.
3 *Ibid.*
4 Wallace-Murphy and Hopkins, *Rosslyn ...*, p 51.
5 Paul Johnson, *op. cit.*, pp 73–4.
6 *Ibid.*, pp 67, 76 and 82.
7 Wallace-Murphy and Hopkins, *op. cit.*, p 71.
8 L David Moore, *The Christian Conspiracy*, p 61.
9 Paul Johnson, *op. cit.*, p 67.
10 Paul Johnson, *op. cit.*, p 76, and David Christie-Murray, *A History of Heresy*, p 1.
11 L David Moore, *op. cit.*, p 62.
12 Paul Johnson, *op. cit.*, p 88.

13 L David Moore, *op. cit.*, p 310.
14 Robin Lane Fox, *Pagans and Christians*, p 655.
15 Eusebius, *Ecclesiastical History*, vol. x.
16 Paul Johnson, *op. cit.*, p 88.
17 L David Moore, *op. cit.*, p 62.
18 Robin Lane Fox, *op. cit.*, p 655.
19 L David Moore, *op. cit.*, p 63.
20 *Ibid.*
21 *Ibid.*
22 Paul Johnson, *op. cit.*, p 92.
23 Robin Lane Fox, *op. cit.*, p 656.
24 Paul Johnson, *op. cit.*, p 88.
25 L David Moore, *op. cit.*, p 310.
26 Nag Hammadi *Codex* VII, 3, cited in Laurence Gardner, *Bloodline of the Holy Grail*, p 99.
27 Laurence Gardner, *op. cit.*, p 159.
28 Declaration of the Council of Hagia Sofia.
29 Ravenscroft and Wallace–Murphy, *The Mark of the Beast*, pp 123–4.
30 Paul Johnson, *op. cit.*, p 117.
31 Betrand Russell, *The Wisdom of the West*.
32 Paul Johnson, *op. cit.*, pp 135–8.
33 R I Moore, *The Formation of a Persecuting Society*, p 12.
34 Paul Johnson, *op. cit.*, p 87.
35 R I Moore, *op. cit.*, pp 12–13.

9 THE RESURRECTION OF REX DEUS

1 Tim Wallace-Murphy, *The Templar Legacy and the Masonic Inheritance within Rosslyn Chapel*, p 44.
2 Tim Wallace-Murphy, *An Illustrated Guidebook to Rosslyn Chapel*, p 34.
3 *Ibid.*, p 31.
4 L–A de St Clair, *Histoire Généalogique de la Famille de St Clair.*
5 *Ibid.*

6   *Ibid.*
7   *Ibid.*
8   *Ibid.*
9   Stephen Runciman, *A History of the Crusades*, vol. I, pp 286–7.
10 Baigent, Leigh and Lincoln, *The Holy Blood and the Holy Grail*, p 85, and Stephen Runciman, *op. cit.*, vol. I, p 292.
11 Stephen Runciman, *op. cit.*, p 292.
12 L–A de St Clair, *op. cit.*
13 Baigent, Leigh and Lincoln, *op. cit.*, p 61.
14 *Recueil des Historiens*, vol. 15, p 162, no. 245.
15 Tim Wallace-Murphy, *The Templar Legacy ...*, p 18.
16 Michel Kluber, *Une Vie pour réforme l'Eglise*, in the journal *Bernard de Clairvaux, Editions de l'Argonante.*
17 *Ibid.*
18 Baigent, Leigh and Lincoln, *op. cit.*, p 59.
19 *Ibid.*
20 Michel Kluber, *op. cit.*
21 Baigent, Leigh and Lincoln, *op. cit.*, pp 36–8.
22 Knight and Lomas, *The Second Messiah*, p 21.
23 Ravenscroft and Wallace-Murphy, *The Mark of the Beast*, p 52.
24 Knight and Lomas, *op. cit.*, p 73.
25 Baigent, Leigh and Lincoln, *op. cit.*, p 59.
26 Graham Hancock, *The Sign and the Seal*, pp 94 and 99, see also Knight and Lomas, *The Second Messiah*, p 26, and Ravenscroft and Wallace-Murphy, *op. cit.*, p 52.
27 Knight and Lomas, *op. cit.*, p 26.
28 Graham Hancock, *op. cit.*, pp 49–51.
29 Ravenscroft and Wallace-Murphy, *op. cit.*, p 52.
30 HRH Prince Michael of Albany, *The Forgotten Monarchy of Scotland*, pp 60–1.
31 Knight and Lomas, *op. cit.*, p 70.
32 *Ibid.*, p 83.
33 Baigent, Leigh and Lincoln, *op. cit.*, p 57.
34 Wallace-Murphy and Hopkins, *Rosslyn ...*, p 97.
35 *Ibid.*, p 98.

10 ACTIONS AND BELIEFS OF THE KNIGHTS TEMPLAR

1   Papal Bull issued by Pope Innocent II in 1139.
2   Research provided by *The European Templar Heritage Research Network*.
3   Baigent, Leigh and Lincoln, *The Holy Blood and the Holy Grail*.
4   Tim Wallace-Murphy, *The Templar Legacy and the Masonic Inheritance within Rosslyn Chapel*, p 19.
5   Consensus document on Templar history compiled by a group of international scholars contributing to the European Templar Heritage Research Network who can be found at http/www.euroknightstemplar.org.
6   Baigent, Leigh and Lincoln, *op. cit.*, pp 42–3.
7   Tim Wallace-Murphy, *op. cit.*, pp 22–3.
8   Fred Gettings, *The Secret Zodiac*.
9   Louis Charpentier, *The Mysteries of Chartres Cathedral*.
10 *Le Règle de Saint Devoir de Dieu et de la Croisade*.
11 Tim Wallace-Murphy, *op. cit.*, p 21.
12 Information kindly supplied from the archives of the *Centre d'Etudes et de Recherches Templières*.
13 *Ibid.*
14 Wallace-Murphy and Hopkins, *Rosslyn ...*, p 100.
15 See Note 5.
16 *Ibid.*
17 Louis Charpentier, *op. cit.*
18 *Ibid.*, and see also The Guidebook to Chartres Cathedral.
19 Ravenscroft and Wallace-Murphy, *The Mark of the Beast*, p 73.
20 Ean Begg, *The Cult of the Black Madonna*, p 103.
21 *Ibid.*
22 Graham Hancock, *The Sign and the Seal*, p 334.
23 The Guidebook to Amiens Cathedral.
24 Pope Pius IX, *The Allocution against the Freemasons*.
25 Magnus Eliphas Levi, *Histoire de la Magie*, Paris 1860.
26 *Ibid.* – A E Waite, trans.
27 *Ibid.* – Albert Pike, trans.
28 Knight and Lomas, *The Hiram Key*, p 269.

29 Graham Hancock, *op. cit.*, p 333.
30 HRH Prince Michael of Albany, *The Forgotten Monarchy of Scotland*, p 61.
31 Robert Graves in his Introduction to Idries Shah's *The Sufis*.
32 G. Quespel, Gnosticism, published in *Man, Myth and Magic*, 40, p 115.
33 Wallace-Murphy and Hopkins, *op. cit.*, p 101.

11 MYTHS AND LEGENDS OF THE MIDDLE AGES

1   Knight and Lomas, *The Hiram Key*, p 111–12.
2   Malcolm Godwin, *The Holy Grail*, p 14.
3   *Ibid.*, p 16.
4   Émile Mâle, *Notre Dame de Chartres*, p 141.
5   Malcolm Godwin, *op. cit.*, p 12.
6   Knight and Lomas, *The Second Messiah*, p 115.
7   *Ibid.*
8   Malcolm Godwin, *op. cit.*, p 18.
9   Andrew Sinclair, *The Discovery of the Grail*, p 27.
10 *Ibid.*, pp 27–8.
11 Knight and Lomas, *The Second Messiah*, p 114.
12 Malcolm Godwin, *op. cit.*, p 6.
13 Andrew Sinclair, *op. cit.*, p 49.
14 Joseph Campbell and Bill Moyers, *The Power of Myth*, pp 197–200.
15 Malcolm Godwin, *op. cit.*, pp 76–7.
16 The Gospel of Thomas from *The Nag Hammadi Library*, John Robinson (ed.).
17 Joseph Campbell and Bill Moyers, *op. cit.*, pp 197–200.
18 Malcolm Godwin, *op. cit.*, p 54.
19 Baigent, Leigh and Lincoln, *The Holy Blood* ..., pp 262–8.
20 Joseph Campbell and Bill Moyers, *op. cit.*, p 163.
21 *Ibid.*
22 Cited in Ted Roszak's *Where the Wasteland Ends*, p 154.
23 Cited in Fritjof Capra's *The Turning Point*, p 410.

24 Joseph Campbell and Bill Moyers, *op. cit.*, p 5.
25 Malcolm Godwin, *op. cit.*, p 8.
26 Andrew Sinclair, *op. cit.*, p 15.
27 N Chadwick, *The Celts*.
28 Andrew Sinclair, *op. cit.*, pp 22–3.
29 T W Rolleson, *Myths of the Celtic Race*.
30 Knight and Lomas, *The Second Messiah*, pp 105–8.
31 *Ibid.*, p 108.
32 *Ibid.*, p 109.
33 *Ibid.*, pp 109 and 111.
34 *Ibid.*, p 115.
35 *Ibid.*
36 Malcolm Godwin, *op. cit.*, p 80.
37 Knight and Lomas, *The Second Messiah*, pp 114–15.
38 Malcolm Godwin, *op. cit.*, p 234.
39 *Ibid.*, p 236.
40 *Ibid.*, p 337.
41 *Ibid.*, p 338.
42 *Ibid.*, p 339.

12 THE ALBIGENSIAN CRUSADE

1 Michèle Aué, *The Cathars*, p 3.
2 Yuri Stoyanov, *The Hidden Tradition in Europe*, p 159.
3 Michael Costen, *The Cathars and the Albigensian Crusade*, pp 32–4.
4 *Ibid.*, pp 37–8.
5 *Ibid.*
6 Yuri Stoyanov, *op. cit.*, p159.
7 Michael Costen, *op. cit.*, p 59.
8 Simon de Vries, *Cathars, Country Customs and Castles*, p 2.
9 Yuri Stoyanov, *op. cit.*, p 160.
10 Arthur Guirdham, *The Great Heresy*, p 15, and Michèle Aué, *Cathar Country*, p 13.
11 Guébin et Moisoineuve, *Histoire Albigeoise de Pierre des Vaux-de-Cerny*.

12 Haim Beinhart, *Atlas of Medieval Jewish History*, p 53, and Yuri Stoyanov, *op. cit.*, p 160.

13 Arthur Guirdham, *op. cit.*, p 16.

14 Michèle Aué, *The Cathars*, p 3.

15 Yuri Stoyanov, *op. cit.*, p 158.

16 Arthur Guirdham, *op. cit.*, pp 35–6.

17 *Ibid.*, p 38.

18 Jesus is reported as saying, in *The Gospel of Thomas*, 'He who drinks from my mouth, will speak as I speak and do as I do' (Nag Hammadi Library).

19 Michael Costen, *op. cit.*, pp 66–7.

20 Arthur Guirdham, *op. cit.*, pp 42 and 45.

21 Yuri Stoyanov, *op. cit.*, p 162, and Michèle Aué, *Cathar Country*, p 10.

22 Arthur Guirdham, *op. cit.*, p 19 and Yuri Stoyanov, *op. cit.*, p 164.

23 Arthur Guirdham, *op. cit.*, p 18.

24 *Ibid.*

25 *Ibid.*, pp 45–7.

26 Picknett and Prince, *The Templar Revelation*, p 88.

27 Yuri Stoyanov, *op. cit.*, p 156.

28 St Bernard of Clairvaux's letter to Alphonse Jordan cited in Wakefield and Evans, *Heresies of the Middle Ages*, pp 122–4.

29 Yuri Stoyanov, *op. cit.*, p 156.

30 Wakefield and Evans, *op. cit.*, pp 140–1.

31 Yuri Stoyanov, *op. cit.*, p 156.

32 Michael Costen, *op. cit.*, p 58.

33 Simon de Vries, *Cathars, Country Customs and Castles*, p 2.

34 Michael Costen, *op. cit.*, p 65.

35 *Ibid.*, p 66.

36 Georges Serrus, *The Land of the Cathars*, p 35.

37 A theory seemingly confirmed by the Templar scholar, Guy Jordan, who claimed that the Templars regarded the reliquary containing the head of John the Baptist as 'la vraie tête Baphometique' and consulted it by means of necromancy. See Wallace-Murphy and Hopkins, Rosslyn ... , p 177.

38 Michael Costen, *op. cit.*, pp 112–14.

39 *Ibid.*, p 114.
40 Georges Serrus, *op. cit.*, p 15.
41 Michèle Aué, *Cathar Country*, p 15, and Arthur Guirdham, *op. cit.*, p 55.
42 Yuri Stoyanov, *op. cit.*, p 173.
43 Arthur Guirdham, *op. cit.*, p 55.
44 Michael Costen, *op. cit.*, p 123.
45 Caesarius of Heisterbach, vol. II, pp 296–8.
46 Guébin et Moisoineuve, *op. cit.*
47 Michael Costen, *op. cit.*, p 125.
48 Georges Serrus, *op. cit.*, p 20.
49 Michael Costen, *op. cit.*, p 128.
50 Michèle Aué, *The Cathars*, p 11.
51 Yuri Stoyanov, *op. cit.*, p 174.
52 Arthur Guirdham, *op. cit.*, p 63.
53 *Ibid.*, p 64, and Michael Costen, *op. cit.*, p 132.
54 Michèle Aué, *op. cit.*, p 12.
55 Georges Serrus, *op. cit.*, p 26, Michael Costen, *op. cit.*, p 140, and Michèle Aué, Cathar Country, p 27.
56 Michael Costen, *op. cit.*, p 151.
57 Arthur Guirdham, *op. cit.*, p 69.
58 Michael Costen, *op. cit.*, p 160.
59 Arthur Guirdham, *op. cit.*, p 83.
60 Michael Costen, *op. cit.*, p 160.
61 Arthur Guirdham, *op. cit.*, p 89.
62 Raimonde Reznikov, *Cathares et Templiers.*
63 Information supplied by Nicole Dawe of the Abraxas Templar Research group
64 Picknett and Prince, *op. cit.*, p 104.
65 See Note 63.
66 Yuri Stoyanov, *op. cit.*, p 178.
67 *Ibid.*, pp 178–84.
68 Michael Costen, *op. cit.*, pp 169–74.
69 Arthur Guirdham, *op. cit.*, p 89.

13 THE END OF THE TEMPLARS?

1   R I Moore, *The Formation of a Persecuting Society*, p 4.
2   Malcolm Barber, *The Trial of the Templars*, pp 33 and 46.
3   Baigent and Leigh, *The Dead Sea Scrolls Deception*, pp 185–93.
4   Malcolm Barber, *op. cit.*, p 15.
5   Knight and Lomas, *The Second Messiah*, p 120.
6   Baigent, Leigh and Lincoln, *The Holy Blood and the Holy Grail*, pp 45–6.
7   Knight and Lomas, *op. cit.*, p 122.
8   *Ibid.*, pp 127–8.
9   *Ibid.*, p 133.
10 Noel Currer-Briggs, *The Shroud and the Grail*, p 95.
11 F W Bussell, *Religious Thought and Heresy in the Middle Ages*.
12 Noel Currer-Briggs, *op. cit.*, p 96.
13 Baigent, Leigh and Lincoln, *op. cit.*, p 46.
14 Lizerand, *Le Dossier de l'Affaire des Templiers*, p 16.
15 Malcolm Barber, *op. cit.*, p 45.
16 *Ibid.*, p 47.
17 *Ibid.*, p 56.
18 *Ibid.*, p 57.
19 Papal Bull *Pastoralis praeminentiae*.
20 Malcolm Barber, *op. cit.*, pp 193–5.
21 *Ibid.*, p 200.
22 Tim Wallace-Murphy, *The Templar Legacy and the Masonic Inheritance within Rosslyn Chapel*, p 22.
23 *Ibid.*, p 21.
24 Knight and Lomas, *op. cit.*, p 174.
25 Anonymous author, *Secret Societies of the Middle Ages*.
26 Ravenscroft and Wallace-Murphy, *The Mark of the Beast*, p 53.
27 Tim Wallace-Murphy, *op. cit.*, p 22.
28 John Robinson, *Born in Blood*, p 137.
29 Malcolm Barber, *op. cit.*, pp 178–93.
30 Louis Charpentier, *The Mysteries of Chartres*.
31 Guidebook to Amiens Cathedral.

32 Reported by Baigent, Leigh and Lincoln.
33 Tim Wallace-Murphy, *An Illustrated Guidebook to Rosslyn Chapel*.
34 Knight and Lomas, *The Second Messiah*, pp 173–4.
35 HRH Prince Michael of Albany, *The Forgotten Monarchy of Scotland*, pp 65 and 150.
36 Tim Wallace-Murphy, *The Templar Legacy and the Masonic Inheritance within Rosslyn Chapel*.
37 J-A Durbec, *Les Templiers dans les Alpes-Maritimes*, published in the journal *Nice Historique*, Jan/Feb 1938, pp 4–6.

14 THE CONTROVERSIAL SHROUD OF TURIN

1 *Memorandum of P D'Arcis*, Herbert Thurston, SJ, trans.
2 Robert de Clari, *The Conquest of Constantinople*, E H Neal, trans.
3 David Sox, *The File on the Shroud*, p 39.
4 Noel Currer-Briggs, *The Shroud and the Grail*, p 106.
5 Ian Wilson, *Blood on the Shroud*, p 117.
6 Pope Sixtus IV, *de Sanguine Christi*.
7 Ian Wilson, *The Turin Shroud*, p 190.
8 Ian Wilson, *Blood on the Shroud*, pp 64–7.
9 Ian Wilson, *The Turin Shroud*, p 193.
10 *Ibid.*
11 David Sox, *op. cit.*, p 17.
12 Ian Wilson, *The Turin Shroud*, pp 14–15.
13 *Ibid.*, pp 19–20.
14 David Sox, *op. cit.*, p 66.
15 Ian Wilson, *The Turin Shroud*, p 21.
16 Giovanni Judica-Cordiglia, *La Sidone*, 1961.
17 Ian Wilson, *The Turin Shroud*, p 22.
18 Robert K Wilcox, *Shroud*, p 136.
19 Ian Wilson, *The Turin Shroud*, p 23.
20 *Ibid.*, p 24.
21 *Ibid.*, pp 24–5.
22 *Ibid.*, pp 25–6.
23 *Ibid.*, pp 26–7.

24 *Ibid.*, p 29.

25 *Ibid.*, p 30.

26 Fr Roland de Vaux, *Fouille au Khirbet Qumran*, published in *Revue Biblique*, vol. 60 (1953), p 102 and plate V.

27 Kert Berna, a German author who claims that the shroud 'proves' that Jesus did not die on the Cross.

28 Ian Wilson, *The Turin Shroud*, pp 52–4.

29 *Ibid.*, pp 60–2.

30 *Ibid.*, p 62.

31 *Ibid.*, pp 196–7.

32 *Ibid.*, p 197.

33 David Sox, *op. cit.*, p 102.

34 Ian Wilson, *The Turin Shroud*, p 202.

35 Ian Wilson, *Blood on the Shroud*, p 185.

36 *Ibid.*, p 8.

37 *Ibid.*, p 9.

38 Kersten and Gruber, *The Jesus Conspiracy*.

39 Ian Wilson, *The Turin Shroud*, p 8.

40 Ian Wilson, *Blood on the Shroud*, pp 225–7.

41 Ian Wilson, *The Turin Shroud*, p 8.

42 L A Garza-Valdes, *The DNA of God?* pp 32–7.

43 Ian Wilson, *Blood on the Shroud*, p 226.

44 L A Garza-Valdes, *op. cit.*, pp 16–19.

45 *Ibid.*, p 69.

46 *Ibid.*, p 26.

47 Pierluigi Bauma-Bollone, 'Identification of the Group of the Traces of Human Blood found on the Shroud', *Shroud Spectrum International*, 6, March 83, pp 3–6.

48 Ian Wilson, *Blood on the Shroud*, p 88.

49 L A Garza-Valdes, *op. cit.*, p 39.

50 *Ibid.*, p 87.

15 THE RELIGIOUS BELIEFS OF REX DEUS

1   *The Allocution against Freemasons* by Pope Pius IX.
2   Magnus Eliphas Levi, *Histoire de la Magie*, A E Waite, trans.
3   Ean Begg, *The Cult of the Black Madonna.*
4   The Acts of the Apostles, ch 2 v 46.
5   The Nag Hammadi Library.
6   The Book of Revelation, ch 6 vs 5, 7, 9 and 12; ch 7, v 2; ch 8 v 1; ch 9 v 4; ch 20 v 3.
7   Genesis, ch 14 vs 18–20.
8   Genesis, ch 12 vs 16–20.
9   *Epiphanus-Haeres*, lxxxviii.
10 Baigent, Leigh and Lincoln, *The Holy Blood and the Holy Grail*, p 52.
11 Ahmed Osman, *Moses, Pharaoh of Egypt.*
12 The Gospel according to Matthew, ch 22 vs 36–40.
13 Ute Ranke-Heinemann, *Putting Away Childish Things*, p 17.
14 Paul Johnson, *A History of Christianity*, p 41.
15 Louis Charpentier, *The Mysteries of Chartres Cathedral.*
16 *Ibid.*
17 Tim Wallace-Murphy, *An Illustrated Guidebook to Rosslyn Chapel*, p 3.
18 Tim Wallace–Murphy, *The Templar Legacy and the Masonic Inheritance within Rosslyn Chapel*, p 21.
19 Ravenscroft and Wallace–Murphy, *The Mark of the Beast.*

16 THE SHADOWY WORLD OF EARLY FREEMASONRY

1   Louis Charpentier, *The Mysteries of Chartres Cathedral.*
2   *Ibid.*
3   Tim Wallace-Murphy, *The Templar Legacy and the Masonic Inheritance within Rosslyn Chapel*, p 22.
4   HRH Prince Michael of Albany, *The Forgotten Monarchy of Scotland*, pp 64–5.
5   Tim Wallace-Murphy, *An Illustrated Guidebook to Rosslyn Chapel*, p 3.

6   The Earl of Caithness, the present hereditary leader of the Clan Sinclair, was the minister for shipping in the Conservative Government at the time of the Brea disaster.
7   HRH Prince Michael of Albany, *op. cit.*, p 120; *see also* Knight and Lomas, *The Hiram Key*.
8   HRH Prince Michael of Albany, *op. cit.*, p 120.
9   Masonic archives in Freemasons Hall, Edinburgh.
10 Knight and Lomas, *The Second Messiah*, p 53.
11 HRH Prince Michael of Albany, *op. cit.*, pp 8–9.
12 Tim Wallace-Murphy, *The Templar Legacy and the Masonic Inheritance within Rosslyn Chapel*, p 31.
13 *Ibid.*, p 31.
14 Knight and Lomas, *The Second Messiah*, p 177.
15 HRH Prince Michael of Albany, *op. cit.*, p 199.
16 Knight and Lomas, *The Second Messiah*, p 197.
17 *Ibid.*, p 197.
18 *Ibid.*, pp 200–2.
19 *Ibid.*, p 203.
20 *Ibid.*, p 204.
21 Wallace-Murphy and Hopkins, *Rosslyn ...*, p 127.
22 Tim Wallace-Murphy, *An Illustrated Guidebook to Rosslyn Chapel*, p 17.
23 Knight and Lomas, *The Second Messiah*, p 207.
24 *Ibid.*, pp 207–9.
25 *Ibid.*, p 209.
26 See Tim Wallace-Murphy, *An Illustrated Guidebook to Rosslyn Chapel* and *The Templar Legacy and Masonic Inheritance within Rosslyn Chapel*.

17 THE CHIVALRIC ORDERS

1   Michael Baigent and Richard Leigh, *The Temple and the Lodge*, p 135.
2   *Ibid.*, p 148.
3   *Ibid.* p 149.
4   *Ibid.*, pp 149–50.

5   HRH Prince Michael of Albany, *The Forgotten Monarchy of Scotland*, p 125.
6   Michael Baigent and Richard Leigh, *op. cit.*, p 150.
7   *Ibid.*, pp 151–2.
8   *Ibid.*, p 152.
9   *Ibid.*, p 151.
10 One livre tournois was the same value as two gold écus. Each écu was 8 g weight of fine gold. In 1999 18ct gold was selling at £4 per gram, therefore one livre tournois was the equivalent of £64 sterling, or approximately 100 US dollars. Therefore 2,000 livres tournois is equivalent to £128,000 or 200,000 dollars.
11 HRH Prince Michael of Albany, *op. cit.*, p 125.
12 Michael Baigent and Richard Leigh, *op. cit.*, p 152.
13 Forbes-Leith, *The Scots Men-at-Arms and Life Guards in France*, vol. I, pp 101–2.
14 *Ibid.*
15 Michael Baigent and Richard Leigh, *op. cit.*, p 155.
16 *Ibid.*
17 *Ibid.*, p 156.
18 Wallace-Murphy and Hopkins, *Rosslyn ...*, p 7.
19 Tim Wallace-Murphy, *An Illustrated Guidebook to Rosslyn Chapel*, p 3.
20 *Ibid.*, pp 13–14.
21 *Ibid.*, p 6.
22 Knight and Lomas, *The Hiram Key*, p 307.
23 Wallace-Murphy and Hopkins, *op. cit.*, pp 202–3.
24 *Ibid.*, p 7.
25 HRH Prince Michael of Albany, *op. cit.*, p 102.
26 Michael Foss, *Chivalry*, p 189.
27 *Ibid.*
28 Laurence Gardner, *Genesis of the Grail Kings*, p 225.
29 Baigent, Leigh and Lincoln, *The Holy Blood ...*, p 106.
30 Ian Wilson, *Blood on the Shroud*, p 117.
31 Tim Wallace-Murphy, *The Templar Legacy and the Masonic Inheritance within Rosslyn Chapel*, p 21.
32 *Ibid.*, pp 24–5.

18 ACTION IS THE MAGIC WORD

1 Wallace-Murphy and Hopkins, *Rosslyn ...*, p 123.

2 *Ibid.*; see also HRH Prince Michael of Albany, *The Forgotten Monarchy of Scotland.*

3 Knight and Lomas, *The Second Messiah*, p 53.

4 Laurence Gardner, *Bloodline of the Holy Grail*, p 322.

5 *Ibid.*, pp 322–3.

6 Tim Wallace-Murphy, *The Templar Legacy and the Masonic Inheritance within Rosslyn Chapel*, p 31.

7 Knight and Lomas, *The Second Messiah*, p 48.

8 HRH Prince Michael of Albany, *op. cit.*, pp 122 ff.

9 Baigent and Leigh, *The Temple and the Lodge*, p 217.

10 Laurence Gardner, *op. cit.*, p 324.

11 Baigent and Leigh, *op. cit.*, p 261.

12 *Ibid.*, p 262.

13 A E Waite, *A New Encyclopedia of Freemasonry*, pp 314–15, and Baigent and Leigh, *op. cit.*, p 255.

14 A. E. Waite, *op. cit.*, p 314.

15 Gould, *The History of Freemasonry*, vol. V, p 88.

16 *Ibid.*

17 Baigent and Leigh, *op. cit.*, p 263.

18 *Ibid.*, p 259.

19 *Ibid.*, p 265.

20 *Ibid.*, p 267.

21 *Ibid.*, p 268.

22 Knight and Lomas, *The Second Messiah*, p 194.

23 Baigent and Leigh, *op. cit.*, p 114.

24 HRH Prince Michael of Albany, *op. cit.*, p 156.

25 *Ibid.*, p 306.

19 REX DEUS AND THE ESOTERIC REVIVAL

1 Baigent and Leigh, *The Temple and the Lodge*, p 351.
2 *Ibid.*, pp 351–2.
3 *Ibid.*, p 261.
4 *Ibid.*, p 262.
5 Colin Wilson, *The Occult*, pp 430–40.
6 Baigent, Leigh and Lincoln, *The Holy Blood ...*, pp 142–3.
7 eg Henry Lincoln, *The Holy Place*.
8 Stella Pates, scholar of medieval church history, who resides in Ottery-St-Mary, Devon.
9 Cited in *The Encyclopaedia of Islam*.
10 See the epilogue by Norman Birks in *The Treasure of Montségur*.
11 *Ibid.*
12 Published by Element Books, Shaftesbury.
13 Published by Element Books, Shaftesbury.

20 REX DEUS – THE EVIDENCE

1 *See* The Gospel of Mary.
2 Published by Element Books, Shaftesbury.
3 Margaret Starbird, *The Woman with the Alabaster Jar*.
4 Wallace-Murphy and Hopkins, *Rosslyn ...*, pp 96–8.
5 See the ETHRN (European Templar Heritage Research Network) Consensus Document, and their website, www.euroknightstemplar.org
6 Wallace-Murphy and Hopkins, *op. cit.*, p 101.
7 *The Allocution against Freemasons* by Pope Pius IX.
8 Louis Charpentier, *The Mysteries of Chartres Cathedral*.
9 Raban Maar, or Maur.
10 Michael Foss, *Chivalry*, p 189.
11 Ravenscroft and Wallace-Murphy, *The Mask of the Beast*, p 52.
12 Knight and Lomas, *The Second Messiah*, p 111.

13 See Knight and Lomas, *The Second Messiah* and *The Hiram Key*; Baigent and Leigh, *op. cit.*; HRH Prince Michael of Albany, *Forgotten Monarchy*; and Laurence Gardner, *Bloodline of the Holy Grail*.

14 Baigent and Leigh, *op. cit.*, p 148–57.

15 Laurence Gardner, *op. cit.*; HRH Prince Michael of Albany, *op. cit.*, and Baigent and Leigh, *op. cit.*

16 Wallace-Murphy and Hopkins, *op. cit.*, and Baigent, Leigh and Lincoln, *op. cit.*

17 Graham Hancock, *The Sign and the Seal*, p 177.

18 *Ibid.*, p 181.

19 *Ibid.*, p 182.

20 Kenneth Mackenzie, *Royal Masonic Cyclopedia*, pp 200–2.

21 Graham Hancock, *op. cit.*, p 182.

22 *Ibid.*, p 183.

23 See Trevor Ravenscroft, *The Spear of Destiny*.

24 Tim Wallace-Murphy, *The Templar Legacy and the Masonic Inheritance within Rosslyn Chapel*, p 39.

25 Tim Wallace-Murphy, *An Illustrated Guidebook to Rosslyn Chapel*, p 17.

26 Laurence Gardner, *op. cit.*, and HRH Prince Michael of Albany, *op. cit.*

21 AT THE DAWN OF THE NEW MILLENNIUM

1 Colin Wilson, *The Occult*, pp 430–40.

2 Trevor Ravenscroft, *The Spear of Destiny*.

3 Guy Jourdan, the Provençal scholar and one-time press attaché to the French Ministry of Defence.

4 See Dr John Robinson's *Honest to God*.

5 Bernard Levin, journalist and author.

6 See Theodore Rozak's *Where the Wasteland Ends*.

7 Elyn Aviva, *Following the Milky Way: a Pilgrimage across Spain*.

8 Epilogue to Norman Birks, *The Treasure of Montségur*.

APPENDIX

Maps and Charts

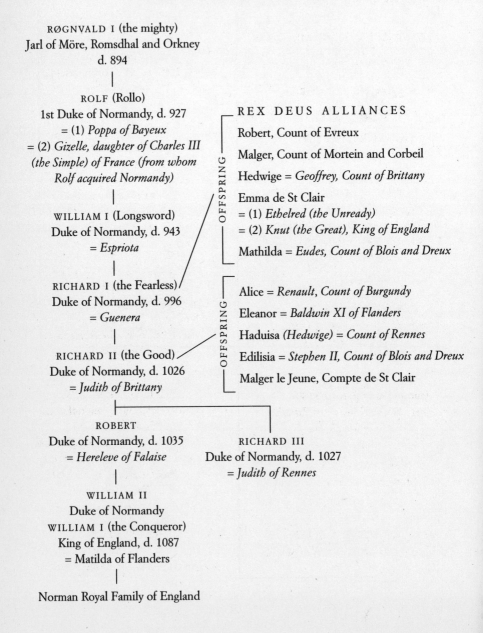

RØGNVALD I (the mighty)
Jarl of Möre, Romsdhal and Orkney
d. 894

ROLF (Rollo)
1st Duke of Normandy, d. 927
= (1) *Poppa of Bayeux*
= (2) *Gizelle, daughter of Charles III*
(the Simple) of France (from whom
Rolf acquired Normandy)

WILLIAM I (Longsword)
Duke of Normandy, d. 943
= *Espriota*

RICHARD I (the Fearless)
Duke of Normandy, d. 996
= *Guenera*

RICHARD II (the Good)
Duke of Normandy, d. 1026
= *Judith of Brittany*

OFFSPRING

REX DEUS ALLIANCES

Robert, Count of Evreux

Malger, Count of Mortein and Corbeil

Hedwige = *Geoffrey, Count of Brittany*

Emma de St Clair
= (1) *Ethelred (the Unready)*
= (2) *Knut (the Great), King of England*

Mathilda = *Eudes, Count of Blois and Dreux*

OFFSPRING

Alice = *Renault, Count of Burgundy*

Eleanor = *Baldwin XI of Flanders*

Haduisa (Hedwige) = *Count of Rennes*

Edilisia = *Stephen II, Count of Blois and Dreux*

Malger le Jeune, Compte de St Clair

ROBERT
Duke of Normandy, d. 1035
= *Hereleve of Falaise*

RICHARD III
Duke of Normandy, d. 1027
= *Judith of Rennes*

WILLIAM II
Duke of Normandy
WILLIAM I (the Conqueror)
King of England, d. 1087
= Matilda of Flanders

Norman Royal Family of England

MALGER LE JEUNE
Compte de St Clair

|

WALDERNE DE ST CLAIR
d. 1047

|

WILLIAM DE ST CLAIR
(the Seemly)
1st Baron of Roslin
(Granted Barony, 1057)
= *Dorothy of Raby*

|

HENRI DE ST CLAIR
Baron of Roslin
(accompanied Godefroi de Bouillon
on the 1st Crusade, 1069)
= *Rosebelle Forteith*

|

HENRI DE ST CLAIR
Scottish Privy Councillor
Ambassador to England, 1156
= *Margaret Gratney*

|

WILLIAM DE ST CLAIR
(succeeded to Barony, 1180)
= *Agnes Dunbar, daughter of Patrick,*
Earl of March

|

HENRI DE ST CLAIR
= *Katherine, daughter of*
Earl of Strathearn

|

HENRI DE ST CLAIR d. 1270
= *Margaret, daughter of Earl of Mar*

WILLIAM DE ST CLAIR
Ambassador to France
= Matilda, daughter of Magnus,
Jarl of Orkney

|

HENRI DE ST CLAIR
(succeeded to Barony, 1297.
Commanded Knights Templar at
Bannockburn, 1314. Signed
Declaration of Scottish
Independence, 1320)
= (1) *Alicia de Fenton*

|

WILLIAM DE ST CLAIR
(died in Spain, 1330, with his
brother John Sir James Douglas and
Sir Robert Logan, while taking the
heart of Robert the Bruce to the
Holy Land)

|

WILLIAM DE ST CLAIR
(succeeded his Grandfather to
Barony c. 1331–35.
Served with Teutonic Knights and
was killed in Lithuania, 1358.)
= *Isabel, daughter of Malise II,*
Jarl of Orkney

|

HENRI ST CLAIR
1st St Clair Earl of Orkney d. 1400
(said to have discovered America)

3 ANCESTRY OF MARGUERITE DE CHARNEY, THE LAST DE CHARNEY TO OWN THE TURIN SHROUD, SHOWING RELATIONSHIP WITH TEMPLAR MARTYR GEOFFROI DE CHARNEY

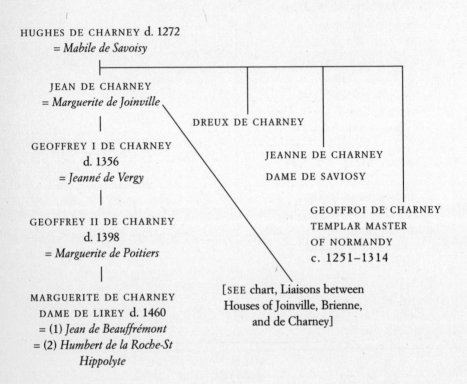

HUGHES DE CHARNEY d. 1272
= *Mabile de Savoisy*

JEAN DE CHARNEY
= *Marguerite de Joinville*

DREUX DE CHARNEY

GEOFFREY I DE CHARNEY
d. 1356
= *Jeanné de Vergy*

JEANNE DE CHARNEY

DAME DE SAVIOSY

GEOFFREY II DE CHARNEY
d. 1398
= *Marguerite de Poitiers*

GEOFFROI DE CHARNEY
TEMPLAR MASTER
OF NORMANDY
c. 1251–1314

MARGUERITE DE CHARNEY
DAME DE LIREY d. 1460
= (1) *Jean de Beauffrémont*
= (2) *Humbert de la Roche-St
Hippolyte*

[SEE chart, Liaisons between
Houses of Joinville, Brienne,
and de Charney]

4 LIAISONS BETWEEN HOUSES OF JOINVILLE, BRIENNE AND DE CHARNEY

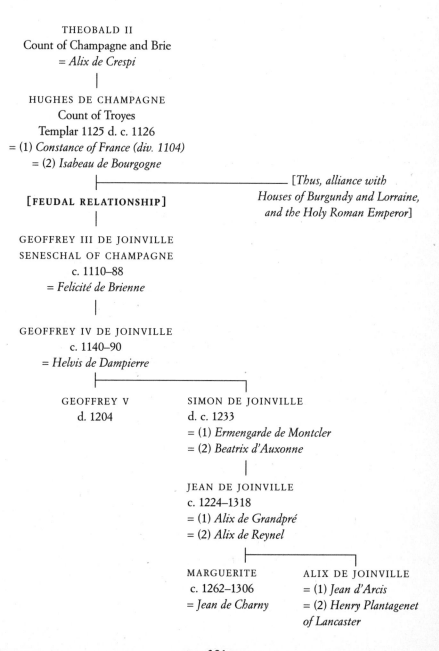

THEOBALD II
Count of Champagne and Brie
= *Alix de Crespi*

HUGHES DE CHAMPAGNE
Count of Troyes
Templar 1125 d. c. 1126
= (1) *Constance of France (div. 1104)*
= (2) *Isabeau de Bourgogne*

[FEUDAL RELATIONSHIP]

[Thus, alliance with Houses of Burgundy and Lorraine, and the Holy Roman Emperor]

GEOFFREY III DE JOINVILLE
SENESCHAL OF CHAMPAGNE
c. 1110–88
= *Felicité de Brienne*

GEOFFREY IV DE JOINVILLE
c. 1140–90
= *Helvis de Dampierre*

GEOFFREY V
d. 1204

SIMON DE JOINVILLE
d. c. 1233
= (1) *Ermengarde de Montcler*
= (2) *Beatrix d'Auxonne*

JEAN DE JOINVILLE
c. 1224–1318
= (1) *Alix de Grandpré*
= (2) *Alix de Reynel*

MARGUERITE
c. 1262–1306
= *Jean de Charny*

ALIX DE JOINVILLE
= (1) *Jean d'Arcis*
= (2) *Henry Plantagenet of Lancaster*

AREAS OF REX DEUS INFLUENCE IN EUROPE:
11TH–15TH CENTURIES

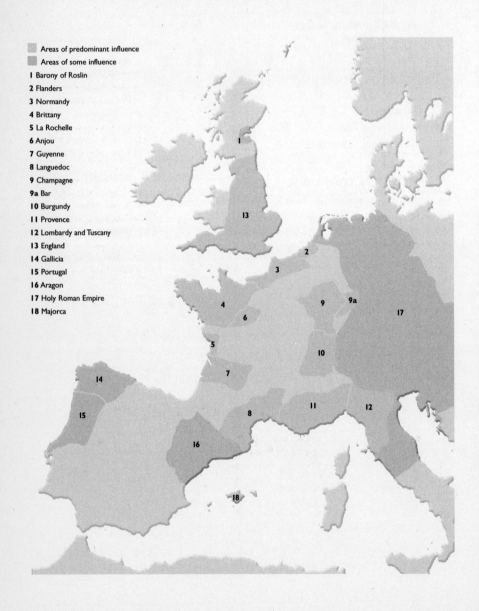

Areas of predominant influence
Areas of some influence
1 Barony of Roslin
2 Flanders
3 Normandy
4 Brittany
5 La Rochelle
6 Anjou
7 Guyenne
8 Languedoc
9 Champagne
9a Bar
10 Burgundy
11 Provence
12 Lombardy and Tuscany
13 England
14 Gallicia
15 Portugal
16 Aragon
17 Holy Roman Empire
18 Majorca

PRINCIPAL TEMPLAR PROPERTIES FROM THE
ORDER'S FOUNDATION PRIOR TO 1150

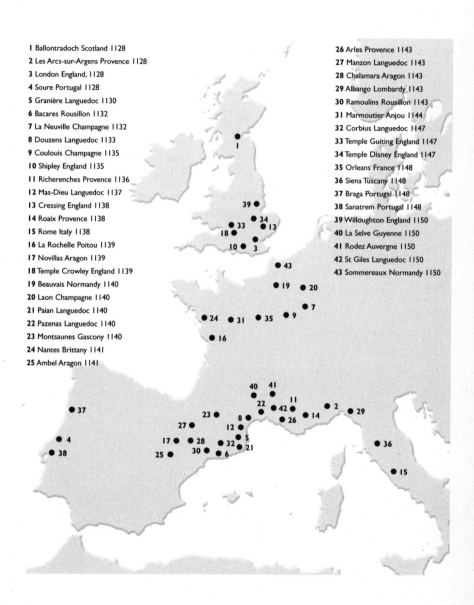

1 Ballontradoch Scotland 1128
2 Les Arcs-sur-Argens Provence 1128
3 London England, 1128
4 Soure Portugal 1128
5 Granière Languedoc 1130
6 Bacares Rousillon 1132
7 La Neuville Champagne 1132
8 Douzens Languedoc 1133
9 Coulouis Champagne 1135
10 Shipley England 1135
11 Richerenches Provence 1136
12 Mas-Dieu Languedoc 1137
13 Cressing England 1138
14 Roaix Provence 1138
15 Rome Italy 1138
16 La Rochelle Poitou 1139
17 Novillas Aragon 1139
18 Temple Crowley England 1139
19 Beauvais Normandy 1140
20 Laon Champagne 1140
21 Paian Languedoc 1140
22 Pazenas Languedoc 1140
23 Montsaunes Gascony 1140
24 Nantes Brittany 1141
25 Ambel Aragon 1141

26 Arles Provence 1143
27 Manzon Languedoc 1143
28 Chalamara Aragon 1143
29 Albango Lombardy 1143
30 Ramoulins Rousillon 1143
31 Marmoutier Anjou 1144
32 Corbius Languedoc 1147
33 Temple Guiting England 1147
34 Temple Disney England 1147
35 Orleans France 1148
36 Siena Tuscany 1148
37 Braga Portugal 1148
38 Sanatrem Portugal 1148
39 Willoughton England 1150
40 La Selve Guyenne 1150
41 Rodez Auvergne 1150
42 St Giles Languedoc 1150
43 Sommereaux Normandy 1150

Bibliography

SACRED TEXTS AND COMMENTARIES ON THE LIFE AND TIMES OF JESUS

Allegro, John, *The Dead Sea Scrolls*, Penguin, 1964.

The Authorized Version Of The Bible.

Baigent, M, and Leigh, R, *The Dead Sea Scrolls Deception*, Corgi, 1992.

Cannon, Dolores, *Jesus and the Essenes*, Gateway Books, 1992.

Crossan, John Dominic, *Jesus – a Revolutionary Biography*, Harper Collins, 1994.

Doresse, J, *The Secret Books of the Egyptian Gnostics*, Librarie Plon, 1958.

Eisenman, R, *The Dead Sea Scrolls and the First Christians,* Element, 1996.

Eisenman, R, *James the Brother of Jesus*, Faber & Faber, 1997.

Eisenman, R and Wise, M, *The Dead Sea Scrolls Uncovered*, Element, 1992.

Fox, R L, *The Unauthorised Version*, Penguin, 1992.

Golb, Norman, *Who Wrote The Dead Sea Scrolls?* Simon and Schuster, 1996.

Gruber, Elmer R and Kersten, Holger, *The Original Jesus*, Element, 1995.

Hassnain, Prof. Fida, *A Search for the Historical Jesus*, Gateway Books, 1994.

Josephus, *The Antiquities of the Jews* and *The Wars of the Jews*, Nimmo, 1869.

Josephus, *The Lost Books of the Bible*, Gramercy Books, 1979.

The Lost Gospel according to St Peter.

Robinson, James M (ed.) *The Nag Hammadi Library*, HarperCollins, 1990.

The Tanakh, Jewish Publications Society.

Thiering, Barbara, *Jesus the Man*, Corgi, 1992.

Wilson, A N, *Jesus*, HarperCollins, 1993.

Wilson, E, *The Scrolls from the Dead Sea*, W H Allen, 1955.

SUGGESTED FURTHER READING

Addison, Charles G, *The History of The Knights Templar*, Black Books, 1995.

Allen, Grant, *The Evolution Of The Idea Of God*, Watts, 1931.

Ambelain, Robert, *Jesus ou le Mortel Sécret des Templiers*, Robert Lafont, 1970.

Andrews R, and Schellenberger P, *The Tomb of God*, LittleBrown, 1997.

Aué, Michelè (Alison Hebborn, trans.) *The Cathars*, MSM, 1995.

Baigent, M and Leigh, R, *The Temple and the Lodge*, Corgi, 1992.

Baigent, Leigh and Lincoln, *The Holy Blood and The Holy Grail*, Book Club Associates, 1982.

Baigent, Leigh and Lincoln, *The Messianic Legacy*, Jonathan Cape, 1986.

Barber, Malcolm, *The Trial of the Templars*, Cambridge University Press, 1994.

Birks, Norman and Gilbert, R A, *The Treasure of Montségur*, The Aquarian Press, 1990.

Burman, Edward, *The Inquisition*, Aquarian Press, 1984.

Bussell, F W, '*Religious Thought and Heresy in the Middle Ages*'.

The Cambridge Illustrated History of the Middle Ages, vol. I, 350–950, (Robert Fossier, ed.), Cambridge University Press, 1989.

Campbell, Joseph and Moyers, Bill, *The Power of Myth*, Doubleday 1988.

Capra, F, *The Turning Point*, Flamingo, 1983.

Charpentier, Louis, *Les Mystères Templiers*, Lafont, 1967.

Charpentier, Louis, *The Mysteries of Chartres Cathedral*, RILKO, 1993.

Christie-Murray, David, *A History of Heresy*, Oxford University Press, 1989.

Costen, Michael, *The Cathars and the Albigensian Crusade*, Manchester University Press, 1997.

Currer-Briggs, Noel, *The Shroud and the Grail*, Weidenfeld and Nicolson, 1987.

de Clari, Robert, *The Conquest of Constantinople*, (E H Neal, trans.), University of Toronto, 1997.

de Sède, Gérard, *Rennes-le-Château, Les Impostures, Les Phantasmes, Les Hypothèses*, Robert Lafont, 1988.

de Sède, Gérard, *Le Trésor Maudit*.

Desgris, Alain, *L'Ordre de Templiers et La Chevalerie Maconnique Templière*, Guy Trédaniel, 1995.

Devcouvoux du Buysson, Fr Philipe, *The Sainte Baume*, Editions PEC, 1992

de Vries, Simon, *Cathars, Country, Customs and Castles,* Comtal Press, 1993.

Dobson, E C, *Did Our Lord Visit Britain?* 1860.

Epstein, Isadore, *Judaism*, Penguin, 1964.

Fedie, Louis, *Le Comte de Razés et le Diocese d'Alet*, Carcassonne, 1880.

Fleming, Ursula (ed.), *Meister Eckhart*, Collins, 1988.

Forbes-Leith, *The Scots Men-at-Arms and Life Guards in France*.

Fortune, Dione, *Esoteric Orders and their Work*, Aquarian Press, 1987.

Foss, Michael, *Chivalry*, Michael Joseph, 1975.

Fox, Mathew, *Original Blessing*, Bear and Co., 1983.

Fox, Mathew, *Creation Spirituality*, Harper, 1991.

Fox, Robin Lane, *Pagans and Christians*, Penguin, 1988.

Franke and Cawthorne, *The Tree of Life and The Holy Grail*, T. Lodge, 1996.

Frazer, Sir James, *The Golden Bough*, Wordsworth editions, 1993.

Fulcanelli, *Le Mystère des Cathédrales,* Neville Spearman, 1977.

Gardner, Laurence, *Bloodline of the Holy Grail*, Element, 1996.

Gardner, Laurence, *Genesis of the Grail Kings*, Bantam, 1999.

Garza-Valdes, L A, *The DNA of God?,* Hodder & Stoughton, 1998.

Gautkin, *Highways of the Faith*, Wellfleet, 1983.

Gettings, Fred, *The Secret Zodiac,* Routledge, Kegan Paul, 1987.

Gimpell, Jean, *The Cathedral Builders*, Cresset, 1988.

Godwin, Malcolm, *The Holy Grail*, Bloomsbury, 1994.

Gould, Robert F, *History of Freemasonry*, Vols I–IV, Caxton, 1956.

Graffin, Robert, *L'Art Templier des Cathédrales*, Garnier, 1993.

Graves, Robert, *The White Goddess*, Faber, 1961.

Guébin et Moisoineuve, *Histoire Albigeoise de Pierre des Vaux-de-Cerny*, Paris, 1951

Guirdham, Arthur, *The Great Heresy*, C W Daniel, 1993.

Hamill, John and Gilbert, R A, *World Freemasonry*, Aquarian Press, 1991.

Hancock, Graham, *The Sign and The Seal*, Mandarin, 1993.

Jackson, J, *The Chivalry of Scotland in the Days of Robert the Bruce.*

Jackson, Keith B, *Beyond the Craft*, Lewis Masonic, 1982.

Jedin, Hubert (ed.), *History of the Church – to Constantine*, Burns and Oates, 1989.

Johnson, Paul, *A History of Christianity*, Penguin, 1978.

Judica-Cordiglia, Giovanni, *La Sidone.*

Kersten, H and Gruber, E R, *The Jesus Conspiracy*, Element Books, 1992.

Knight, Chris and Lomas, Robert, *The Hiram Key* Century, 1996.

Knight, Chris and Lomas, Robert, *The Second Messiah*, Century, 1997.

Knoup, James, *The Genesis of Freemasonry*, Manchester University Press, 1947.

Lacroix, P, *Military and Religious Life in the Middle Ages*, Chapman and Hall, 1874.

Lamas, *Guide to Compostela*, 1996.

Levi, Magnus Eliphas, *Histoire de la Magie*, 1860.

Lewis, L, *St Joseph of Arimathea at Glastonbury*, 1922.

Lincoln, Henry, *The Holy Place*, Jonathan Cape, 1991.

Lionel, Frederic, *Mirrors of Truth*, Archedigm, 1991.

Lizerand, *Le Dossier de l'Affaire des Templiers*, 1923.

Mackenzie, Kenneth, *The Royal Masonic Cyclopedia*, Aquarium Press, 1987.

Mâle, Émile, *Notre Dame de Chartres*, Flamarrion, 1983.

Miller, Malcolm, *Chartres Cathedral*, Pitkin Pictorials, 1992.

Mitchell, Ann, *Cathedrals of Europe*, Hamlyn, 1968.

Montfull, *Les Grand Cathédrales*, PML, 1995.

Moore, L David, *The Christian Conspiracy*, Pendulum Press, 1983.

Moore, R I, *The Formation of a Persecuting Society*, Basil Blackwell, 1990.

Mullins, Edwin, *The Pilgrimage to Santiago*, Secker and Warburg, 1974.

Nieuwbarn, M C, *Church Symbolism*, Sands and Co., 1910.

Osman, Ahmed, *Moses – Pharaoh of Egypt*, Paladin, 1991.

Picknett, Lynn and Prince, Clive, *The Templar Revelation*, Bantam, 1997.

Querido, Rene, *The Mystery of The Holy Grail*, Rudolf Steiner College, 1991.

Ranke-Heinemann, Uta, *Putting Away Childish Things*, HarperCollins, 1995.

Ravenscroft, Trevor, *The Cup Of Destiny*, Samuel Weiser, 1982.

Ravenscroft, Trevor, *The Spear Of Destiny*, Samuel Weiser, 1982.

Ravenscroft, Trevor, and Wallace-Murphy, T, *The Mark Of The Beast*, Sphere Books, 1990.

Reznikov, Raimonde, *Cathares et Templiers*, Editions Loubatières, 1993.

Richards, M C, *The Crossing Point*, Wesleyan University Press, 1973.

Rigby, Greg, *On Earth as it is in Heaven*, Rhaedus, 1996.

Robinson, John, *The Priority of John*, SCM Press, 1985.

Robinson, John J, *Born in Blood*, Arrow, 1993.

Roszak, Theodore, *Where The Wasteland Ends*, Faber & Faber, 1978.

Runciman, Stephen, *A History Of The Crusades*, 3 vols, Pelican, 1971.

Russell, Bertrand, *Wisdom of the West,* Macdonald, 1959.

Serrus, Georges, *The Land of the Cathars,* Editions Loubatières, 1990.

Schonfield, Hugh, *The Passover Plot*, Element Books, 1985.

Schonfield, Hugh, *The Pentecost Revolution*, Element Books, 1985.

Schonfield, Hugh, *The Essene Odyssey*, Element Books, 1993.

Secret Societies of the Middle Ages, Nattali and Bond, London.

Shah, Idries, *The Way Of The Sufi*, Penguin, 1982.

Sinclair, Andrew, *The Discovery of the Grail*, Century, 1998.

Sizekely, E B, *Essene Teaching from Enoch to the Dead Sea Scrolls*, C W Daniel.

Sox, David, *The File on the Shroud,* Coronet, 1978.

Starbird, Margaret, *The Woman with the Alabaster Jar*, Bear and Co., 1993.

Stevenson, David, *The First Freemasons*, Aberdeen University Press, 1989.

Stourm, *Notre Dame D'Amiens*, Hachette, 1960.

Stoyanov, Yuri, *The Hidden Tradition in Europe*, Arkana, 1994.

Thomas, Keith, *Religion and the Decline of Magic*, Penguin, 1991.

Thurston, Herbert (trans.), *Memorandum of P. D'Arcis*.

Trevor-Roper, Hugh, *The Rise of Christian Europe*, Thames and Hudson, 1965.

Upton-Ward, G M, *The Rule of The Templars*, The Boydell Press, 1992.

Waite, A E, *The Holy Kabbalah*, Oracle, 1996.

Wakefield, Walter and Evans, Austin P, *Heresies of the Middle Ages*, Columbia University Press, 1991.

Wallace-Murphy, T, *An Illustrated Guidebook to Rosslyn Chapel*, Friends of Rosslyn, 1993.

Wallace-Murphy, T, *The Templar Legacy and the Masonic Inheritance Within Rosslyn Chapel*, The Friends of Rosslyn, 1994.

Wallace-Murphy, T and Hopkins, M, *Rosslyn – Guardian of the Secrets of the Holy Grail*, Element, 1999.

Welburn, Andrew, *The Beginnings of Christianity*, Floris, 1991.

Wilcox, Robert J, *Shroud*, Bantam, 1977.

Wilson, Colin, *The Occult*, Grafton, 1979.

Wilson, Ian, *The Turin Shroud*, Weidenfeld & Nicolson, 1978.

Wilson, Ian, *Blood on the Shroud*, Book Club Associates, 1998.

Index

Rhedae *see* Rennes-le-
Château
Rhodes 168
Rigaux, B 59
Riggi Numana, Professor
Giovanni 194, 195
Rite of Strict Observance
219, 251
Robert I, Duke of Bar 238
Robert III, Emperor of
Bavaria 239
Robert the Bruce 176–7,
217, 219, 230, 276
Robert de Clari 181–2
Robert of Gloucester 146,
147
Robin, Jean 135
Robin Hood legends 241,
242, 272
Robinson, John 216, 276
Robinson, Bishop John 59
Robinson, Dr John 190–1,
196
Rocamadour 125
Rollo (Hrolf), Duke of
Normandy 107
Røngvald the Mighty 107
Rose-Croix 20
Rosicrucian Manifestos 273
Rosicrucianism 245, 247,
272
Rosicrucians 23–4, 133,
219, 240, 241, 273
Roslin 108, 116–17, 118,
165, 241, 242
Roslin Castle 241, 272
Rossal (Knight Templar)
23, 112, 113, 114, 226
*Rosslyn – Guardian of the
Secrets of the Holy Grail*
284
Rosslyn Chapel 36, 37, 38,
174, 175, 177, 222,
225–6, 228, 234–6, 241,
242, 276–9
Rosslyn Hay manuscript
234–5

Roussillon 6, 7
Royal Arch degrees 218–19
Royal Society 223, 244,
248, 273
Russell, Bertrand 98–9

S

Sadducees 57, 67
Sainte Baume mountains
82
Sainte Chapelle, Paris 142
Salome 131–2
Samson 51
Sanhedrin 66, 69
Santa Anna, General 258
Sarah, wife of Abraham 51
Sarah the Egyptian (Sara
Kali) 80–1, 83
SAS 231
Saunière, Abbé Bérenger
ix, 7–13, 15, 17, 18, 20,
22, 32, 33–6, 37, 260,
261
Saunière Society 36, 37
Sava, Dr Anthony 185, 187,
196
Savoy, Duke of 215
Savoy, House of 183, 184,
233, 270
Schellenberger, Paul 32
Schidlof, Leo 21
Schonfield, Hugh 50, 174
Scotland, Lord Steward of
249
Scots Guards 230–2,
233–4, 272
Scottish Rite Freemasonry
218–19, 223, 228, 245,
249–50, 252, 253, 259
*Search for the Historical
Jesus, A* 76
Seborga 113
Second Messiah, The 200,
223
Second World War 5, 281

Secret Dossiers 20–1, 22,
23, 24–6, 26–7, 31, 33,
34, 35, 113, 142, 251
Sède, Gérard de 15–16, 32
Sens, Archbishop of 171–2
Sermon on the Mount 61
Serpent Rouge, Le 21
Seton, Alexander
(Alexander
Montgomery) 251
Seton, Sir William 230
Seton family 231
*Shadow of the Templars,
The* (television
documentary) 17
Sheba, Queen of 276
Shroud and the Grail, The
182
Shroud of Turin 174–5,
177, 181–98
Sicarii 57, 78
Sieyès, Abbé 257
Sigismund, Archduke 260
Sigismund von
Luxembourg, King of
Hungary 238
*Sigismundis dei rex
Hungaraie* 238
Simon de Montfort 159,
160
Simon Peter *see* Peter, St
Sinai, Mount 213
Sixtus IV, Pope (Francesco
della Rovere) 183
Smith, Professor Morton
59
Socrates 98
Sol Invictus 89, 93
Solomon, King 122, 205,
276, 224, 225
Solomon's Temple 10, 224
Song of Songs 75, 111,
130
Sons of Zadoc 224
Sophia (Wisdom) 142, 174,
210